TREATING INFIDELITY

OTHER BOOKS BY GERALD WEEKS AND NANCY GAMBESCIA
with Norton Professional Books

Erectile Dysfunction: Integrating Couple Therapy, Sex Therapy, and Medical Treatment

Hypoactive Sexual Desire: Integrating Sex and Couple Therapy

A NORTON PROFESSIONAL BOOK

TREATING INFIDELITY

Therapeutic Dilemmas and Effective Strategies

GERALD R. WEEKS, PH.D.

NANCY GAMBESCIA, PH.D.

ROBERT E. JENKINS, M.S.

W.W. Norton and Company
New York • London

For information about permission to reproduce
selections from this book, write to
Permission, W. W. Norton & Company, Inc.,
500 Fifth Avenue, New York, NY 10110

Production Manager: Leeann Graham
Manufacturing by Haddon Craftsmen, Inc.

Library of Congress Cataloging-in-Publication Data

Weeks, Gerald R., 1948–
Treating infidelity : therapeutic dilemmas and effective strategies /
Gerald R. Weeks, Nancy Gambescia, Robert E. Jenkins.
        p.   cm.
   ISBN 0-393-70388-6
   1. Marital psychotherapy. 2. Adultery. I. Gambescia, Nancy.
II. Jenkins, Robert E., 1951–   III. Title.
RC488.5.W4435 2003
616.89'156—dc22   2003060787

W. W. Norton & Company, Inc., 500 Fifth Avenue, New York, N.Y. 10110
www.wwnorton.com

W. W. Norton & Company Ltd., Castle House, 75/76 Wells St., London W1T 3QT

1 3 5 7 9 0 8 6 4 2

Contents

Acknowledgments

THE AUTHORS WOULD LIKE TO GRATEFULLY ACKNOWLEDGE the many individuals and couples who have contributed to this text. The personal experiences of our clients helped us to refine and elucidate our approach to treating infidelity. During the past decades, we have witnessed the devastation as well as the survival of numerous relationships affected by intimacy transgressions. Treatment was often arduous for all of us, but there were countless rewards in the process.

We are especially grateful for the invaluable assistance of those who have been involved in research and editing. Susanne Methven contributed countless hours by helping us to refine the manuscript and prepare it for publication. Her unwavering devotion is greatly appreciated. Lisa Paolina played a significant role in reviewing the research on trust. Also, we value our ongoing relationship with Norton through the publication of *Erectile Dysfunction, Hypoactive Sexual Desire,* and now, *Treating Infidelity.*

Finally, the enduring support and understanding of our families and loved ones is vital to our work as therapists, educators, and authors. We thank them for their patience and understanding.

Preface

THROUGHOUT THIS BOOK, WE DEFINE INFIDELITY AS A VIOLATION of a couple's assumed or stated contract regarding emotional and / or sexual exclusivity. We broaden traditional definitions of infidelity because they do not begin to capture the great variety of presentations a therapist will encounter, such as same-sex partners, emotional affairs, and Internet infidelity. For example, through cybersex it is possible to experience all phases of the sexual response cycle (desire, arousal, and orgasm) without touching another individual. Differences exist between and among couples in their agreements about sexual and emotional exclusivity. Couples often disagree about behavior that falls within the gray area of the intimacy agreement. A partner crosses the line by secretly diverting intimacy from the relationship and redirecting it into other sexual and / or emotional outlets (Shaw, 1997). Such partners use deception to conceal the transgression, minimize the impact on the relationship, and create confusion in their partners (Pittman, 1989). Infidelity creates a betrayal of trust and a resulting crisis in an exclusive, committed relationship. Various degrees of deception, confusion, and disagreement about the intimacy violation are operative at the onset of treatment. Instability, volatility, uncertainty, and pessimism about the future of the relationship typically characterize the emotional state of the partners. Most therapists feel emotionally and intellectually taxed when treating infidelity. The relationship is extremely fragile, and there is a great likelihood that divorce will result from the infidelity and / or underlying factors that triggered it (Drigotas & Barta, 2001). Furthermore, infidelity challenges the ethical and moral assumptions in the therapist, and countertransferential reactions will require careful scrutiny.

Infidelity is common in clinical practice and notoriously difficult to treat successfully. The actual prevalence is unknown, particularly because there are inconsistencies in how researchers define affairs and other betrayals of intimacy. Research methods also add to the confusion. Surveys typically ask about the incidence of extramarital sex (EMS), a term that is extremely ambiguous. Many respondents interpret EMS to mean coitus with someone other than the spouse; thus, they may not report other forms of intimate or sexual behavior such as sex without coitus, cybersex, emotional affairs, or flirting. In addition, unmarried or same-sex partners in exclusive dyadic relationships might not be included in the sample pool and may deny or justify the intimacy infraction because they are not married.

Nonetheless, Choi, Catania, and Dolcini (1994) conservatively estimated that roughly 26%–50% of men and 21%–38% of women have engaged in EMS at some point in their lifetimes. Others (Nass, Libby, & Fisher, 1981) have reported higher prevalence rates of EMS, such as 50–65% of men and 45–55% of women. The noted incidence of infidelity in clinical populations is considerably higher than in the general population (Humphrey, 1985; Humphrey & Strong, 1976; Marett, 1990). In our experience, it is one of the leading presenting problems for couples counseling.

Infidelity is a relationship problem and requires a flexible regimen that combines elements of individual and conjoint therapy. In many cases, couples are unable to survive the ravages of infidelity when employing nonsystemic treatment strategies. The authors have devised a comprehensive clinical approach to infidelity that addresses the individual risk factors, family-of-origin influences, and relational conditions that contributed to the intimacy violation. This intersystems approach has been used by the authors for years in the successful treatment of relational and sexual dysfunctions (Weeks & Gambescia, 2000, 2002). In addition, the powerful influence of forgiveness is an integral component of the intersystemic treatment of affairs and other intimacy transgressions.

The chapters in this volume address numerous forms of intimacy violations in committed, exclusive relationships. Although most of the couples we treat are in heterosexual marriages, the principles in this book are applicable to other forms of committed unmarried partnerships, including same-sex unions. The purpose of this volume is to provide the clinician with the most effective strategies and techniques for understanding and treating infidelity. We commence with a brief review of each chapter.

The volume begins with an overview of the meaning, prevalence, mani-festations, and definitional issues regarding infidelity. Any violation of the couple's agreement about intimacy—regardless of the presentation—is viewed as a relationship problem. The intersystems conceptual framework is introduced as the most comprehensive approach to the therapeutic chal-lenges of infidelity.

Chapter 1 organizes infidelity into types or categories, each with common elements and unique features. The typologies of eight authors, representing a variety of clinical viewpoints, are examined.

Chapter 2 reviews the existing body of literature that identifies many risk factors or conditions commonly associated with infidelity, with particular sensitivity to gender issues. Topics that have relevance to clinical practice are highlighted: marital satisfaction, sexual permissiveness, type of involvement with the affair partner, justifications, marital equity, social and cultural norms, courtship and cohabitation attitudes and behaviors, biological fac-tors, and relationship to the affair partner.

Chapter 3 builds on information concerning both research and typologies, by identifying some of the more common dimensions of infidelity that are encountered in clinical practice. The multidimensional approach does not attempt to classify or categorize, but instead promotes a deeper understand-ing of the many presentations and components of the infidelity.

Chapter 4 discusses the immediate and postdiscovery consequences of infidelity, with particular emphasis on gender differences. Reactions to infi-delity are intense and varied, yet they often fall within a range of predictable behaviors for both the unfaithful and the betrayed partners. At the appro-priate time, a therapist who is familiar with the consequences of infidelity can normalize the emotional reactions in order to promote the best thera-peutic outcome.

Chapter 5 addresses some of the more difficult and perplexing issues encountered when treating infidelity. These include countertransference, troubling tactical issues (e.g., when a partner or couple attempts to minimize the infidelity), and ethical concerns. In particular, three alternative ways of dealing with the issue of confidentiality are presented. The goal is to increase therapist awareness and competence in dealing with the quandaries, predic-aments, and other complexities of infidelity.

Chapter 6 describes many of the tools needed for the initial phases of treatment. The couple must commit sufficiently to the relationship and make a genuine investment in treatment. The method of discovery of infidelity affects the way that therapy is conducted. Common clinical presentations of infidelity, as well as strategies to help the couple recover from the resulting emotional trauma, are explored. Topics including the judicious use of individual sessions and therapeutic separation, and the need for accountability and trust, are also reviewed.

Chapter 7 provides the reader with the basic principles and strategies used throughout the duration of treatment. A systemically oriented integrative model is detailed that will enhance the effectiveness of the therapist and promote a positive outcome more often than traditional individual or psychodynamic approaches to treating infidelity. Intersystemic strategies, such as the therapeutic reframe, will defuse many of the painful and intense emotions surrounding infidelity while circumventing the destructive effects of blame or moral righteousness. Moreover, each partner, not just the unfaithful partner, colludes and assumes some responsibility in the infidelity.

Chapter 8 is the first of three chapters to incorporate the notion of forgiveness into the treatment of infidelity. Forgiveness is defined. Its use helps to rebuild the damaged relationship, promote optimism, and interrupt deadlocks.

Chapter 9 identifies the factors that help to unify and strengthen the couple, such as empathy, humility, and hope. These factors set the stage for constructing a genuine apology and eventual forgiveness. Effective apologies are difficult to compose and require direction and rehearsal in order produce forgiveness.

Chapter 10 outlines common barriers to forgiveness, such as narcissism, shame, accusatory suffering, anger, and fear. The therapist will learn strategies for recognizing and removing the obstacles to forgiveness when couples are refractory to the customary treatment for infidelity and where forgiveness is difficult yet nevertheless possible.

Chapter 11 promotes strategies for relapse prevention. As the underlying risk factors that contributed to the infidelity are identified and eliminated, the couple experiences a stronger relationship, one with greater satisfaction and intimacy.

Chapter 12 continues with an intimacy-based approach to the treatment of infidelity. The communication problems that typically interfere with intimacy are corrected. Techniques and strategies commonly used to promote and improve communication will reduce the risk of the infidelity recurring.

Treating infidelity is a complicated and arduous process that challenges even experienced therapists. Couples enter treatment in crisis, and fear that the relationship will not survive the betrayal of intimacy. Typically, emotions are intense. The betrayal reveals that the couple's prior assumptions about the relationship are no longer true. Traditional couples therapy techniques are insufficient to the task, and a comprehensive systemic approach is necessary. This book provides the tools that will help the therapist and couple to examine each facet of the betrayal, correct the factors that triggered the infidelity, and build a strengthened relationship.

Overview

IN EVERY COMMITTED RELATIONSHIP, THERE IS A STATED or assumed contract regarding sexual and / or emotional intimacy. This contract guides and regulates the expression of intimacy within and outside of the primary relationship. The parameters of such an agreement may vary among and between couples; however, sexual monogamy is typically a condition. A couple usually perceives a breach of any part of the intimacy contract as a violation, which threatens relationship stability. Moreover, it negatively affects other assumed dimensions of the relationship, such as honesty, trust, and loyalty.

Infractions of intimacy are given a variety of labels. Often, a sexual boundary violation in a marriage is called *extramarital sex* (EMS) or perhaps *extradyadic sex* (EDS) if it occurs within the context of a committed relationship. The terms *affair* and *adultery* can refer to any number of transgressions that violate emotional and / or physical intimacy, such as flirting, sexual relations, emotional affairs, or Internet infidelity. These ambiguous labels often generate confusion and disagreement because they do not render a precise description of the specific conduct in question. Furthermore, they typically pertain to a narrow range of couples (usually married and heterosexual) in exclusive relationships.

In an effort to generate an operational definition for intimacy violations, we found that the term *infidelity* is more comprehensive than other commonly used labels such as *affair, adultery,* or *EMS.* A review of the empirical literature revealed that some or all of the following criteria may represent infidelity:

- Emotional and / or physical intimacy secretly diverted from the primary relationship (Shaw, 1997).
- Emotional and / or physical intimacy expressed through other relationships or outlets without the consent of the partner (Shaw, 1997).
- A betrayal of partner's trust (Glass & Wright, 1997).
- Deception to circumvent discovery of boundary violations (Pittman, 1989).
- Deliberate efforts to conceal secrets from the partner (Lusterman, 1998).
- Secrecy and lies to create confusion and pain in the partner (Brown, 1991b.)
- Denial of the detrimental impact of the boundary violation and deception on the relationship (McCarthy, 2002).
- Threat to the security of the relationship (Spring, 1996).
- Damage to the relationship (Whisman, Dixon, & Johnson, 1997).

We use *infidelity* frequently throughout this volume to depict a wide range of betrayals of intimacy, whether physical, emotional, or both. We use *affair* to specify infidelity within a heterosexual marriage.

Definitional Issues

Researchers are well aware of the need to use operationally precise language when describing events. Clinicians confront the same issue when working with clients. They must ensure that all parties are employing language in the same way and that there is a shared understanding or meaning. Historically, defining infidelity has been a difficult matter. One of the earliest writers to address the terminology was Thompson, who constructed a behavioral denotation. According to him, "extramarital sex is defined as genital sexual involvement outside the marriage without express knowledge or consent of one's partner. An extramarital crisis occurs for many married couples when the uninformed partner becomes aware of the extramarital involvement" (1984, p. 240). Despite Thompson's efforts, definitional ambiguity remained. The term *genital sexual involvement* has a wide variety of meanings, including heterosexual intercourse, noncoital genital contact, or homosexual contact. Partners can have different definitions and may dispute whether a specific act is a betrayal of the intimacy contract. Sometimes, the unfaithful partner may wish to deny that a violation has occurred by contending that the intimate behavior was not significant. No one is fooled by this spurious argument.

Thompson (1984) used the expression *outside of marriage* as a defining property of an affair. This aspect of the terminology raises questions about other types of committed relationships that place a value on monogamy, including gay and dating partnerships or cohabitating unmarried couples. The definition must be broadened to include these types of relationships. In addition, Thompson stated that the spouse has not given consent for the extramarital relationship. Partners may be perplexed about how to determine the boundaries of intimate exclusivity and the vague area where acceptable and unacceptable behaviors overlap, particularly in relationships that permit sexual intimacy with persons outside of the primary relationship. Couples may stipulate that the partner will have to tell the other person about the relationship and not get emotionally involved. Sometimes, the requirement of sexual exclusivity can be broken only with partners of the same gender. Because these agreements are idiosyncratic, the therapist must discuss and understand the couple's definition of the conditions constituting infidelity. It is often difficult to determine when a requirement has been violated.

Another definitional issue raised by Thompson (1984) is whether the committed partner is ignorant about or has tacitly sanctioned the infidelity. Charny and Parnass (1995) produced the only study to examine this issue. They surveyed therapists who had extensive experience in treating affairs. These therapists believed that, in the vast majority of cases, betrayed partners unconsciously collude with their partners to allow the affair. Even though they may suspect or consciously oppose the affair, they covertly communicate that they tolerate the infidelity by not addressing noticeable signs that intimate energy is being diverted from the relationship. Many partners we have treated choose to deny the existence of an affair due to the emotional, marital, familial, and economic consequence that would follow from confronting the issue. They are afraid to confront the issue because conflict will ensue or the marriage will end. If there is implicit approval or if the partner is in denial of the infidelity, has an affair occurred according to Thompson's definition? Experimental studies have also shown that in well-established relationships there is a strong cognitive bias toward judging the partner's statements as truthful (Stiff, Kim, & Ramesh, 1992). Apparently, as the couple spends more time together it is important for them to believe each other to be truthful. Thus, a truth bias develops in well-established relationships that may account for some of the denial or lack of ability to see what is obvious to strangers.

Glass and Wright (1992) expanded Thompson's (1984) view of infidelity to include affairs that were primarily sexual, primarily emotional, and a combined emotional / sexual type. These categories make sense from a clinical and intuitive perspective, because many therapists see affairs that do not involve sex but possess a strong emotional component. Again, it is often difficult to determine what constitutes an emotional affair and to settle on when such a relationship crosses the line of acceptability for a given couple. We know that emotional affairs are characterized by:

- A great deal of intimacy.
- A strong sense of commitment.
- Sharing of thoughts and feelings that are not revealed to one's committed partner.
- A powerful urge to spend time with the affair partner.
- Secrecy surrounding this relationship.
- A sense in the betrayed partner that matters that are private to the couple are being discussed with the affair partner.

The problem with an emotional affair is that the couple can dispute these criteria, particularly when deciding if a friendship has become too familiar (Glass & Staehel, 2003). Furthermore, jealousy is a factor that sometimes confuses this issue. At the extreme are partners who are so suspicious that looking at or conducting a brief conversation with other people is interpreted as a violation. In one case, a man brought his wife to therapy accusing her of having multiple affairs. He complained that she talked to men at parties for too long and, when she arrived late from work, he accused her of seeing her lover. She attempted to point out the irrationality of his accusations, yet he could not let go of the idea that she was having an affair. In this case, the problem was not in the marriage but instead in the husband's expectation of an affair due to experiences in his family of origin.

Assessing emotional infidelity can be more complex and arduous than a physical affair. The therapist must get an accurate picture of whether jealousy is involved and whether the relationship fits the criteria mentioned previously, and then determine how this relationship violates the couple's intimacy contract. These clients usually do not enter therapy unless the partner believes that the relationship is inappropriate. Given the previous criteria, the partner is usually correct in labeling the behavior as infidelity. Interestingly, once the therapist and the spouse confront the partner in the emotional affair, usually there is agreement that a line has been crossed. This partner often agrees that the relationship is a diversion from the marriage and feels a sense of relief in knowing that the inappropriate association must end.

More recently, the clinical literature has addressed newer or emerging versions of intimacy transgressions involving the Internet (Cooper, Delmonico, & Burg, 2000; Schneider, 2000; Young, Griffin-Shelly, Cooper, O'Mara, & Buchanan, 2000). Some of the presentations include viewing pornography on the Internet and using the images for purposes of sexual stimulation; visiting chat rooms for interactive or solo sexual arousal; using video cameras for viewing, exhibiting, or exchanging sex; and conducting Internet affairs. One of the most unsettling issues regarding cybersex is determining when the couple's contract regarding sexual or romantic exclusivity is breached. Typically, cybersex is a solitary activity that involves deception and secrecy. Furthermore, it diverts intimate energy from the relationship without the consent of both partners (Shaw, 1997). In some cases, viewing Internet pornography is acceptable if it is done infrequently. In others, a partner crosses the line when entering a chat room. In one example, the couple enjoyed using the Internet to share their own videotaped sexual practices and to view those of other couples. A violation occurred when the husband engaged in this activity without his wife.

In our experience, cybersex can be highly addictive and might be a symptom of an undiscovered sexual addiction. Another couple sought treatment when the husband was found engaging in live cybersex on the family's computer. In this case, the Internet infidelity was only one manifestation of an insidious sex addiction. He spent increasing amounts of time at home and at work exchanging sexual stimulation with others online. In addition, he sometimes arranged physical meetings with the women he met online. The Internet activities were destructive to his productivity at work and damaged his marital and family relationships. He was so consumed by the addiction that he failed to cover his tracks and felt relieved when discovered by his wife. This couple required treatment for sex addiction, which involved extensive individual and group therapy. The treatment plan involved a return to the marital therapist after the sex addiction was under control.

Whether or not infidelity has occurred largely depends on how the clients define the situation. The key is to determine whether or not the transgression is experienced as a betrayal of the couple's intimate relationship, based on their definition. Couples are usually not interested in how the therapist defines infidelity, or in debates about the dimensional aspects of the affair or behavioral definitions. When infidelity is the couple's presenting problem, the partners usually agree that something inappropriate has happened. Once there is some agreement that a boundary has been crossed, the therapy can proceed to discover the nature of the violation and acceptance of responsibility for it. An admission to any wrongdoing opens the door for greater disclosure and acceptance of responsibility in the future.

Our Definition

We have developed a definition that combines a number of the aforementioned theories with our clinically based formulations. We define infidelity as a violation of the couple's assumed or stated contract regarding emotional and / or sexual exclusivity. Our definition is broader and more comprehensive than others for many reasons. First, the couple need not be married or heterosexual to fulfill the criterion of belonging to a committed, intimately exclusive relationship. Next, the parameters of exclusivity are specific to each couple; for some, infidelity can occur in an open relationship when a partner is intimate without the consent of the other. Finally, the behaviors in question do not necessarily involve physical contact or sex, provided that they are considered a breach of the couple's covenant regarding intimacy. For example, Internet infidelity, flirting, non-coital sex, viewing of pornographic magazines or movies, or emotional affairs often cross the line of acceptability.

With infidelity, intimacy—whether emotional, physical, or both—is diverted from the primary relationship and expressed through other outlets or relationships without the partner's consent. The partners often disagree about the exact point of departure from the intimacy contract. Typically, the line is crossed when deception is used to conceal the transgression, thereby confusing the partner, creating mistrust, and inflicting pain. The relationship is challenged, weakened, and / or damaged by the betrayal of trust and violation of the intimacy contract. There are numerous dimensions of infidelity, each with a particular presentation. Every couple is unique in their definition of exclusivity; the way in which the transgression is understood ultimately determines the treatment.

Often, it is difficult to know the point of departure from the couple's agreed-on contract regarding intimacy. Typically, this is an area of contention between partners. One way of determining that a line has been crossed is to trace the onset of deceptive communication. Hiding behaviors, secrecy, lies, and other forms of deception are harbingers of infidelity, even if no physical contact has occurred. When a partner systematically needs to conceal thoughts, emotions, and behaviors from the other, a violation of the couple's intimacy contract has taken place. Our definition does not apply if the partners agree about intimate expression outside of the primary relationship, and deception is not involved.

Discovery or disclosure of infidelity precipitates a crisis in the relationship. Previously held assumptions about loyalty, love, and the couple's sense of "we-ness" are destabilized. The partners urgently attempt to deal with the dilemma and the events surrounding the discovery as the relationship rapidly moves from a context of security to uncertainty. Moreover, the underlying conditions that made the partnership vulnerable to infidelity quickly rise to the surface. Many are unable to recover from the assault to the relationship and, therefore, the underlying relational problems are never addressed.

Joe and Kate met in college and were married for 14 years. They believed that their marriage was exceptional and that they possessed a bond that was stronger than most. One of the unique features of their partnership was their openness regarding physical intimacy and willingness to experiment with new and creative behaviors. They had always been physically monogamous. Six years ago, Joe began to amuse himself with Internet pornography. Occasionally, he would share some of his downloaded images with Kate. Over time, however, he developed a library of favorites that he would surreptitiously return to periodically. Kate began to notice that Joe was distracted and emotionally distant. She gradually became resentful that he was less involved in household responsibilities and always on the computer. In addition, the couple's sexual frequency progressively diminished over several years. Eventually, she discovered the collection of Joe's Internet pornography and learned that he often masturbated while viewing the images. She was hurt and enraged when she realized that for years Joe had violated their agreement about sexual exclusivity. He justified his actions by stating that he had never entered a chat room nor had physical intimacy with another woman. He denied the detrimental impact of his behaviors on the relationship, and assumed that as long as his activities were secret they could not adversely affect Kate. His primitive excuses frustrated her and provoked more anger. She became hypervigilant and preoccupied with collecting evidence of his infidelity, noting the dates and times that he logged on to pornographic sites, and discovered that he had been online on special occasions such as birthdays and anniversaries. Kate doubted the specialness of the marriage, her identity as a sexual partner, and the security she assumed by virtue of their relationship.

PREVALENCE

The incidence of infidelity in the general population is significant despite clear social disapproval for this behavior (Smith, 1994). Infidelity has been monitored throughout the past five decades by empirically studying the correlates and predominance of EMS in nonclinical populations. There has been considerable variation in the recorded prevalence of EMS throughout the years. Kinsey, Pomeroy, and Martin (1948) and Kinsey, Pomeroy, Martin, and Gebhard (1953) obtained the highest rates through the earliest large-scale research. These data estimated that 50% of husbands and 26% of wives had experienced EMS during the course of their marriage. Throughout the next three decades, numerous sex surveys were conducted, revealing findings that were consistent with Kinsey's group (Wiederman, 1997). These include:

- 40% for males and 36% for females (Athanasiou, Shaver, & Tavris, 1970).
- 41% for men and 18% for women (Hunt, 1974).
- 20% for men and 10% for women (Johnson, 1970).
- 47% for men (Yablonsky, 1979).
- 32% for women (Maykovich, 1976).

Most of the research on extramarital infidelity that was conducted after 1990 produced significantly lower prevalence rates than reported in earlier studies. Several national studies designed to investigate a variety of opinions and behaviors recorded incidental findings related to the frequency of EMS. These include:

- 0.8% of married women and 2.1% of married men had had more than one sexual partner during the past 12 months (Smith, 1991).
- 4% of married men had more than one sexual partner in the past year (Billy, Tanfer, Grady, & Klepinger, 1993).
- 4% of married women had more than one sexual partner in the past year (Forste & Tanfer, 1996).
- 1.2% of subjects had more than one sexual partner during the past 30 days, 3.6% during the past 12 months, and 6.4% during the past 5 years. In each time period, men were twice as likely as women to have an extramarital sexual encounter (Leigh, Temple, & Trocki, 1993).
- 2.2% of respondents had more than one sexual partner in the past year. Men were two times more likely than women to have EMS. It is estimated that roughly 26%–50% of men and 21%–38% of women have engaged in EMS at some point (Choi, Catania & Dolcini, 1994).

Two large-scale studies conducted in the 1990s provide useful information about infidelity. In 1993, the National Opinion Research Center collected data from approximately 1,200 respondents nationally. The survey was based on a stratified sample and consisted of both face-to-face and paper-and-pencil surveys. Laumann, Gagnon, Michael, and Michaels (1994) analyzed these data and published a major text in the field, *The Social Orga-*

nization of Sexuality: Sexual Practices in the United States. The major finding of this study was that 24.5% of married men and 15% of married women reported having an affair at some point in their marriage. In another well-designed study, Wiederman (1997) focused exclusively on the prevalence of extramarital sex. He used data from a nationally representative sample of 884 men and 1,288 women. As with the other studies, men were about two times more likely to have had an affair (22.7% vs. 11.6%). The reader will note that this rate is slightly lower than that reported by Laumann and colleagues (1994).

We know from our clinical experience that couples who seek therapy often present with the complaint of infidelity. The prevalence and nature of infidelity in clinical practice has not been systematically investigated, however. Humphrey and Strong (1976) conducted a survey of clinical members of the American Association of Marriage and Family Therapy. The therapists reported that 46% of the couples coming for help reported having an affair. A replication of this study revealed higher rates, with some therapists recounting that the majority of their caseload had experienced an affair (Humphrey, 1985). Our clinical experience of over more than 25 years is consistent with the two studies of therapists. In fact, over half of our couples have reported some form of infidelity currently or in the past.

It is difficult to assess the actual prevalence of infidelity due to the many methodological and design problems in the existing body of research. The sample sizes vary from small studies that tend to represent one socioeconomic group to larger, stratified samples. Of course, the smaller samples limit generalizability of results and the larger samples carry other methodological problems. For instance, many of the studies used personal interviewing to ascertain extremely sensitive information. This approach could cause subjects to underreport or suppress acknowledging an affair due to embarrassment or shame. Even when a survey method was used, some subjects would not respond honestly for fear of the consequences of discovery.

The age of the subjects was another confounding problem. Often, the incidence of EMS was reported in a younger cohort during a limited time span such as a year. Thus, the actual prevalence of EMS is distorted because the frequency over a given year is low compared to the lifetime of the couple (Wiederman, 1997). Moreover, the rate of occurrence of infidelity increases with marital duration for men (Kinsey et al., 1953; Laumann et al., 1994). This tendency is also true for women, with the highest rate of occurrence among women in their 40s, although the frequency declines after then (Wiederman, 1997).

Another problem with the existing body of research, as we discussed earlier, is the way in which an affair is defined. Most of the prevalence statistics are obtained from studies that operationalize the definition of affair globally as extramarital sex, leaving room for definitional inconsistencies. For instance, if a subject is asked to report the number of sex partners within a given time frame, they could interpret sex to mean coitus and omit other noncoital extramarital sexual relationships that included masturbation, fantasy, or oral sex. Furthermore, information about emotional affairs, Internet adultery, sex with prostitutes, and so on might be suppressed due to the nature of the questions used.

Most of the reported prevalence of infidelity pertains only to marital relationships, omitting extradyadic sexual behavior in other committed, cohabitating couples. Sexual exclusivity is an expected norm in these groups; therefore, data about them could enrich our understanding of infidelity (Choi et al., 1994). For example, the available research on cohabitating couples reveals a higher incidence of infidelity than in married couples (Dolcini et al., 1993; Treas & Giesen, 2000).

The reported prevalence of EMS over the last four decades has declined, yet a significant number of married and committed Americans have experienced sexual intimacy with someone other than their partner. We know from the available data and our clinical experience that infidelity is a common problem with devastating consequences. Considering that emotional and Internet affairs were not reported in these studies, it is likely that the actual prevalence of infidelity (emotional and sexual) is significantly greater than presumed.

How can this information help us to comprehend and better predict the prevalence of infidelity? We are beginning to gather information about the risk factors that increase the likelihood of EMS, such as a high degree of sexual interest, permissive sexual values, marital dissatisfaction, and racial correlates (Treas & Giesen, 2000). What other relational, individual, and intergenerational factors could place a committed couple at risk for infidelity? Our conceptual framework will help define the idiosyncratic factors for specific couples.

CONCEPTUAL FRAMEWORK

Infidelity is difficult to treat effectively and requires a comprehensive, systemic approach that addresses cognitive, affective, and behavioral dimensions. We believe that the intersystemic approach offers the best possibility for treatment because it is contextual, inclusive, and involves the theoretical and technical integration of various schools of therapy, treatment approaches, and techniques (Weeks, 1977, 1986, 1994). This model subsumes three interlocking foci of assessment and treatment: the couple's relationship, the individual risk factors of each partner, and influences from the families of origin on the present relationship.

The couple is comprised of two individuals. Each partner brings history, defense mechanisms, beliefs or irrational ideas, expectations, and so on to the relationship. The couple also possesses their own unique system of dynamics such as communication style, the interplay of expectations, roles assumed, conflict resolution ability, and so on. Finally, partners have a personal history embedded in their families of origin. Using a genogram can provide the historical foundation for the couple's current problems (DeMaria, Weeks, & Hof, 1999).

The intersystem approach also includes six integrative concepts borrowed from the work of Strong and Claborn (1982): definition, interpretation, prediction, congruence, interdependence, and attribution. The first three concepts are intrapsychic in nature, and the last three are interactional.

Definition refers to how each partner determines the boundaries of the couple's relationship. Every partnership searches for definition. A basic model that we use in our theory was developed by Sternberg (1986) and called the *triangular theory of love*. According to this theory, love consists of three components—commitment, intimacy, and passion. Weaknesses or problems in any of the three areas can predispose a couple to the ravages of infidelity.

Interpretation concerns how events, actions, or behaviors are seen and understood by each partner. Sometimes the intent of a behavior is far from its effect due to the way the other partner interprets the behavior. Cognitive distortions may affect the way behaviors are perceived. In the case of an affair, for example, a partner may constantly feel criticized, even though it is not the partner's intent. The criticized partner may then feel angry and resentful, which could contribute to an affair.

Prediction occurs gradually as a relationship develops and the partners may conceive the idea that they can foresee the other's actions. When an action is inconsistent with what was predicted, the couple's equilibrium is disturbed and conflict arises. In some cases we have treated, unpredictable behavior such as staying out late, talking excessively to someone of the opposite gender at a party, or not being accessible by phone can lead to automatic accusations of an affair.

Congruence pertains to the degree to which partners share the same definitions and expectations, and is correlated with relationship satisfaction. If partners discover highly incongruent beliefs, they will be less satisfied, frustrated, and wondering why they married. For example, one couple married thinking they both wanted to have children. After a few years, the wife brought up the topic of starting a family and her husband flatly refused. She personalized his statement by feeling rejected, lost her desire for him, and started to think about divorce and other men.

Interdependence in a healthy relationship means that the partners depend on each other for meeting their needs. The more they expect in this regard, the more interdependent they become. If the partners start to believe that the other cannot or will not meet their needs, the sense of appropriate dependency is lost and the relationship becomes more tenuous. Men, for example, assume that they can be dependent on their partners to fulfill their sexual needs. When this need is not met, they sometimes believe they can no longer count on their partner and may consider looking elsewhere.

Attribution can be linear or circular (see Weeks & Treat, 2001). Linear attribution involves all-or-none thinking; for instance, if one partner is wrong, the other is right. Ideally, couples are able to view their relationship in terms of circular attribution. This concept means that partners see their part in the origin and / or maintenance of the problem. They can communicate about how one individual influenced a reaction in the other that triggered a reaction in the first partner, and so on. Partners must be helped to accept the systemic nature of infidelity. Thus, it is viewed as a symptom of a dysfunctional relationship or an intimacy problem for the couple, rather than as something for which only one partner can be blamed.

The six integrative concepts can be used to help understand the intrapsychic and interactional factors that made the relationship vulnerable to an affair or other versions of infidelity. Once the clinician has completed the assessment, treatment can begin. Treatment involves correcting each factor that contributed to the infidelity. For example, if an affair is partly due to a bipolar illness, then the clinician can diagnosis this disorder, discuss its impact on the partner and the relationship, and explain that affairs are sometimes related to the manic phase of behavior. Treating the bipolar illness eliminates one factor that contributes to having extramarital sex.

Unique Aspects of Treatment
Barriers to Seeking Treatment

It is impossible to estimate how many individuals actually consult with a therapist for treatment of infidelity. Given the prevalence of affairs, it is safe to say that many do not, due to barriers to seeking help. For instance, unfaithful partners often want help in ending affairs yet avoid treatment for fear that discovery could exacerbate relational conflict and dissatisfaction, and possibly precipitate a divorce. They also fear that the therapist will have a judgmental or punitive attitude about a behavior that is socially unaccepted. In other cases, one or both partners do not consider therapy because they are trying to minimize the meaning and impact of the affair.

In instances of long-term or emotional affairs, motivation to end the secret relationship is usually low despite the fact that the unfaithful partner is in violation of his or her ethical and moral standards. Sometimes unfaithful partners believe that they are in love with two people and are in a quandary about losing one or the other. They might even visit a therapist without telling their partner in order to understand better the motivations for the affair. However, this effort will do little to improve the relationship because it excludes the spouse from the treatment.

If a couple is able to overcome the barriers to seeking treatment, several emotional obstacles must be anticipated. First, there is often an underlying atmosphere of pessimism and skepticism about resolution of the infidelity and the future of the relationship. These intransigent emotions can challenge even the most experienced therapist. In this text, we offer strategies for infusing optimism into the treatment. Next, if the couple enters treatment during the crisis of the disclosure of the infidelity, emotions are intense and disorganized. Typically, the partners are extremely distressed and inconsolable. Specific organizing strategies must be initiated immediately. Another obstacle is the reluctance of one or both partners to freely discuss their feelings. As a rule, they feel shame, embarrassment, and discomfort discussing a sexual or intimate betrayal. The couple may also be disinclined to talk to a therapist about infidelity because they are unfamiliar with the limits of confidentiality. They may fear the therapist might "leak" this information, their secret would be discovered, and social embarrassment would result. It is important to reassure couples that affairs are commonly seen in our practices and that whatever is revealed is strictly confidential (barring the usual statement regarding spouse abuse and a duty to warn).

Therapeutic Issues

Infidelity is commonplace in clinical practice, yet many practitioners feel ill prepared to deal with it. Therapists experience endless challenges to their knowledge base and value system. Moreover, the risk of marital dissolution is higher than with most other relational problems, a factor that weighs heavily on therapists. In addition, intricate interpersonal or countertransference issues often emerge when treating infidelity. These issues have not received much attention in the clinical and research literature. In fact, much more has been published in scientific journals about the etiology, typology, and other aspects of infidelity than about practical information regarding treatment. Of the texts available on the topic, most are dated or offer approaches that are nonsystemic or nondynamic in orientation (Lawson, 1988; Strean, 1980, 2000). In this volume, we discuss many tactical issues such as countertransference issues, secret affairs, and concerns about confidentiality.

One of the ways we approach infidelity is to consider the many dimensions of an intimacy transgression and the specific treatment required for each dimension. Researchers have largely circumvented such an approach. If physical contact is a dimension, we are interested in assessing parameters such as duration, frequency, type, risk of discovery, degree of emotional involvement, gender, and other dimensions of an affair or the affair partner. For instance, we know that casual infidelity violates the couple's expectation about exclusivity and damages their intimate relationship. Likewise, if the affair involves an emotional, romantic, or loving relationship, the couple often has more difficulty in recovering from the multiple levels of betrayal. A further dimension that can complicate recovery is how well the affair partner is known to the couple. The betrayal is often greater if this person is a neighbor, friend, or coworker (Glass & Staehel, 2003). Another frequently overlooked dimension is the possibility that both partners are involved in some form of intimacy violation, even if one partner is not physically intimate with his or her affair partner. Therapists should also be sensitive that some types of infidelity, such as virtual infidelity or cyberinfidelity, do not fit the traditional stereotype of an affair.

Our approach recognizes that some aspects of infidelity are distinctive whereas others are to be expected. The therapist must be familiar with emotional experiences of the unfaithful partner, how to keep this partner committed to treatment, and how to address these feelings with sensitivity. Simultaneously, the intense emotional responses of the betrayed partner must be anticipated and moderated. Throughout the text, we emphasize the necessity of the partners' commitment to the therapy and to the relationship. However, the specific presentation of infidelity will have a strong bearing on the treatment plan designed for each couple. Furthermore, we recommend specific strategies for the various postdiscovery phases. In the intermediate phases, for instance, we recommend a number of strategies for seeking and receiving forgiveness. We devote three treatment chapters to forgiveness to emphasize the importance of understanding the numerous and complex components of the forgiveness process. For example, we recommend strategies that will strengthen unifying factors in the relationship, such as empathy, humility, and hope. These unifying factors must outweigh the barriers to forgiveness, such as anger, fear, and shame.

Often, infidelity requires a combination of individual, sex, and marital therapy. For example, an affair might have grown from sexual frustration or lack of desire on the part of one partner. Based on our experience, very few therapists know how to treat the lack of desire. They tend to use generic couple therapy techniques and their own intuition rather than follow a treatment program with various guidelines. Our approach emphasizes the necessity of recognizing and treating the underlying risk factors such as the lack of sexual desire and other conditions that make the relationship vulnerable to infidelity.

In the final phases of treatment, the therapist concentrates on the couple's intimate relationship. Our approach is intimacy based, because infidelity represents violations in the couple's contract regarding intimacy. We use the Sternberg (1986) model of love as a foundation for this phase of treatment. This model incorporates three equally important aspects of any loving relationship: intimacy, commitment, and passion.

We believe that the best way to repair intimacy problems and strengthen the relationship is through a combination of techniques that rely on clear, precise communication between partners. Often, misunderstandings in communication can create a breeding ground for conflict, mistrust, and a lack of commitment, all factors associated with infidelity. Our approach recognizes, strengthens, and teaches couples about the five essential ingredients of intimacy, levels of communication (Bernal & Barker, 1979), and recognizing barriers to communication. Finally, we recommend basic techniques for facilitating intimate communication.

CONCLUSION

This text provides the therapist with valuable tools for assessing and treating a wide variety of intimacy violations in committed relationships. We offer an operational depiction of infidelity that will aid in evaluating the exact nature of the transgression and developing a unique treatment plan for each presentation. Our therapeutic strategies are intimacy based; repairing the damage to the couple's intimate relationship is an essential objective. In order to accomplish this, underlying problems that made the relationship vulnerable to infidelity must be recognized and addressed. We recommend systemic strategies that help the couple frame the infidelity as a relationship problem, regardless of the ostensible guilt of one partner. Nonsystemic approaches are not adequate to this task. We promote an understanding of the stages of healing, as well as the more typical reactions of the unfaithful and the betrayed partners. In addition, the reader will learn to assess and treat diverse manifestations of infidelity through applying the definitional criteria to each situation. This text will help even the most experienced therapists increase their knowledge, comfort, and effectiveness when working with the challenges of infidelity.

TREATING INFIDELITY

1

❀ ❀ ❀

Typologies of Infidelity

INFIDELITY IS A COMPLICATED AND MULTIFACETED PHENOMENON. In every occurrence, the attributes of each partner, influences of each partner's family of origin, and relational issues are distinctive. In spite of this, shared elements exist among the various presentations. In an effort to understand the common features of infidelity, a number of clinicians have created organizational models that provide types or categories. This typological approach incorporates certain identifying characteristics such as motivational factors, precipitating events, relational vulnerabilities, expected treatment outcomes, and prognoses. Typologies, however, have limitations, because they tend to be somewhat loosely defined and based on clinical observation rather than empirical study. Thus, the clinician may attempt to fit intimacy transgressions into general categories and therefore miss the salient nuances of each situation. Another issue that creates confusion is that typologies are typically about extramarital sex and do not necessarily address other behaviors that constitute a violation of the couple's intimacy contract, such as cyberinfidelity. Although typologies can provide useful information to the clinician, one must never lose sight of the fact that infidelity is complex and therefore defies oversimplification.

In this chapter, we review and contrast eight typologies that represent a variety of clinical viewpoints. These include the works of Brown (1991b),

Charny (1992), Lawson (1988), Levine (1998), Humphrey (1987), Strean (1976), Lusterman (1995, 1998), and Pittman (1989).

Brown's Typology

We begin with Emily Brown, who developed one of the earliest and more popular models. She devotes an entire chapter of her 1991 book, *Patterns of Infidelity and Their Treatment,* to exemplify various types of affairs. A number of parameters are employed, such as range of feelings, behavior manifestations, age, gender, and treatment prognosis. Brown's (1991b) stated purpose was to help the clinician understand the "hidden message" or the underlying emotional reason for infidelity. Her highly descriptive system comprises five types of affairs, which are described in great detail.

Conflict-Avoidant Affairs

When one partner is clearly more dissatisfied than the other is, and previous attempts to get the conflict-avoidant partner to talk about the problem have failed, an affair sometimes occurs. Although this is not viewed an adaptive strategy, an affair offsets the balance of the relationship, precipitates a crisis, and forces the couple to deal with the problem. In Brown's (1991b) experience, this type occurs equally between men and women and often takes place early in marriage. The duration of the affair tends to be brief, with a minimum of emotional involvement. Although betrayed partners are angry about such affairs, they sometimes attempt to circumvent the crisis by ostensibly appearing overly understanding about its occurrence. According to Brown (1991b), the probability of divorce is low for this type of couple. Our experience further suggests that the unfaithful partner did not intend to have an affair in the first place and often unconsciously wishes to be caught or stopped.

Jim, 51, and Melinda, 48, fit this particular pattern. Married for over 30 years, the couple had three adult children. Their marriage was traditional, as Melinda had primary responsibility for childcare and homemaking until the last child was gone. She then started working outside of the home and was rapidly promoted. Throughout the marriage, Jim controlled family decisions and Melinda acquiesced. They could rarely, if ever, recall having a fight. In fact, they were very polite in the session to each other and toward the therapist. When Melinda became involved in an extramarital affair, Jim discovered it almost immediately. She felt remorse over the affair and could not understand what would drive her toward such an unacceptable behavior. He wanted only to forgive Melinda.

From the first session, it was clear that Melinda's role in the couple's marital system was that of the underassertive partner. The marriage was of such a long duration, and the patterns so well entrenched, that she could not offset the established blueprint. However, in the workplace Melinda began to feel a greater need to speak up for herself. Without fully understanding her motivation, Melinda essentially took charge by having an affair in a manner that ensured she would be discovered. It was a revelation to both to learn that they avoided conflict, and that Melinda needed a change in the standard operating procedure of the marriage. The crisis of the infidelity made it possible for the preexisting struggles over power and control to be addressed in the therapy.

Intimacy-Avoidant Affairs

The real issue with this type of infidelity is that the partners do not know how to be emotionally and / or sexually close to each other. The only intensity experienced by the couple occurs through chronic conflict and episodic fighting. The unfaithful partner triangulates the couple and hinders intimacy by acting as an emotional buffer. As with the previously mentioned type, Brown (1991b) maintained that the intimacy-avoidant affair occurs equally between men and women, is more common in younger marriages, and tends to be brief with minimal emotional involvement. Although this kind of affair sometimes involves bilateral infidelity, the prognosis is good in terms of the marriage surviving the affair.

Prior to meeting each other, Jerry, and Susan, both 29 and professionals, had been involved only in short-term relationships. They entered therapy for premarital counseling in order to resolve issues over power, control, and roles in the relationship. Although this work went well, it was apparent that the couple was unable to articulate the larger issue regarding their inability to be intimate. They were both raised in cold and distant families who valued intellectual achievement. After a number of sessions their therapist attempted to illustrate the deeper predicament with intimacy, but the couple was unable to accept this notion, remaining focused only on the problems they had presented. They were warned that failing to resolve this underlying issue was certain to cause future trouble. Nonetheless, the therapy ended after a few sessions.

Two years later, the couple returned to therapy after Susan had been discovered having an affair. Although this was the first time she had acted in this manner, Susan confessed the almost constant wish to have romantic liaisons with other men. Jerry had remained monogamous, but he often worked to the exclusion of his wife. They were a bit embarrassed about not accepting the therapist's earlier recommendation. In fact, they both knew immediately that the infidelity was a warning that their intimacy issues needed to be addressed.

Sexual Addiction Affairs

Brown (1991b) asserted that the sexual addict experiences a disquieting sense of emptiness and seeks sexual conquests to palliate this uncomfortable feeling. Typically, attention is diverted from healthy ways of fulfilling needs in exchange for the excitement gained from sexual seduction. In Brown's clinical experience, the addict is driven by a need for power and thus seeks public positions or political employment for the sake of personal gratification. Sometimes the affair(s) become a public scandal when discovered.

The characteristics of this type of infidelity contrast significantly from the first two already described. The unfaithful partner is often grandiose, male, has multiple brief affairs, and lives a life separate from his spouse. Understandably, the prognosis for such a couple is poor and couple therapy is not an appropriate choice of treatment, particularly in the beginning.

Our experience with infidelity driven by sexual addiction is somewhat different from Brown's on a few points. The sex addict need not be a high-powered political figure or anyone seeking public recognition. In fact, sex addicts come in all sizes and shapes. The best form of treatment is a combination of group and individual therapy for both partners, as described by Carnes (1991) and Turner (1995). We agree with Brown (1991a,b) that the spouse is usually in denial of the problem for an extended period of time, and often finds the behavior so extreme that it is not understandable or forgivable. Thus, the vast majority of sex addicts we have treated have lost their partners. If the marriage manages to survive, we find that ongoing conjoint therapy is necessary after a period of addressing the addiction, codependence, and relapse prevention.

Dan, 42, and Nancy, 40, had been married for about 20 years. Dan was an executive and Nancy managed the home and other domestic responsibilities. Dan traveled extensively and spent a good deal of time in New York City. When on business trips, he would sometimes use cocaine, frequently hire prostitutes, or alternatively have liaisons with women from work. Dan had known for some time that he could not stop himself from acting out sexually. He was extremely conflicted because this behavior was contrary to his ethical and moral code of conduct. The precipitating incident occurred when his wife discovered that she had contracted a sexually transmitted disease. Consequently, the couple entered treatment for the addiction. The program involved individual and group therapy and required attendance in

SLAA (Sex and Love Addicts Anonymous) meetings several times a week. After a 2-year period of treatment, they were referred for marital therapy.

Dan learned about family-of-origin factors that contributed to his addiction. Although he was the favored child, he was also expected to live up to incredibly high standards. From childhood and beyond, he never felt able to meet the high expectations of his parents. As an adult, the addictive behaviors temporarily distracted Dan from the pain of feeling like a failure. His sexual addiction had gradually escalated to the point that he was cross-addicted to pornography, women, and drugs by the time he entered treatment.

Initially, he attempted to blame his wife for not being sexual enough. She was able to help him realize that she almost never withheld sex and approached sex with passion. His continuing individual treatment, attendance in SLAA, and the conjoint sessions quickly moved the therapy to a different level. His spouse was helped to understand sexual addiction and we regarded the situation as a special type of infidelity. Both partners took responsibility for their unique contributions to the marital problems. Much of the work was centered on her denial of the obvious cues and her need to be viewed as the faultless partner. Dan worked on understanding the motives for his sexual behavior. His work now provided a window that Nancy had never before been able to penetrate. They began to understand each other as whole people for the first time.

Empty-Nest Affairs

According to Brown (1991b), the empty-nest affair is not simply an affair to fill up the purposelessness one feels after the departure of children from the family. It occurs most often in relationships that are emotionally barren from the inception, not only after the children have left. In part, the relationship is vulnerable because it is built on expectations rather than a genuine attachment. In the case of the male partner, a family is formed even if he is not in love with his mate. Thus, the level of emotional attachment appears to be strong as long as the children are present to replace what is missing in the marriage. Men, who according to Brown are more prone to this type of infidelity, are typically in their later years when the children have departed. Women, on the other hand, usually wait to embark on such affairs until the children are older but not necessarily out of the house. Empty-nest affairs tend to be very discreet and may last for many years. In fact, the affair becomes an integral part of the marriage; without it, the marriage could not thrive. Sometimes the affair ends only when one of the partners dies or if the spouse finds out. The affect of the couple is usually depressed, because they are attempting to revitalize a dead relationship. Thus, the prognosis for the marriage is poor.

One of our cases illustrates this type of infidelity. Harry entered individual therapy when he was 55. He had been a successful businessman for a number of years, retired early, and then entered public service. He was regarded as a model of success and integrity, and had a sterling reputation. After a few unfocused sessions of therapy, he admitted to his real problem: an affair for over 20 years with his former secretary. She was single and beginning to pressure him about marriage. Harry did not want to "go public" with a divorce, fearing that his affair partner would want to marry quickly and his reputation would be lost.

Harry was never interested in couple therapy, although he focused much of his concentration on relationship dissatisfaction. He reported that his marriage had been dead for many years and he saw no benefit in trying to revive it. One justification for having an affair was that his wife was a self-centered woman who was more interested in keeping her inheritance and using his wealth to live a lavish lifestyle than in embracing a positive relationship with Harry. This was a marriage of appearance, with little emotional substance. For as far back as he could remember, Harry did not recall loving his wife. Ironically, he married her because of her family name and wealth. The couple had two grown daughters who were not married or successful in careers. Harry had many reasons for not divorcing, such as saving face with his daughters and maintaining the pretense of a happily married man.

Out-the-Door Affairs

These affairs typically occur within the first 15 years of marriage, tend to be of longer duration (6 months to 2 years), and involve both genders in equal proportions. There is a high level of emotional involvement with the affair partner, and thus the affair often hastens an end to the marriage. The person having this affair unconsciously wants to leave the marriage without attempting to repair the preexisting problems. In fact, many are caught by their partners who are so hurt by the long-term betrayal that there is no chance for forgiveness or reconciliation. In essence, there is little desire to assume responsibility for the demise of the marriage (Brown, 1991b). The betrayed spouse typically enters therapy angry and remains angry. Affair partners often become the next marital partners, because they are better matched to the betraying spouses.

Henry and Marge, both 48, entered therapy ostensibly to work on their marital problems. Marge was psychologically and financially dependent on Henry, although he was emotionally detached from her. Furthermore, Henry was openly involved in an affair with a single woman. Marge hoped that, through treatment, the affair would cease and the marriage would return to "normal." She minimized the significance of the infidelity by declaring that Henry was suffering from a midlife crisis. Henry had no intention of stopping the affair, which had been going on for 3 years. Moreover, he had made it clear that if Marge were to leave the marriage he would almost certainly marry the affair partner. Essentially, Harry had been hoping that Marge would become so frustrated with the situation that *she* would end the marriage.

CHARNY'S TYPOLOGY

Charny (1992) offered a unique set of systemic concepts promoting a more comprehensive understanding of the marriage or primary partnership. He focused on the motivations for the infidelity and the distinctive relational dynamics that perpetuate it. Charny (1992) used unique terms for the unfaithful and betrayed partners (*affair-er* and *affair-ee*) to emphasize the interlocking roles of each spouse in the infidelity. This system, like all others in the literature, is based on clinical observation. Charny's (1992) typology consisted of 18 general types of affairs classified into 3 broad categories with 6 types within each.

In Types 1–6, there is a lack of commitment and emotional intimacy in the primary relationship; thus, it is not treated as exclusive or sacred. The affair-ee is exploited and viewed as an object to be used by the affair-er.

- *Type 1: Corruption, including sadism / masochism.* The affair-er, meeting his or her narcissistic needs through the affair, is unable to consider the primary partner's needs, and cannot be empathic. The affair is often enacted openly in an intentionally hurtful manner. Moreover, the acting out occurs when the partner is most in need of support. The affair-ee accepts this abusive behavior in order to avoid being alone or to preserve property and financial status.

- *Type 2: Superficiality and apathy.* In this presentation, there are a series of affairs for the purpose of sex and recreation. The relationship to the affair partner lacks depth and commitment. Both the affair-er and the affair-ee maintain a position that the affairs are of no real consequence. The affair-ee defends against being hurt, appears apathetic, or in some instances has a personality disorder.

- *Type 3: Escapism.* The primary motivation of the affair-er is to escape from the difficulties of the marriage rather than confronting the spouse. The affair-ee also avoids conflict by minimizing statements made by the spouse about the affair.

- *Type 4: A matter of no importance.* Sexual pleasure is the primary motivation for this type of infidelity. Both the affair-er and the affair-ee view sexuality as simply meeting a physiological need and depreciate the impact of the affair on the primary relationship.

- *Type 5: Search committee—falling in love to find a replacement spouse.* This affair is designed to end the marriage. The affair-er finds a new partner to replace the existing spouse, who is seen as being incapable of meeting the affair-er's needs. Unconsciously, the affair-ee colludes in the process by overlooking and thereby enabling the affair. Each wants the marriage to end, but neither can assume any responsibility.

- *Type 6: Falling in love to threaten spouse—if there is no change, we separate.* The affair-er is trying to precipitate a crisis in order to force change or to separate from the marital partner. The affair-ee allows the affair in order to fulfill the same motives.

In the following discussion, Types 7–12 exemplify commitment to the marriage but failed attempts to resolve differences. The affair is an attempt to fill the void within the marriage and thereby help it to continue.

- *Type 7: Falling in love to complete qualities missing in oneself.* The affair-er feels personally unfulfilled in the marriage, so he or she searches elsewhere. Sometimes such partners seek to prove their masculinity or femininity or to find in others what is missing in themselves. The affair-ees recognize that they cannot give their partners what is needed, and compensate by enabling the affairs.

- *Type 8: Enables continuation of the marriage, including settling the score for the other's infidelity.* The affair-er does not intend to end the marriage, but is compelled to turn the tables or reestablish equity for the spouse's affair. The affair-ee allows the infidelity to continue to preserve the marriage and maintain equity if his or her own affair is known.

- *Type 9: Challenge to improvement and recreation of the marriage.* The affair-er is attempting to create a crisis in the marriage that will produce change. Past protests have been ineffective; thus, the affair is designed as a wake-up call. The affair-ee also understands there will not be movement in the marriage unless there is a crisis.

- *Type 10: Renewal of excitement and adventure.* In these marriages, the sense of excitement and passion has diminished. The affair-er is attempting to import passion or excitement from an external source. The affair-ee also wants greater excitement and may vicariously enjoy the infidelity.

- *Type 11: Desire-daring-survival—a test of courage and power.* Affair-ers are trying to prove that they are capable of greater passion, possess more courage, and can survive *not* following the rules or what is proper. The motives of affair-ees are complex: They, too, want to test their ability to survive the thing they fear the most and their own reactions to being hurt and betrayed.

- *Type 12: Sexual excitement plus "safe" opportunity.* The affair-er is motivated to express sexual passion, but only under a condition perceived to be safe, such as brief physical affair. The affair-ee either accepts that passion can sometimes become unrestrained or proceeds in denial that it could or has occurred.

The third major class of affairs, Types 13–18, is motivated primarily by hedonism. This group is characterized by a lack of commitment to the sacred relationship bond. Typically, such couples are unable to tolerate or resolve the normal tensions that build in a relationship.

- *Type 13: Fun and variety, antiboredom, social contagion.* The affair-er and affair-ee assume that marriage is boring and lacking in variety. Thus, affairs are viewed as a necessary part of life. Such couples often believe that others have the same attitudes about marriage and infidelity.

- *Type 14: Release of nonmarital tensions.* Affair-ers are stressed by tensions at work or other nonrelational areas, and thus seek affairs as a distraction or release. Affair-ees feel inadequate to help their partners cope with their problems and thus collude with the infidelity.

- *Type 15: Hope at difficult moments.* This type of infidelity occurs when affair-ers feel vulnerable in a life-and-death situation. They may be responding to a death in the family or to a feeling of their own mortality resulting from age or illness. Affair-ees sense the pain of their affair-ers and feel inadequate to handle it.

- *Type 16: Freedom and independence.* The affair-er perceives marriage as restrictive or confining. Intimacy is viewed as smothering and resulting in a loss of freedom. The affair-ee also has similar fears. The infidelity allows the marital partners to maintain their independence and avoid intimacy.

- *Type 17: Open marriage.* The affair-er and affair-ee operate with an intimacy contract that allows outside intimate relationships. These couples usually agree to the circumstances and conditions of these affairs.

- *Type 18: Hedonism—an insistence on the pleasure principle.* The couple believes that the most important principle in life is the pursuit of pleasure. The intent is not to hurt the partner, but to fulfill hedonistic urges.

Charny (1992) promoted a systemic understanding of infidelity; however, this typology has a number of problems beyond being observational rather than empirical. Some of the types do not seem consistent with the headings. For example, "falling in love to threaten spouse" represents an affair that is exploitative, manipulative, and indifferent to the marriage. Our experience shows that this assumption is too global. In fact, this type of infidelity often forces a change in the spouse that could actually improve the marriage. In another section, Charny stated that affairs are generally enacted to replace missing parts of the self or the marriage. Moreover, he believed that the affair eventually recreates the marriage, weakness for weakness. We do not find this to be true of many affairs that we have treated.

A major supposition of Charny's (1992) typology is that the spouse is aware of the infidelity and either consciously or without realization colludes to facilitate it. This assumption is based on clinical observation and is supported by a small sampling of psychotherapists who participated in a study of extramarital affairs conducted by Charny and Parnass (1995). Although we tend to agree that in many affairs (discovered or undiscovered) the betrayed partners are consciously or unconsciously aware, we do not always see evidence of such conscious collusion.

LAWSON'S TYPOLOGY

Lawson (1988) specified three types of affairs in her book, *Adultery: An Analysis of Love and Betrayal.* A brief description follows.

- *Parallel*: The parallel affair is known and tacitly approved by the spouse. In some cases, both partners might be having affairs.
- *Traditional*: In the traditional affair, the partner is unaware that it is happening, would not approve of it, and views the infidelity as a violation of the marital agreement.
- *Recreational*: Recreational affairs are consensual and constitute a defining characteristic of "open marriages."

LEVINE'S TYPOLOGY

In the journal article *Extramarital Sexual Affairs*, Levine (1998) presented a typology with four classifications. These include the following.

- *Affairs*: This is a liaison that begins with an emotional attachment and develops into a sexual relationship.

- *Just sex*: Partners meet in order to have sex without the constraints of an emotional attachment.
- *Making do*: The "making-do" affair is actually an abortive relationship that never manages to take off. The partners are temporarily occupied until someone better appears. Levine (1998) noted that these relationships are sometimes referred to as "casual" or "convenient sex."
- *Imaginary partner sex*: The use of pictures, videotapes, strip shows, masturbation, phone sex, and the various forms of Internet sex constitutes imaginary sex. Levine's article was published in 1998, when this type of behavior was beginning to gain more recognition, especially with respect to the Internet-mediated affairs.

HUMPHREY'S TYPOLOGY

In the article *Treating Extramarital Sexual Relationships in Sex and Couples Therapy,* Humphrey (1987), offered another typology that embodies six criteria representing the fundamental issues in most affairs. These include:

- Duration of the affair.
- Degree of emotional involvement of the partners.
- Amount of sexual involvement.
- Secret or revealed affair.
- One or both partners having affairs.
- Sexual orientation of the affair partners.

In addition to the six more common causative factors, Humphrey (1987) also noted that unusual circumstances may be present in the etiologies, such as physical or mental health problems in the partner, periods of separation, and alternative lifestyles.

STREAN'S TYPOLOGY

The psychoanalytic view is represented in Strean's (1976, 1980) classification of affairs into four, broad categories. Each type is not necessarily mutually exclusive.

- *The Spouse as incestuous object*: In this category, the spouse is unconsciously experienced as the powerful parent who is nurturing, understanding, comforting, and so on. Unfortunately, sexual relations with the spouse are perceived to be incestuous and therefore forbidden. The extramarital partner is seen as a "love object" with whom sex can be enjoyable, as opposed to a parent.

- *Fighting the superego*: Another function that is projected onto the partner is that of the omnipotent conscience. The spouse looks to the partner for regulation of ethics, morals, and so on. Independence is acquired by rebelling against the powerful spouse through acts of infidelity. An interesting case involved Karen, who admired her husband, a respected attorney and prominent lay figure in his church. In fact, his moral superiority was a factor that caused her to be attracted to him. After 10 years of marriage, serious sexual problems, and three children, Karen felt smothered by her husband's omnipotence. She sought independence at age 40 through an affair with another man who was equally intelligent and powerful in his profession. Unfortunately, he had a reputation as a philanderer and managed to remain married although he periodically had affairs. Eventually, she divorced her husband, hoping to marry her affair partner.

- *Expression of bisexuality*: One facet of the bisexual sexual orientation is enacted through the marriage and the other through an affair. Furthermore, Strean (1976) believed that the individual with a bisexual orientation needs two partners, one who is seen as masculine and the other who is seen as feminine.

- *Defense against symbiosis*: Two dependent individuals cling to each other and need to view their experiences in the same way in order to validate their weak identities. They are extremely sensitive to criticism, and each seeks to be powerful and controlling of the other. The infidelity represents an escape from the symbiotic ties, victory over the other, and an attempt at autonomy.

A review of the popular literature reveals numerous texts about adultery, extramarital affairs, infidelity, and betrayals of committed relationships. Many of these offer typological approaches. We next discuss two of the more popular books.

LUSTERMAN'S TYPOLOGY

Lusterman (1995) viewed infidelity as a fundamental breach of the core component of the marital contract, fidelity. He used the term *infidelity* to convey this breach of faith. The person involved in the affair is seen as the *infidel* and the spouse / partner is considered the *victim*. These forceful terms are used in order to help the couple understand the traumatic effects of the infidelity on the relationship. More specifically, Lusterman brought into focus the discovery and resultant emotional turmoil subsequent to the violation of trust. In the book *Infidelity: A Survival Guide*, Lusterman (1998) offered a typology of eight components that deal primarily with the motivations for having affairs.

- *Midlife events*: The normative events of midlife—such as children leaving the home, death of a parent, or unemployment—may prove to be too taxing for the individual. The infidelity is an attempt to cope with or insulate oneself from acutely feeling these situational stressors. An example is Max and Stephanie, both in their mid-30s, who presented for marital therapy after the birth of their first child. Max became involved in an intense, romantic affair and attempted to leave the marriage in order to live with the affair partner. Fortunately, each spouse entered individual therapy and the couple attended joint sessions. Max was able to end the affair and examine the reasons that contributed to it. He recognized that the responsibility of parenting was overwhelming, and he feared he would act abusively, as his father had. Also, the relationship was extremely stressed by the couple's inability to work together effectively with the added responsibilities of childrearing.

- *Entitlement*: The "infidel" feels at liberty to have the affair due to personality predisposition, not getting one's needs met in the marriage, or a search for pleasure.

- *Sexual identity*: Heterosexual partners may not be sure of their sexual identity and decide to have a homosexual relationship to test their feelings.

- *Sexual addiction*: The partner is compelled to engage in compulsive sexual acts often escalating to a habitual pattern of acting out with others.

- *Exploratory affairs*: The unfaithful partner is in a primary relationship that is not working, and has not decided whether to stay or leave. The purpose of the affair is to help clarify this question.

- *Tripod affairs*: These affairs depict classic triangulation. The partners cannot tolerate too much intimacy, so they allow a third person into their relationship.

- *Retaliatory affairs*: One partner has an affair in order to strike back against the other partner having an affair. We have seen a couple in which the male partner punished his wife's flirtation by having sex with a prostitute while she was away from the home and then immediately confessing his indiscretion.

- *Exit affairs*: The partner having the affair has decided to leave the marriage.

PITTMAN'S TYPOLOGY

Pittman (1989) wrote of infidelity as a betrayal of trust in a monogamous relationship. Dishonesty and secretiveness characterize it. Any form of sexual dishonesty is viewed as disorienting and potentially destructive to the marriage. First, there is the assault of the infidelity. Next, a web of secrecy and lies is used to conceal the breach of the couple's intimacy agreement. In his text *Private Lies: Infidelities and the Betrayal of Intimacy*, Pittman (1989) presented a typology consisting of the following four categories.

- *The accidental encounter*: This is a one-time rendezvous that usually occurs while drinking, and / or with friends at a bachelor party, strip club, and massage parlor. Sometimes this type of infidelity occurs if one takes advantage of a "safe" opportunity of a proposition while away from home on a business or similar trip.

- *Habitual philandering*: A chronic or addictive pattern of having affairs is a way of life for some.

- *Romantic affairs*: These relationships are about the wish or need to experience the intense emotion of being "in love" in order to escape from life's difficulties. Laurence and Brit, both 35, were unhappily married for 7 years and had two children. In his job, Laurence often traveled for long periods of time. Brit felt abandoned, unappreciated, and angry with her spouse. Lawrence tolerated her dour moods and remained in the marriage although miserable. Both conceded that they did not like the other. He suspected that she was having an affair, and eventually she confessed, anticipating that the marriage would end. In marital therapy, they were able to examine the relational problems and life stressors that precipitated the infidelity. Today, they have constructed a new marital agreement and genuinely enjoy each other for the first time in their marriage.

- *Marital arrangements*: The partners implicitly collude in order to create distance and avoid the problems of the marriage. One or both partners may engage in affairs to accomplish this goal.

CONCLUSION

The typological approaches may help us to understand something about the motivations and the variety of presentations of infidelity. We have attempted to present some of the many theoretical approaches from systemic to psychoanalytic viewpoints. There is considerable overlap among the typologies we reviewed. However, each represents a unique and original approach. The clinician who has not seen a vast range of infidelity will find this information useful, yet the more experienced therapist might discover the typological approaches too confining, because the categories do not always capture the intricacies of affairs or other forms of infidelity. In fact, the category becomes the defining characteristic, often truncating the process of gaining a deeper understanding. We believe that typologies aid in the comprehension of infidelity and provide a considerable initial step in assessment and treatment.

2

❀ ❀ ❀

Empirical Perspectives on Infidelity with Treatment Implications

THE RESEARCH LED BY KINSEY INITIATED AN ERA of scientific attention to sexual behavior (Kinsey et al., 1948, 1953). In the decades that followed, numerous surveys and other studies examined various aspects of sexuality, often using convenience samples. Researchers collected a substantial amount of information about the incidence, prevalence, and correlates of infidelity through these studies. Interestingly, the recorded prevalence of infidelity has varied somewhat throughout the years and it is believed to be underreported for reasons related to study design, statistical analysis, and other social and experimental variables (see Christopher & Sprecher, 2000; Drigotas & Barta, 2001; Thompson, 1983; Wiederman, 1997). Nonetheless, an estimated 26%–50% of men and 21%–38% of women have engaged in EMS or other forms of infidelity at some point in their lifetimes (Choi et al., 1994).

We reviewed the existing body of literature that identifies many risk factors or conditions commonly associated with infidelity, and selected the issues that have relevance to clinical practice. Some of these include marital satisfaction, sexual permissiveness, type of involvement with the affair partner, justifications, marital equity, social and cultural norms, courtship attitudes and behaviors, biological factors, and the relationship to the affair partner. We were particularly interested in gender differences with respect to the risk factors associated with infidelity. Our practices are filled with examples of relational unhappiness that triggered or resulted from affairs and other forms of infidelity. The existing data assist us to better understanding infidelity and better tailoring treatments to meet the needs of each couple.

CORRELATES OF INFIDELITY

Women and Infidelity

Historically, articles and books about infidelity have focused on extramarital affairs. Also, they have blended the experiences of men and women together or they have had a stronger focus on the male perspective. Researchers are now beginning to unravel the puzzle about how men and women view affairs differently, often focusing on the viewpoint of the woman. One of the earliest and most comprehensive efforts of this type was a study published by Atwater (1979). This study included 40 women—representing a wide range of educational, occupational, and socioeconomic backgrounds—who had experienced EMS. The semi-structured interview format was used to facilitate a detailed subjective account of the extramarital experiences of these women. In Atwater's (1979) study of women's first EMS experience, the following factors were associated with deciding to have an affair:

- Eighty percent of the women had sex with their husbands before marriage, and 50% of these had additional premarital sexual experiences with other men. In other words, these women had decided not to conform to the socially sanctioned norm of remaining virgins before marriage.

- Ninety-five percent of the women stated that they had no conscious intent of having an affair at the start of their marriages. The male affair partner usually initiated the first affair. Only 7 of the 40 women in the study originated the sexual interaction.

- About half the subjects knew another woman who had had an affair; sometimes, that woman was their mother. Merely knowing another woman who had an affair seemed to have a permission-giving effect. Whether the experience of the other woman was positive or negative apparently made no difference.

- The women usually talked to someone, frequently a friend or coworker, before having the affair. One fourth of the women also reported having conversations with their spouses in some general or hypothetical way, to test their husband's reactions.

- These women contemplated the affair and did not react impulsively. The modal time to reflect on the infidelity was 1 month.

Next, Atwater (1979) examined motivations for infidelity. Half the women reported being "emotionally involved" with a male friend before he became a lover. The friendship became a risk factor, which increased the likelihood of an emotional attachment and ultimately EMS. The theme of emotional involvement is often a component of the affair process for women (Glass & Wright, 1985; Humphrey, 1987). Interestingly, only a few of the women who were emotionally attached reported being in love with their affair partner.

Another motivational element involved an exquisite combination of two factors—the right person at the right time of life. Life situations such as an unhappy marriage, the need for personal growth, a quest for greater knowledge, or the desire for sex created vulnerability in these women.

The last area studied by Atwater (1979) was the women's reactions after the affair. In almost every case, the reaction was positive, ranging from enjoyment to extreme pleasure. Moreover, the women believed they had learned something about themselves that increased their self-identity. Three fourths of the women justified the infidelity by emphasizing their need for self-fulfillment. Although these women assumed responsibility for their actions, they apparently rejected the anticipated societal sanctions against infidelity, especially for women. A minority of the subjects reported negative feelings such as guilt and anxiety after their first affair.

Finally, Atwater (1979) found that the experience of having one affair predisposed the women to have subsequent infidelity. Sixty-three percent of Atwater's subjects had more than one affair; (20 women had 2–6 affairs; 5 women had 11–30 affairs). The modal length of the affair was 1 year, with a range of 10 months to 17 years. Half the women also reported that at some time they had been simultaneously involved with two men in addition to their husbands. Finally, 84% of the women intended to have future affairs.

The Atwater (1979) investigation provided a comprehensive view of women's infidelity and demonstrated that cultural norms did not hold up for women choosing to have an affair. These women sometimes were driven to infidelity by unhappy or unfulfilling marriages and / or were attracted by the thrill of the personal growth that resulted from an affair. In fact, this study illustrated how strongly women tended to integrate emotional involvement with sexual fulfillment. Furthermore, once the women experienced this form of excitement and growth, they were attracted to future affairs.

Larry and Barbara, both in their mid-30s, requested marital counseling after Larry discovered Barbara had been having a 6-month affair with a man who was physically and psychologically different from him. Larry and Barbara had been dissatisfied for long periods during their 10-year marriage. Barbara's perspective on the infidelity confirmed much of Atwater's (1979) research, because her motivations included the need for greater intimacy, an emotional connection, sexual fulfillment and growth, and a quest for knowledge about her own experience as a woman. She was able to terminate the affair in time to address in conjoint sessions many of her and Larry's relationship problems. In addition, Barbara used individual sessions to examine her motivations for having an affair. Even though it had been extremely positive personally, she was not interested in repeating the affair experience because she recognized the detrimental effect on the marriage.

The Atwater (1979) study did not investigate a woman's decision to end an affair. Hurlbert (1992) examined some of the personal factors associated with the termination of an affair. His sample consisted of 60 young women (the mean age was 28) who had been married about 4 years. He divided the affairs into two types—emotional and sexual.

The best predictor of the duration of an affair was the woman's sexual attitude. Those women with more positive attitudes toward sex had longer affairs, especially for the sexual type. In addition, Hurlbert (1992) suggested that the influence of sexual attitudes might be more powerful early in the relationship. At the extreme statistical ranges of the sexual affair group, 16 of the women maintained the infidelity for at least a year whereas 7 reported that they stopped the affair immediately. Hurlbert (1992) speculated that these 7 women might have had less positive attitudes about sex or might not easily have tolerated a sexual relationship outside of marriage. The author commented that women who continued their affairs possibly became emotionally attached to their affair partners after the initial period of sexual enjoyment, making it difficult to end the affair.

Another factor that proved important was the length of time the affair partner was known before the woman crossed the line from friendship to affair. The longer the woman had known the man, the longer the affair tended to continue. Given the ages of the women, some of the men clearly were known before the marriage and may have been past lovers.

Unfortunately, Hurlbert (1992) did not include older women. Other researchers have noted that women in their 60s were least likely of any age group to have affairs (Wiederman, 1997). When infidelity occurs in older women, it is usually associated with marital dissatisfaction (Glass & Wright, 1977). Little is known about the distribution of emotional versus sexual affairs, the duration of these affairs, and the reasons why older women terminate them.

Marital Satisfaction and Infidelity

Glass and Wright (1977) investigated the relationship between infidelity and marital satisfaction in a large study that reexamined previous research findings by Athanasiou and colleagues (1970). The authors noted gender differences. In general, EMS was considered the criterion for infidelity. It was clearly associated with lower marital satisfaction in men and women. Moreover, contentment decreased with the duration of marriage for all respondents but one. Men who had experienced EMS reportedly were dissatisfied early in the marriage and remained so throughout the duration. In addition, having an affair was generally correlated with divorce for the men in this study.

Of the women who had experienced EMS, those in older marriages were most dissatisfied when compared to all other respondents, male or female. In fact, the later in marriage a woman first had an affair, the lower her marital satisfaction was inclined to be. Clearly, in this group of older women, marital unhappiness was a justification for having an affair. However, these women were not likely to divorce their husbands. The authors suspected that many women remained in unhappy marriages for reasons of financial security and social status while satisfying their emotional needs through affairs. Perhaps these women were more committed to remaining in the marriage than younger wives were because of the length of time they had invested in their unions. Conversely, women experiencing EMS in younger marriages did not complain of dissatisfaction. Although it seems counterintuitive that more fulfilled women would have more affairs, the authors suspected that the affairs were more often of a purely sexual nature and did not result from dissatisfaction. However, considering the high divorce rate in this group, it could be surmised that the younger wives divorced if they were unhappy.

Glass and Wright (1977) noted the high percentage of male EMS beginning within the first 5 years of marriage, and speculated that this might be related to the pressures of work, parenthood, and the attention that the wife gives to the children. The incidence of affairs among wives in their late 30s and early 40s might be associated with loneliness stemming from children leaving home. As women continue to enter the work force and the gender gap narrows, however, their affairs might increasingly be motivated by risk factors more commonly associated with male EMS.

In a later study, Glass and Wright (1985) investigated marital satisfaction in men and women who had affairs. They found that, in general, women who had affairs were more dissatisfied with their marriages than men who had affairs were. These women apparently were motivated to seek a greater level of emotional involvement than they experienced with their husbands. Sexual factors rather than marital dissatisfaction motivated the men who had affairs.

In an effort to organize the developing body of research on infidelity, Thompson (1983) reviewed 12 different surveys. Some of his findings are pertinent to our discussion, although they do not necessarily discriminate between genders. First, marital and sexual dissatisfaction were most strongly related to EMS, particularly when combined with other negative factors such as feeling isolated in the marriage. Second, a group of characteristics called "personal readiness factors" also covaried with the incidence of EMS. Some of these factors included the need for emotional independence, a sense of alienation, perceived opportunity for involvement, knowing someone who has engaged in EMS, and perceiving sexual activity as separate from love.

Overall, however, it is difficult to understand exactly how each of the previously mentioned variables relates to EMS. For example, does personal readiness actually promote EMS? Does it lead to another variable, or does EMS lead to the variable? Nonetheless, the reader can begin to see a relationship between certain conditions and the likelihood of having an affair, although the direction of the relationship is not always clear.

Thompson found that there were significant gender differences in attitudes as well as occurrences of infidelity among the respondents. However, these differences varied from study to study. For instance, in one investigation, employment status influenced EMS behavior for wives but not husbands. In another study, financial status was related to EMS behavior for men but not women. Although Thompson noted the contradictions between the genders with respect to some of the variables in the surveys, there was no "convergence of results" (1983, p. 13).

Sexual Permissiveness and Infidelity

On an attitudinal level, most people claim disapproval of infidelity, yet empirical studies have shown that denunciation of such behavior does not serve to reduce its incidence. For instance, a permissive attitude toward infidelity has emerged as an important covariate in much of the research (Glass & Wright, 1992; Singh, Walton, & Williams, 1976; Thompson, 1983; Treas & Giesen, 2000). Moreover, men gave more approval for affairs than women did. In general, permissive attitudes toward EMS are more likely to occur in liberally minded, sexually permissive individuals with low religiosity, premarital sexual experience, and premarital sexual permissiveness (Christopher & Sprecher, 2000; Thompson, 1983). Also, according to Smith (1994), living in a big city, being male, being African American, and having more education are covariates of EMS.

Saunders and Edwards (1984) examined the relationship between sexual permissiveness and EMS and found some interesting gender differences. They developed a model that expanded on the Reiss, Anderson, and Sponaugle (1980) multivariate model of extramarital permissiveness. The most important findings of this study suggested that permissive attitudes toward EMS are significantly affected by the following four factors:

1. "Diffuse intimacy conception"—the degree to which individuals focus the satisfaction of intimacy needs on only their mates—was the strongest predictor for extramarital permissiveness for men and women in this study. Male and female partners who were inclined to share personal and private information with persons other than their spouses tended to be more permissive in their attitudes toward EMS. Women in this group were more likely to have an affair.

2. "Comparison level of alternatives" refers to the process of comparing one's marriage to other available relationships. If the marriage was perceived as better than other alternatives, the probability of EMS was low. The comparison level of alternatives was a strong predictor of attitudes among women but a much weaker one for men.

3. "Autonomy of heterosexual interactions" is the sense of freedom from social constraints or the ability to govern the self with respect to heterosexual interactions. This factor was more strongly related to permissive attitudes toward EMS in men alone.

4. Marital satisfaction is defined in the Saunders and Edwards (1984) study as a "function of comparison between one's marital expectations and one's marital outcome" (Lenthall, 1977). The degree of perceived satisfaction with one's marriage influenced permissive attitudes toward EMS more strongly for the men than the women in this study.

The marriage of Davis and Beth reflects some of the conditions identified by Saunders and Edwards (1984). Before returning to work 2 years ago, Beth had been the primary caretaker of their two children, an arrangement the couple had agreed on early in their 15-year marriage. During her "confinement" at home, Beth reported feeling extremely unhappy due to limited interactions with her peers. She believed that returning to work provided opportunities for intellectual stimulation and socialization. Recently, Beth often compared her marriage to other couples' relationships and concluded that she would be happier with almost anyone other than Davis. She reported feeling resentful that Davis was unable to meet her emotional needs and complained of increasing marital dissatisfaction because of personal differences.

The couple entered therapy at Davis's insistence, because he discovered Beth having an emotional relationship with a colleague that had progressed to EMS. Beth and Davis had had a mutually satisfying sexual relationship until 3 months prior. Davis reported feeling alienated from Beth and, in fact, her affair partner had been Beth's main confidante for the previous 8 months. Davis did not know how to correct the situation and felt helpless to alter the course of their marriage. This couple continues in ongoing concurrent marital therapy with mixed results, as she is uncertain about remaining in the marriage.

Type of Infidelity

Glass and Wright (1985) explored the kind of involvement (emotional vs. sexual) that occurred in extramarital affairs, the amount of such involvement, and the differences between men and women with respect to these parameters. Roughly 300 White, middle-class participants (153 women and 148 men) volunteered to complete Glass and Wright's questionnaire. The authors speculated and found that men and women approached affairs in ways that paralleled gender role expectations.

On a continuum from sexual to emotional involvement, male infidelity was likely to be characterized as more sexual and less emotional. Women reported emotional motivations for infidelity. If the extramarital relationship endured, it often progressed to encompass both emotional and sexual components. It appeared that the men and women proceeded through different phases as they approached a combined-type extramarital affair. Men often began with sex and advanced to emotion, and women did the opposite. The authors suggested "that men and women follow different codes in behavior or paths in the development of extramarital relationships, and that these paths or codes reflect sex roles in our culture" (Glass & Wright, 1985, p. 1118). Furthermore, men and women who were involved both emotionally and sexually in an affair experienced the greatest degree of marital dissatisfaction when compared to those whose involvement was primarily emotional or sexual. Emotional involvement with the affair partner served as a predictor of marital dissatisfaction for both sexes, but only after accounting for sexual involvement.

The study also proposed that men did not necessarily view extramarital relationships as representative of an unhappy marriage, particularly if the affair was strictly sexual. In fact, 56% of men who experienced extramarital sexual intercourse reported happy marriages, compared with only 34% of the women. For women, marital dissatisfaction was significantly related to the degree of emotional attachment to their affair partners. For men, extramarital relationships appeared more closely "associated with their attitudes, beliefs, and values than with their marital dissatisfaction" (Glass & Wright, 1985, p. 1115).

Justifications for Infidelity

Glass and Wright (1992) investigated the justifications for having an extramarital affair and the gender differences in the justifications offered. The volunteer sample was composed of 148 male and 155 female subjects who completed a questionnaire. Respondents were White, highly educated, mostly professional, and similar in religious beliefs; thus, the results are not largely generalizable. At least 25% of women and 44% of men in this study had had one or more extramarital affairs.

Both men and women who had experienced an extramarital affair were more likely to use justifications than were those who had never been involved. The most commonly used justifications were sexual gratification, romantic love, and emotional intimacy. Women used love as a justification more than men did. As expected, men offered sex as the primary justification for having an affair, a finding also noted by Humphrey (1987). Women were most approving of love justifications, next approving of emotional justifications, and least approving of sexual justifications. Men did not differ in their approval levels of the justification factors.

Men and women in the study used a sexual justification more often when involved in sexual rather than emotional types of affairs. However, the love justification was associated more with emotional than sexual involvement for men. Women commonly used love to justify their involvement in both sexual and emotional types of affairs.

There was no gender difference in the use of emotional intimacy as a justification for having an affair, and this justification was cited less often. However, the authors suggested that the likelihood of an actual affair was greater for subjects who approved of emotional intimacy in opposite-gender friendships, and viewed "falling in love" as a valid reason for an extramarital relationship.

A Dutch study by Van den Eijnden, Regina, Buunk, and Bosveld (2000) shed light on the relationship between justifying having an affair and actually engaging in one. A sample of almost 400 Dutch participants might not reflect the American experience, yet it is interesting to note two findings with respect to justification and gender. Men who had engaged in affairs (or unsafe sex) estimated that a higher percentage of others engaged in the same behavior than did men who had not engaged in these behaviors. The former group saw themselves as similar to those in the same situation and perhaps projected their own acceptance of this practice onto other men. Conversely, women who had affairs perceived themselves as relatively unique in comparison to faithful women and men who engaged in extramarital behavior. The researchers offered two possible explanations. First, they speculated that the women took greater responsibility for their behavior or saw it as internally motivated. Second, the women's self-perceptions may have reflected a double standard that sanctions marital fidelity for women.

An individual therapist referred a female client for conjoint therapy. The couple had been married for 10 years and had a 6-year-old son. They were in crisis because Joan had been discovered having an affair. She vehemently denied the infidelity until her husband produced irrefutable evidence. She then admitted to having an affair but insisted that it had ended. She offered a number of justifications for her affair. She stated that she was "in love" with her affair partner. Furthermore, she deserved to be happy because her husband, Tom, had "ignored" her intimacy needs over the years. In some very emotional interchanges, Joan stated that she was entitled to "fill the voids" in the marriage with another relationship. Tom suspected that the affair had not ended and again discovered that his suspicions were correct. Joan continued to be absorbed emotionally and physically with her affair partner, offering numerous justifications for her actions. The couple's marital therapist referred her back to her individual therapist until she could decide to work on or end the marriage. Tom filed for divorce.

Marital Equity and Infidelity

Evaluating fairness in marital relationships is a completely subjective phenomenon. Individuals usually do not agree on the parameters that define equity or the relevance of these factors to the relationship. Even objective observers will have subjective opinions as to the level of impartiality in a given relationship. We have learned from equity theory that partners who perceive their relationships as unfair become distressed, whether they are the one getting too much (overbenefiting) or too little (underbenefiting) gain. The more inequitable the relationship, the more distressed the person feels. The only way to reduce or eliminate this distress is to try to reinstate equilibrium to the relationship. If balance cannot be restored psychologically or physically, the individual will attempt to exit the relationship. Equity theory has been a useful framework for understanding contractual relationships such as exploiter–victim, philanthropist–recipient, employer–employee, or husband–wife.

Walster, Traupmann, and Walster (1978) hypothesized that infidelity might be an "equity restoring mechanism." They presumed this was true of those overbenefiting as well as underbenefiting from the marriage. For example, the more deprived a partner feels in marriage, the more likely he or she is to seek equity in other, supplementary relationships, at times engaging EMS. Theoretically, the underbenefited partner resents contributing far more to the marriage and may feel there is not much to be lost if the spouse discovers the infidelity and, consequently, seeks divorce.

As expected, Walster and colleagues (1978) found the highest incidence of affairs among partners who felt deprived in the marriage. In addition, the underbenefited group began their extramarital activities earlier than did those in the equitable or overbenefited groups. An interesting finding occurred in spouses who viewed their relationships as equitable: They had a slightly greater percentage of extramarital affairs than did the over-benefited group. The authors controlled for two possible variables—age of the respondent and length of the relationship—and found each to have an insignificant impact on the results.

Prins, Buunk, and Van Yperen (1993) also examined the relationship between perceived equity and infidelity; they considered factors such as social disapproval and marital satisfaction. The subjects were respondents who completed a questionnaire, using Buunk and Van Yperen's (1989, 1991) sample. Of the 80 couples in this study, neither partner in 47 couples had engaged in an extramarital affair; in 20 couples, one of the partners had had an extramarital affair; and in 13 of the couples, both partners had engaged in affairs.

The desire to have an affair was found less often in the equitable rela-tionships compared to those who felt either overbenefited or underbenefited in the marriage. Furthermore, normative approval of infidelity appeared to be the most significant covariate to affect the desire for and participation in extramarital relationships, independent of those of dissatisfaction and ineq-uity (Prins et al., 1993)

Overall, men in the study reported a higher degree of relationship satis-faction than women did. However, they expressed a stronger desire than women did to have an affair. The desire for EMS was related to dissatisfac-tion within the marriage as well as to moral approval of such behavior for men in the study. Although the men felt more overbenefited in their mar-riages than women did, feelings of equity or inequity appeared to have little to no effect on their desire for EMS.

The women in this study felt more underbenefited in their marriages than the men did. Nonetheless, women's feelings of inequity—whether from under- or overbenefiting—were related to actual extramarital involvement, not the mere desire for it. In addition, feelings of dissatisfaction in their marriages (including sexual aspects) and moral approval of extramarital relationships strongly correlated with actual EMS. For women, the desire for EMS was related to the perceived level of relationship satisfaction, sexual satisfaction, and norms toward extramarital sex. Additionally, women who expected direct reciprocity in their marriages were more inclined to engage in EMS.

Social Norms and Infidelity

Buunk and Bakker (1995) investigated some of the social factors that could predispose an individual to be unfaithful. The authors considered variables such as attitudes toward infidelity, past nonmonogamous behaviors, and perceptions of others' beliefs and behaviors regarding infidelity. In this study, an affair was defined as a sexual relationship outside of the primary monogamous relationship or extradyadic sex (EDS). The study was conducted once, then 15 years later, using 250 White Dutch citizens (125 men and 125 women) each time. There were more cohabitating unmarried couples in the second round. A substantial number of the participants had experienced EDS. We use the acronyms *EDS* and *EMS* (extramarital sex) to distinguish unmarried from married cohorts.

The main gender difference found in the Buunk and Bakker (1995) study was that men were more willing to engage in EDS than women were. In the first study, this gender difference was significant and independent of other factors that could influence an individual to have an affair. In the second study, the gender difference endured but was more dependent on other elements that might inspire an individual to engage in EDS, such as relationship status and attitudes toward EDS. Those who cohabitated rather than married were somewhat more inclined to have affairs; this finding is consistent throughout the empirical literature (Forste & Tanfer, 1996; Treas & Giesen, 2000). Individuals who felt that, given the opportunity, they could have an affair often perceived social approval for it. They also assumed that others had also engaged in EDS, a clear projection of their intentions on others. Those who had a positive attitude toward EDS and had been involved in such behavior in the past were more willing to engage in an affair. Age did not contribute significantly in either study.

Culture, Race, Ethnicity, and Infidelity

Our review of the empirical literature on infidelity did not reveal very much information about race, culture, and ethnicity. In fact, we found no texts and few journal articles that examined these correlates directly. The scant available information was often a by-product of larger studies and surveys of sexual attitudes and behaviors. Therefore, it is essential that the therapist learn as much as possible from the couple about these issues to avoid stereotypical assumptions.

Wiederman (1997) reviewed the General Social Survey, conducted in 1994, which collected data from over 2,000 Americans, at least 18 years of age, who had been or were currently married. Although this large-scale study did not focus exclusively on infidelity, Wiederman (1997) noted a higher incidence of EMS in the preceding year among African American men and women than among White men and women. However, according to this study, the lifetime incidence of EMS was the same for Black and White respondents.

Treas and Giesen (2000) examined sexual infidelity among married and cohabiting Americans. They used a multivariate model to analyze the findings of the 1992 National Health and Social Life Survey about sexual attitudes and behavior in the United States. The survey included over 3,000 male and female respondents between the ages of 18 and 59. Regarding race, the survey indicated that African American men were considerably more likely to engage in EMS when compared to African American women or White men or women.

Choi and colleagues (1994) used the data from a subset of 2,350 married respondents between the ages of 18 and 49 from the National AIDS Behavioral Survey to examine the social distribution of infidelity. They assessed three groups—Whites, African Americans, and Hispanics—and noted that correlates of EMS differed by race and ethnicity. In all three groups, a stronger belief in monogamy was associated with less EMS. African American men and women had higher rates of EMS during the preceding year than White men or women had, a finding consistent with that of Wiederman (1997). Among African Americans and Hispanics, EMS occurred more frequently in men than in women. The gender differences in the two groups might reflect a greater adherence to traditional sex roles that promote sexual freedom for men and virginity and fidelity for women (Choi et al., 1994; Penn, Hernandez, & Bermudez, 1997).

Attending church was correlated with lower levels of EMS for Hispanic men and African Americans but not for Whites. In terms of indices of sexual satisfaction, African Americans experiencing sexual problems and Hispanics with sexual communication dissatisfaction were more likely to have affairs than were Whites with similar complaints (Choi et al., 1994).

Penn and colleagues (1997) provided a framework to assist the therapist in understanding the diverse meanings of infidelity for clients of different cultures, religions, and ethnic backgrounds. Although generalizations may be helpful, it is important to remember that the amount of acculturation and the stage of ethnic identity development may affect an individual's behavior. For Hispanic Americans, the authors suggested several factors that are related to infidelity. Gender roles are one such factor. The cultural expectation is that men are dominant, whereas women are submissive. Another factor, family loyalty, is emphasized in the Hispanic culture. Thus, the child, rather than the couple, is the focal point of the marriage. In addition, although fidelity is hoped for at the time of marriage, it is almost expected that the man will, at some point, be unfaithful.

Penn and colleagues offered four main factors that contribute to infidelity among African Americans: history of slavery, present and past discrimination, uneven ratio of men to women, and chronic financial and relational stress. First, the very essence of slavery attempted to "destroy the kinship bonds and the cultural system of African Americans" (1997, p. 173). Slaves

were not allowed to marry, family members were sold to various slave owners, and men and women were sexually abused (men as breeders and women
as sexual objects for their owners). The authors stated, "spousal love and
commitment were not allowed to develop properly among the slaves. This
shaky foundation created by slavery is what African Americans attempt to
build monogamous relationships on today" (1997, p. 173). Second, because
of discrimination in the workplace and increased employment opportunities
for women, African Americans have been forced to be flexible in their roles,
leading to role confusion. Some men find it impossible to adequately support
their families and thus feel "forced to leave their household to ensure that
their family will receive government assistance and medical benefits" (1997,
p. 174). Third, the number of African American women far exceeds that of
the men due to high infant mortality, substance abuse, hazardous jobs, poor
health care, incarceration, military service, and homicide. Fourth, chronic
financial and relational stresses contribute to conflict and instability in marriage and other relationships.

Penn and colleagues (1997) also discussed the cultural values of Asian
Americans regarding marriage and EMS. First, each partner's family still
heavily influences the selection of a spouse. The main purpose of marriage
is to carry on the husband's family line. The wife's status is lower than her
husband's. Because of this unequal status, the blame for infidelity is placed
either on the wife for not being available enough or on the affair partner for
drawing the husband away from his family. If the wife is the unfaithful
spouse, she brings shame to her family. According to Penn and colleagues
(1997), shame plays such a large role that this belief is thought to actually
help to substantially limit the occurrence of affairs. Naturally, the degree
that these suggestions hold true for Asian Americans largely depends on their
level of acculturation.

Courtship and Infidelity

The present review of gender differences and EMS would be incomplete
without discussion of premarital or dating relationships. Typically, casual or
early dating is not defined in terms of relational or sexual monogamy. It is
commonly assumed that each couple decides when sexual exclusivity defines
the courtship relationship. Three studies addressed this particular issue; all
used college students as participants.

Hansen (1987) investigated EDS during courtship among college students
reportedly in committed relationships. The sample consisted of 215 students
(93 men and 122 women) who voluntarily completed anonymous question-
naires measuring extradyadic relations, religiosity, sexual attitudes, extra-

dyadic permissiveness, gender-role orientation, and years dating. The subjects were an average of 20.8 years old, predominantly White, and 85.6% had never been married.

For this sample, social approval of EDS was not evident for either gender despite the prevalence of the behavior. During courtship, 70.9% of men and 57.4% of women engaged in EDS while in committed relationships. In terms of attitudes toward EDS, the men were more permissive than women were. Two conditions were related to the incidence of EDS in men: years of dating and permissive attitudes toward affairs. For women, EDS was positively related to liberal sexual attitudes and nontraditional gender-role orientation. Hansen (1987) suggested that perhaps the reason permissive attitudes toward EDS were not as prevalent for women may be because women are still operating according to a sexual script that includes passivity, particularly in the extradyadic area. If men are taking the lead in initiating their extra-dyadic relations and women are relatively passive in theirs, it is not surprising that attitudinal variables like permissiveness are less predictive of female than of male extradyadic relations. Extradyadic relations during courtship may be something that happens to women rather than something they consciously initiate.

In a series of two tightly controlled experiments, Seal, Agostinelli, and Hannett (1994) investigated romantic and sexual behavior outside of the exclusive dating relationship. They found that EDS was pervasive among unmarried dating couples despite the disapproval of this practice. The subjects consisted of undergraduate college students (32 males and 24 females) who were single, noncohabiting heterosexuals in exclusive dating relationships. The ethnic background of the subjects was predominantly White and Hispanic.

Two factors—"sociosexuality" and gender—were isolated. *Sociosexuality* refers to the individual's willingness to engage in uncommitted sexual relations (Simpson & Gangestad, 1992). Specifically, Seal and colleagues focused on the individual's willingness to "disregard relational boundaries" that would serve to inhibit extradyadic affairs (1984, p. 2).

Relative to restricted individuals, sociosexually unrestricted individuals, were more willing to pursue extradyadic relationships despite being involved in monogamous dating relationships. It was also found that relationships of increasing duration only had an inhibitory effect on restricted individuals' willingness to enter into extradyadic relationships, and had little to no effect on unrestricted individuals' willingness. Seal and associates concluded that the unrestricted individuals were less concerned with issues of faithfulness and loyalty. In the sociosexually restricted group, individuals waited longer before engaging in sexual intimacy, and were more inhibited by the loyalty boundaries of the exclusive relationship.

With respect to gender differences, men reported greater willingness than women did in pursuing extradyadic relationships. This finding was in harmony with traditional gender scripts for romantic behavior that depict men as the primary initiators (McCormick, Brannigan, & LaPlante, 1984; Rose & Frieze, 1989).

Another finding revealed that men and unrestricted individuals were more willing to engage in physically intimate extradyadic behavior on a hypothetical first date. Further analyses revealed that as dating relationships increased in length, women and sociosexually restricted individuals became increasingly less willing to engage in physically intimate EDS behavior. The length of the relationship did not necessarily correspond to the level of commitment. However, an increased level of commitment inhibited one's willingness to engage in extradyadic relationships.

In general, the empirical research has consistently demonstrated the disparity between the occurrence of infidelity and the social disapproval of this practice (Singh et al., 1976). Sheppard, Nelson, and Andreoli-Mathie (1995) conducted a study focusing on the relationship between dating attitudes and EDS, including the gender differences that might exist. Fifty male and 147 female college students recorded their opinions about scenarios depicting varying degrees of emotional and sexual infidelity.

As expected, men tended to rate infidelity in dating and marriage relationships as more acceptable than women did. Additionally, men who engaged in EDS tended to be involved in the more physical aspects of infidelity, whereas women were more likely to be emotionally unfaithful. The participants rated committed dating infidelity as significantly more acceptable than marital infidelity. In dating or marital relationships, the most acceptable form of infidelity was emotional. This raises the issue of how infidelity is defined and how this definition might be different for men and women. This group of students most strongly disapproved of infidelity for purely sexual purposes without an emotional involvement.

Singh and colleagues also found a relationship between low self-esteem and dating infidelity. Self-esteem scores were significantly higher in the group who did not have EDS. The authors speculated that low self-esteem might motivate an individual to engage in EDS in order to enhance a sense of self-worth. The implications for counseling are obvious. The therapist must understand the motivations for having an affair before being able to assist the person in changing behavior.

Cohabitation and Infidelity

In addition to the single college student cohort, researchers have examined unmarried cohabiting couples in committed relationships with respect to infidelity. As a group, cohabitating couples are less conventional than married couples in their family values (Clarkberg, Stolzenberg, & Waite, 1995). Also, they are described as having a lower level of commitment to the relationship because they are less likely to have children, buy a home together, or legalize their union (Bumpass, Sweet & Cherlin, 1991; Treas & Giesen, 2000).

Christopher and Sprecher (2000) reviewed the empirical literature of the preceding last decade on sexuality in marriage, dating, and cohabitating relationships. They concluded that the incidence of EDS is higher in cohabitating couples than in married couples. Forste and Tanfer (1996), using a national sample of women between 20 and 27 years of age, also found a higher incidence of EDS in cohabitating couples. Treas and Giesen (2000), using data from the National Health and Social Life Survey of over 3,000 Americans, found that cohabatitors were slightly less likely than married couples to expect sexual exclusivity in their relationships. Other investigators (Dolcini et al., 1993; Laumann et al., 1994) have reported similar results. Because the level of commitment to the relationship is lower for the cohabitating couple, the costs of exiting the relationship are not as great as for the married couple (Dolcini et al., 1993). Thus, based on the available information to date, cohabitating couples are at a greater risk for infidelity, and this factor should be considered and explored with the couple in treatment.

Biological Factors and Infidelity

An interesting study addressed the connection between biology and behavior. Booth and Dabbs (1993) wondered if the body of research about testosterone levels and behavior (aggression, antisocial acts, sensation seeking) could be examined within the context of marriage. They investigated the relationship between testosterone levels and the choice to marry, marital happiness, and duration of marriage. Thousands of former servicemen were interviewed and examined in 1985 and 1986 as part of a study regarding the effects of service in Vietnam on mental and physical health. The participants were representative of the U.S. population in race and education. Testosterone levels were measured using one single serum sample taken in the early morning.

The findings revealed a consistent negative relationship between testosterone levels in men and indices of marital success, satisfaction, and stability. Men with higher levels of testosterone were less likely to marry and more likely to have experienced a divorce at some time in their lives. Moreover, these men were inclined to have hit or thrown things at their spouses and spent time apart from their wives because they were not getting along. As expected, infidelity was correlated with testosterone levels in men, with the most affairs occurring in the high-range group. Men with mid-range levels of testosterone reported lower marital success, and men with the lowest levels of testosterone were most successful in the marital indices measured.

This exploratory study underscores the need to include biological variables in the assessment of infidelity; however, it illustrates that isolating a single biological factor can lead to overgeneralizations and undue concern about men as marriage partners. Reports from spouses would be helpful in explaining the results within an intimate relational context. In addition, the effects of habituation (boredom) and other individual variables should be considered in any discussion of biological factors and infidelity. The authors warned that this study "raises as many questions as it answers" (Booth & Dabbs, 1993, p. 475). For instance, what is known about testosterone levels in women with respect to marital satisfaction and stability? Also, how does the testosterone level of one partner interact with that of the other in terms of hormonal synchrony? Furthermore, do opposites attract in terms of testosterone levels?

Moreover, most of the literature on infidelity does not show a direct relationship between biological factors and the incidence of affairs. In fact, the correlates of EMS are exclusively emotional and relational (Glass & Wright, 1992; Treas & Giessen, 2000). For instance, we know that the biological effects of aging have a profound influence on testosterone levels and the subjective experience of sexual desire (Weeks & Gambescia, 2002). For example, do higher testosterone levels in younger men partially explain the incidence of infidelity in this group? We know that the number of sex partners declines over the lifetime of the individual (Dolcini et al., 1993; Treas & Giessen, 2000). Does this fact reflect biological as well as social conditions related to infidelity? What effect would declining testosterone levels have on the tendency toward infidelity in men and women over the stages of life?

Ray, a 61-year-old executive who had been married twice, was currently in a long-term relationship and was considering marriage. He sought treatment for an erectile dysfunction. The treating therapist referred him for a urological evaluation because of his age and other nonspecific medical factors. The medical evaluation revealed that Ray had an unusually high testosterone level for a man of his age.

He reported that it had always been difficult to resist sexual temptation despite the realization that infidelity was inappropriate. One of Ray's affairs had lasted for 15 years. In fact, it continued through both of his marriages. He had recently met a woman whom he found compatible and wanted to marry. This relationship was obviously new, and he enjoyed sex with her. Nonetheless, he continued to see various partners for EDS. At this point, the affairs were producing guilt and raising questions about whether he was marriage material. Ray wondered why he could not exercise better control over himself. An examination of his pattern did not show that he was using the affairs for psychological purposes such as triangulation. In this case, one can only wonder about the extent to which his high testosterone level motivated him to continue to act out sexually.

Relationship to the Affair Partner

Wiggins and Lederer (1984) investigated several antecedents of EMS by examining the differences between those involved in liaisons with coworkers and those involved in liaisons with noncoworkers. Participants were 32 female and 27 male clients voluntarily seeking marital counseling for marital infidelity at a medical center in a large, mid-Atlantic city. Needless to say, generalizability of results is limited because of the small number of participants. However, there were some interesting findings from this correlational study. First, those with the greatest incidence of EMS did not report lower levels of sexual satisfaction; they were more dissatisfied with their marriages. This finding supports Thompson's (1983) research. Additionally, these individuals had lower levels of self-acceptance.

Probably the most significant result was that participants who had been sexually involved with coworkers seemed to have much more rewarding marriages than did those who were involved with noncoworkers. In addition, these individuals had only half as many affairs and were married almost twice as long before an affair took place when compared to the group who had EMS with noncoworkers. The authors suggested that these individuals were happily married but were drawn into relationships because of proximity and common interests. The relationship between opportunity and infidelity has been replicated elsewhere (Christopher & Sprecher, 2000; Drigotas & Barta, 2001; Treas & Giesen, 2000). The counselors of these clients saw substantial evidence that they cared for both their spouses and their affair partners and were distressed that their actions had hurt others greatly.

The group who sought EMA with noncoworkers were relatively low on marital compatibility, had decided early in marriage that "something else" was better, sought sexual liaisons with others, and were primarily concerned with how their actions "would look" if their significant others discovered what had happened. It could easily be speculated that those who had affairs with coworkers were more at risk for being caught and perhaps even wanted to be caught.

CONCLUSION

The empirical research about infidelity raises and answers many questions; nonetheless, gaps continue in our understanding of this phenomenon. First, there is a need for an ongoing gender-sensitive exploration that differentiates more explicitly the experiences of men from women regarding all forms of infidelity. In addition, research dealing with attitudes and behaviors regarding infidelity over the lifetime of the individual is essential. When is a partner more likely to be unfaithful? What factors in the individual's development influence decisions to stray from the couple's understanding of exclusivity? To date, this sort of issue has been explored as a small part of larger studies of sexual behavior in general (Kinsey, Pomeroy, & Martin, 1948; Kinsey, Pomeroy, Martin, & Gebhard, 1953; Laumann, Gagnon, Michael, & Michaels, 1994; Wiederman, 1997). Longitudinal research could address the interface of adult development and infidelity more precisely. Thus far, only a few longitudinal studies conducted in the 1980s examined broad aspects of sexual behavior. While they have reached maturation, little information was gathered about infidelity (see Christopher & Sprecher, 2000).

There is an added weakness in current research on infidelity concerning the many intergenerational influences on marital behaviors, values, and expectations. We know from our clinical work that people learn how to behave in intimate relationships by observing interactions of parents and others within the family of origin. Moreover, we have seen repeatedly that affairs often reflect an intergenerational legacy. How do such learnings and messages from families of origin occur and influence decisions regarding affairs?

The empirical research on infidelity clearly demonstrates that affairs take place in particular situations and under certain conditions of vulnerability for the individual or couple. Furthermore, infidelity is considered a major factor in marital dissolution and divorce (Penn et al., 1997). To date, however, the body of information on infidelity consists of studies that typically employ small numbers of participants who are predominantly White; thus, ethnic minorities are underrepresented. Retrospective, self-report data were analyzed in most of the research, and many factors can influence reliability of these data. For instance, social sanctions against infidelity, particularly for women, can lead to distortion or deceit in the responses. Sometimes, errors in reporting were made because of faulty recall of events or embarrassment.

Often, exploratory and correlational research modalities were used in the studies we reviewed; therefore, this body of research does not actually predict infidelity. Moreover, the definitional criteria for infidelity and the time period in which it occurred were inconsistent and varied from study to study. In some, the reported EMS was recent or had occurred during the preceding last year. In others, the lifetime occurrence of EMS was used to determine incidence. All of these factors served to limit the generalizability of the results. See Thompson (1983), Wiederman (1997), Christopher and Sprecher

(2000), Treas and Giesen (2000), and Drigotas and Barta (2001) for a more detailed discussion of the limitations of the existing research on infidelity. Nonetheless, the studies we reviewed were extremely helpful in broadening our understanding of why and when affairs occur, and treatments that might be effective.

3

❋ ❋ ❋

The Multiple Dimensions
of Infidelity

DEFINING AND ASSESSING UNFAITHFULNESS FROM A CLINICAL perspective is
often a laborious task. Not all instances are alike, and each variation influences the way in which infidelity is understood and ultimately treated. Moreover, individuals often disagree about whether an intimacy violation has
actually occurred. For example, in the case of emotional infidelity, there is
often denial of the magnitude of actual involvement and the extent to which
the relationship in question interferes with the marriage. In addition, our
clients often disagree about the specific physical behaviors that constitute
infidelity. Some individuals do not admit that they are having an affair unless
coitus has occurred; others recognize that kissing the affair partner is a violation of a sacred covenant regarding fidelity.

Existing research on infidelity has increased our understanding of this
phenomenon, but also has inherent limitations. Clinical research tends to
examine infidelity from various perspectives: Descriptive research looks at
demographic data retrospectively, normative research observes the societal
factors that can predispose an individual to infidelity, and evolutionary
research embodies many assumptions about human behavioral correlates of
infidelity. Each viewpoint examines only some of the dimensions of intimacy
betrayals. Other approaches consider the conditions that can cause an individual to disengage from a committed relationship. For a more detailed dis-

cussion of the scientific explorations of infidelity, see Drigotas and Barta (2001).

Various typologies have been developed as a way of viewing and organizing different categories of infidelity. The typologies are useful, but do not present a detailed and systematic method of assessment and treatment. Instead, they tend to describe the motivational factors that predispose an individual to have an affair or a set of objective criteria for defining an infidelity. This approach forces the clinician to categorize infidelity into one of many predetermined classifications. Often the fit is not good.

The studies we reviewed often employed a self-report method, the honesty of which is limited, particularly in circumstances of embarrassment and shame. To address the limitations in both research and typologies, we have identified a compilation of some of the more common dimensions of infidelity. This collection resulted from our combined years of clinical experience and through the available clinical and research literature (Humphrey, 1987; Sprenkle & Weis, 1978; Westfall, 1989, 1995). The multidimensional approach facilitates a deeper look into the many presentations and components of the breach of the couple's intimacy contract. It does not attempt to classify or categorize, but instead treats each instance of infidelity as a unique situation involving interlocking and reciprocal structural elements.

DURATION OF INFIDELITY

Duration is a dimension that refers to the time frame within which the intimacy betrayal occurred. Often it is viewed as the length of an extramarital affair, Internet infidelity, or other secret disloyalty. This may be difficult to ascertain because, in the case of an affair, it may have begun as a friendship or working relationship. Commonly, it is difficult to establish the exact point at which the relationship crossed the line of acceptability. For instance, the clinician must help the unfaithful partner to estimate as honestly as possible when a friendship transitioned into an affair and, if appropriate, when it ended. It is also helpful to establish when this partner began to hide his or her activities involving another person, the Internet, pornography, and so on from the primary partner or spouse. Secrecy is a good indicator that intimate energy has been extracted from the primary relationship and diverted into a covert affiliation or activity. When individuals examine the time periods involved, they can begin to identify and accept responsibility for the actions that led to and precipitated infidelity.

In the cases we have treated, most instances of infidelity have been extramarital affairs. Less frequently, the transgressions involved visiting prostitutes or engaging in Internet unfaithfulness. Many of the affairs we have treated have been short term, ranging from several weeks to a few months.

Usually, the situation ends of its own accord or is discovered by the partner. Less commonly, we have treated affairs that have lasted for several years. Recently, one of the authors worked with a couple in which the husband had been seeing prostitutes for the entire duration of the marriage. In another instance, the husband had been secretly viewing Internet pornography for half of a 15-year marriage. We must be mindful not to generalize too heavily from our clinical experience regarding duration, yet unfortunately the clinical studies on infidelity do not reveal the percentage of longer-term affairs. It may be that the protracted affairs are more common than seen in clinical practice because the partners are skilled at not being caught. The unfaithful partners may also be in relationships with impaired spouses who are not aware enough to realize that something is amiss or who are comfortable with a limited amount of intimacy.

In one such case, a woman had an affair with her husband's best friend for more than 20 years. She left the home every Sunday using the excuse of going to church, but actually met her affair partner in a motel. Her husband was a polysubstance abuser during the duration of this affair and was too impaired to notice. Rather than address his substance abuse problems, the wife circumvented conflict by having an affair.

FREQUENCY OF COMMUNICATION

Sexual Contact

Once again, the term *sexual contact* can have ambiguous meanings. Typically, this dimension refers to actual physical communication between persons. In the case of infidelity, the number of actual sexual encounters between the partners within a given time frame constitutes this dimension. However, in instances of cybersex, the contacts might not involve touching another person, yet they constitute occurrences of infidelity. Often, masturbation accompanies the interaction within a chat room or while viewing pornography. The frequency of sexual contacts is typically erratic and intermittent, and ranges from a single instance to more common occurrences. The regularity of contact often depends on availability, privacy, and opportunity.

One of the most unusual betrayals that we treated involved a single meeting between a married man and a prostitute. The man left his home for work one morning and, as he entered his car, a woman approached him, offering oral sex for $20. The man was shocked that the prostitute solicited business in a residential area outside his home with his wife inside. Nonetheless, without much hesitation, he directed the prostitute to meet him down the street in an alley, where the act was completed. As soon as he arrived at work, he began to worry that his wife might have seen him and that he could have acquired a disease. He had been faithfully married for years. He panicked over his transgression and high-risk behavior. Moreover, his actions did not make sense to him.

Similarly, infidelity may occur when a spouse or committed partner is traveling and is approached by a prostitute, sex addict, or someone who just seems to catch one's eye in a way that has "never happened before." Money may be exchanged for the single sexual encounter, but is not a necessary criterion. In another case, friends invited a man to a legal brothel in Nevada. He expected to sit at the bar while they spent some "private time" with the prostitutes. Once the group arrived at the brothel, his friends told him that they were going to buy him a prostitute so that he could be fully initiated into their crowd. With some reluctance, he agreed, in spite of the fact that it was his first time ever engaging in EMS. When he got home, he felt so guilty about what he had done that he immediately told his wife. Initially, he tried to blame his friends for what happened, but his wife held him accountable and suggested that they seek therapy immediately.

Total Number of Transactions

Another component of frequency involves the number of actual contacts between the affair partners, regardless of whether intimate contact occurs. The couple having an affair may work together and see each other repeatedly throughout the day. They often communicate through telephone, cellular telephone, e-mail, or even voice mail. Obviously, the degree of involvement between the affair partners becomes proportionately detrimental to the primary relationship. In some cases, there is more tangible daily contact between the affair partners than between the spouses. Many times, the emotional involvement of the affair partner surpasses that of the spouse. In fact, as the affair partners eventually develop their own unique frame of reference, the viewpoint of the spouse becomes more foreign.

Thus, when determining the frequency dimension, assessment should always incorporate the amount of actual communication between the couple rather than intimate interactions alone. One of our most interesting cases involved a couple who met while attending a party with their respective spouses. They managed to sneak away for a few moments and engage in what she called "petting" behavior. Before long, they started a voice mail affair with multiple messages per day. They both had extremely busy work schedules and found that communicating by voice mail worked best. Thus, their physically intimate encounters were far less frequent than their private messages to each other. Nonetheless, their level of intimacy became very threatening to each marriage.

Another affair involved a clergyman with a woman from his congregation. Because his schedule was unstructured, the clergyman could visit her house almost every day during the time when her husband was working outside of the home. This couple had frequent intimate contact that was sometimes sexual.

In another case, a couple sought therapy for the husband's lack of sexual desire. They had sex a few times per year. His desire did not improve, nor did it appear that it would. His wife started a very discreet affair with a man she saw every few months at regular meetings out of town.

In the last few years, we have encountered many instances of infidelity that began or survived through frequent Internet or e-mail contact. In some of these cases, the unsuspecting spouse inadvertently discovered a correspondence from the affair partner and traced a chain of communications that revealed an ongoing affair. In another case, the husband frequently viewed pornographic images on the computer. The suspicious wife discovered an exhaustive trail of contacts of several years' duration.

The frequency and duration of infidelity provides clues about emotional involvement with the affair partner or activity. Affairs of long duration with frequent contact possess the greatest probability of significant emotional involvement. Potentially, they are most destructive because they represent considerable disengagement from the marriage. However, extreme damage to the marriage may also result from a sexual encounter with a prostitute or opportunistic stranger. Such a betrayal of trust leaves the uninvolved partner wondering about the meaning and significance of the marital bond.

LOCATION OF ENCOUNTERS

The availability of a safe, private, and economically affordable location for encounters is another dimension of infidelity. The most common meeting places are a hotel, motel, or one or both partners' homes or offices. As we have suggested previously, not all affairs take place in a physical location. Technologically mediated affairs are becoming more common and often take place in cyberspace. The partners may never meet but exchange hundreds of e-mail messages, including photographs. Some of these affairs may graduate to physical encounters, but others exist exclusively online. In fact, on some websites, participants can specify the type of desired relationship, and some members will seek an Internet relationship and nothing more. Others might specify that phone contact, including phone sex, is permitted.

Tim was a very busy physician. During the day, he never had a minute alone because he was always with patients and staff. In the evening, he spent hours "surfing the web" in his study. Eventually, his wife discovered that he regularly contacted women online for sexual conversation. He never actually met any of the women, because they were scattered across the country. Another interesting case involved a woman who was in denial that her husband was having an affair. The couple had been married for many years and the wife had a variety of psychosomatic symptoms. Her husband went out by himself every Friday and Saturday night until early morning. He claimed he was going out to bars with his male friends. In fact, he was going to a large nightclub, picking up women, and having sex with them in his car behind the club. A different case involved a highly visible couple in a small community. While their spouses were at home, they met regularly in a secluded spot in the woods to talk and have sex.

Like all of the dimensions of infidelity, the location is particularly important to the betrayed spouse. They usually persist in seeking information about the setting of the encounters. The worst situations occur when the affair takes place in the marital home, especially when the marital bed or family computer is used for infidelity. Betrayed spouses find this particularly distasteful and painful, and often question their sanity or intelligence in not detecting what has occurred. They experience a sense of shame or embarrassment contemplating whether the neighbors might have known about the affair.

RISK OF DISCOVERY

Another dimension of infidelity involves the possibility that the partners will be detected during their meetings. The risk of discovery varies along a continuum from absolute discretion to open or obvious affairs. The participants who use absolute discretion are careful to conceal their relationship because they truly do not want to be caught or they do not want to hurt their spouse(s). In a case mentioned earlier, the woman met her affair partner while traveling. She was very prudent not to arouse suspicion or leave any kind of paper trail, e-mail, or telephone records of her encounters. She rationalized her affair using sexual justification, claiming that she was satisfied with every other aspect of her marriage and did not wish to jeopardize the union.

As we mentioned in Chapter 1, the discovery of infidelity is sometimes an attempt, consciously or unconsciously, to bring about a crisis in the marriage. We have often heard that a betrayal served as a "cry for help" or a "wake-up call" for the ostensibly unconcerned partner. In these instances, dormant but destructive marital conflicts, which may have been circumvented by the couple for years, are brought to the surface through discovery of an affair or another type of infidelity. On occasion, the betrayal causes so much guilt and conflict that discovery is a relief—the partner having the affair has been unable to stop and relies on intervention from an outside source. Less frequently, the unfaithful partner uses disclosure to punish or hurt the partner.

Regardless of the motivation, however, the unfaithful person often becomes careless, leaving a trail of evidence behind. We have heard many stories of discovery and some themes are more common: cellular phone bills with the same number repeated many times, e-mail messages, receipts from hotels, clothing with lipstick stains or perfume (even missing clothing), or a history of Internet pornography site and chat room visits. In cases of sex addiction, the spouse may unearth several sources of Internet evidence. Unfortunately, the crisis of discovery rather than the preexisting marital problems often brings the couple to the therapist's office.

One client was discovered when she forgot to erase from her e-mailbox some e-mail messages from her lover. When her husband used the family computer, the letters shocked him and brought about a crisis in the marriage that eventually led to divorce. In a different case, the woman kept a handwritten journal of the infidelity in her briefcase and although a friend warned her that her suspicious husband might look for evidence, she did not hide the journal. Subsequently, he found it and used the information in an extremely distasteful letter that he wrote to all of her friends and colleagues, exposing the affair.

Occasionally, a change in typical behavior or unaccounted-for time arouses the suspicions of the spouse. In one case, the distrustful husband used a hidden voice-activated tape recorder to listen to telephone conversations held by his wife at home while he was at work, because he desperately needed confirmation of his suspicions. He discovered that she was having a torrid affair and, when she denied it, he presented the evidence. In other instances, we have heard that the doubting partner found a way to listen to private voice mail messages or to read e-mail correspondence in the spouse's private account. Not infrequently, the partner is so suspicious that a detective is hired.

Many of the cases we have treated have been conducted with some discretion, but not enough to evade detection. In fact, discovery occurs commonly enough in clinical couples about whom we hypothesize that the partners actually want to be caught. In one such case, the couple sought therapy because the husband was no longer interested in having sex. Although he denied having an affair, the suspicious wife found his cellular phone personal identification number and checked his messages regularly. On one occasion, she heard an extremely sexual communication from his affair partner. He immediately confessed and was visibly relieved about the discovery, reporting that he felt so guilty about the infidelity that he actually wanted to be stopped. Another client was conflicted about having an affair but could not end it. She was ambivalent about choosing between her affair partner and her spouse. She loved both and hoped that one would force a decision that she could not make herself. Finally, she told her husband about the infidelity, hoping that he would deliver an ultimatum. Instead, he gave her time to "make up her mind!"

Sometimes the trail of evidence is so overwhelming and apparent to the therapist that it is impossible to accept that the spouse did not realize what was happening. Obviously, the partner was in denial about the infidelity, thereby overlooking the obvious signs of indiscretion. Nonetheless, we believe that there are always reasons for denial in noninvolved spouses. Perhaps they are afraid that a confrontation will precipitate a separation or divorce. In other cases, the noninvolved spouses might not desire sexual intimacy and the infidelity enables the partners to fill their sexual needs outside of the marriage. Dependency needs also come into play when a spouse unconsciously colludes in overlooking the affair. The spouse might be financially or emotionally dependent on the partner and not able to withstand the tremendous financial or social loss of a separation or divorce. Regardless of the cause of the denial, we believe that there is agreement at some level between the partners that an affair is happening, that it will not be discussed openly, and that the marriage will remain intact. This strategy "works" until a dynamic within the system changes.

Finally, some affairs involve a high level of risk discovery or are conducted openly. (We are not referring to "open marriages," in which spouses agree to have affairs. In open marriages, there is little deception, because both partners know about the EMS.) The phenomenon of obvious adultery is quite common in our clinical experience. In the openly conducted affair, the EMS is so flagrant that discovery is inevitable. One couple is illustrative of this pattern. The husband had multiple affairs throughout the marriage. He always chose a partner from the many women with whom he worked. Coworkers quickly discovered the most recent affair and notified his wife. She knew of his philandering and observed his pattern of spending an inordinate amount of time or traveling with a particular female coworker. Whenever caught, he never denied the affair; instead, he admitted it and stated that he would stop when he was ready. His wife frequently retaliated by having an affair with men far beneath her socially, hoping that her husband would be upset and embarrassed by her choice of affair partner.

In a few couples we have treated, the partner unreservedly had an affair and announced that he or she was in the process of choosing between the affair partner and the spouse. Such patients proclaim that they are torn between the spouse and the affair partner, love them both, and do not wish to hurt either. Somehow, they cannot perceive that the infidelity itself is causing injury to both partners. The apparent disconnection between their behavior and the emotional consequences is a component of this pattern. They are consumed and exhausted by the intensity and excitement generated by living each day in crisis. Like addicts, they are unable to make the choices necessary to reduce the excitement and return to a more stable lifestyle. In addition, they seem to derive narcissistic pleasure from knowing that both partners desire them. Usually, the cycle ends when the affair partner or the spouse ends the affair or the marriage.

The method of discovery is often a determinant of the degree of damage to the betrayed partner. The more public instances of infidelity precipitate shame and embarrassment; this adds to the other devastating emotions that betrayed spouses usually feel. They are often painfully aware that they are the "last to know" and wonder how to save face when the affair is so public. These spouses are in a state of shock, and question assumptions about their marriages and their lives in general. Often, they feel betrayed, obsessively question how they could have been so thoroughly fooled, and despair that they really do not know their mates or the meaning of the relationships.

THE DEGREE OF COLLUSION BY THE BETRAYED PARTNER

The uncertainty of whether or not the betrayed spouse knows about the infidelity is always an issue for the therapist. The greater question is whether or to what degree the unknowing partner implicitly tolerates, approves of, or consents to the infidelity is a controversy that researchers and clinicians have not been able to resolve. Occasionally, betrayed partners will assert that there was absolutely no warning until they were confronted with an undeniable piece of evidence. An extremely traumatic mode of discovery is the diagnosis of a sexually transmitted disease (STD) in the intimate partner who was not having the affair. The infidelity is unexpected and the level of deception is great. It is believed by some (Glass & Wright, 1997; Stiff et al., 1992) that if the unfaithful person is extremely discreet and maintains a loving relationship with the spouse, there is little reason for mistrust or suspiciousness. Our clinical observations, however, support the systemic perspective that some awareness of the infidelity and, moreover, collusion by the uninvolved spouse, whether conscious or unconscious, is operating. In fact, in a number of marriages the partners are comfortable with the homeostasis although it is less than optimal in terms of intimacy. A survey of therapists by Charny and Parnass (1995) supported our clinical observation in that the vast majority of therapists participating in the survey believed that at some level the spouse or committed partner knows about the infidelity.

There is no doubt that when couples enter treatment, the majority of betrayed partners express robust surprise as well as verbal disapproval of the discovered infidelity. One of the most difficult tasks of therapy is to help wounded, betrayed spouses to see that they were a part of the affair. This must be done skillfully, nonjudgmentally, and with precise timing. This therapeutic strategy is addressed in Chapter 7, in the section on reframing the infidelity. Typically, as the therapist listens to each story, it is obvious that suspicions should have been aroused, pointing toward an affair or another type of infidelity. Our experience suggests that, in most cases, such spouses could or must have known if they were attentive to their partners.

We have encountered only a few cases in which the unfaithful spouse was very intelligent, manipulative, or had a sociopathic personality. The infidelity was compartmentalized so well that the unfaithful spouses' behavior toward their spouses remained the same. Often, this strategy is demonstrated in other areas of the unfaithful partner's life; they are typically seen as credible and honest people. One case example involved a man who had held several key positions in business and politics. He was widely known as a person who could not be bought or bribed. Colleagues and the media perceived him as the quintessentially honest man and supported him throughout his career. He was also known as a strong family man and a church member. Eventually, a 13-year affair was discovered. His relationship with his wife had always been stable but somewhat distant, with sexual intimacy occurring at regular but infrequent intervals. He had few close friends, always feared criticism and punishment for not being perfect, and suffered from long-term dysthymia. His wife felt that the distance in their relationship was due to her husband's depression and events in his background. She never truly understood her unconscious reasons for marrying him and for remaining in the relationship, nor did she see that she had been naïve about his loyalty.

This is not the situation with most of our couples. The evidence usually ranges from subtle to obvious, but it is always present in retrospective stories of infidelity. In an example of Internet infidelity, the husband used the computer in the couple's living room for over 2 years to communicate regularly with his affair partner and enjoy pornography. The wife had difficulty giving up her anger at his betrayal in order to address her lack of attentiveness to the relationship. The therapist was challenged to help her to see that she did have a part in the situation. Timing, empathy, discretion, and patience are necessary when presenting such a systemic viewpoint.

LEVEL OF DECEPTION

This dimension is interwoven with the risk of discovery and the degree of collusion by the betrayed spouse. Any act of infidelity takes on two aspects: the infidelity itself and the dishonesty needed to carry it out. Secrecy, deception, and lies overlay almost all forms of infidelity. Accordingly, the unfaithful partner begins to lead a double life. This partner may disappear frequently for encounters, and uses cover stories such as meetings, errands that take hours, recreational activities such as biking trips, or church activities. Sometimes secretaries, colleagues, or others are involved in the deception or inadvertently protect the unfaithful partner. Over time, the person having the affair usually cannot tolerate the levels of deception and the double life.

For many we have treated, infidelity is easier to justify or rationalize than the dishonesty employed to distract the betrayed partner. Although extremely damaging, infidelity makes some sense to the wounded partner. However, the lies employed to conceal the infidelity are infinitely more destructive to the intimate partner and the relationship. In fact, the degree of deceitfulness is often related to the level of damage to the marital bond. The betrayed spouse begins to question the foundation on which the marital relationship is grounded. The assumptions of trust, loyalty and honesty are shattered. Regaining trust, if it is possible at all, may take a considerable amount of effort and time. This issue is revisited and discussed more thoroughly in Chapters 6 and 7.

History of Past Infidelity

This dimension involves acts of physical unfaithfulness with another partner. The typical couple seeking treatment for infidelity will report one or two prior affairs with the current one still in progress or having ceased due to discovery. In some of the more exceptional cases, there have been multiple sexual partners. Lusterman (1995) and Pittman (1993) described this type of infidelity as philandering, because there is little or no emotional involvement with the affair partners. In general, the number of sexual partners appears to be most related to the needs of the unfaithful partners and the opportunities they have been afforded, including the norms of their social groups. One couple in their mid-30s entered therapy because the wife had learned about an affair her husband was having. After initially rebuffing the EMS, he was forced to concede when confronted with undeniable proof. Then the wife recounted other suspicions she had had in the past and the many opportunities he had for infidelity while working and traveling in the entertainment industry. In a private meeting, the husband admitted that he had over 100 sexual relationships prior to marriage and 150 since he and his wife had been married 12 years ago. He attributed the premarital affairs to being single and having a high sex drive. He justified the EMS by saying that everyone in his social group had many affairs while they were traveling. In other words, he was doing what everyone else did. He even asked his colleagues whether they thought his behavior was inappropriate, and they had said it was what guys do when they travel and "what wives don't know won't hurt them." Further exploration confirmed a pattern of sexual behavior that was driven, problematic, obsessive, and compulsive. The couple's therapy had to be expanded to include treatment of his sex addiction (See Carnes, 1992, for a detailed description of sex addiction).

Another couple had a similar pattern and problem. They were in their mid-40s and the husband was a highly successful businessman who traveled extensively. When he traveled, he used cocaine, picked up women in bars, and / or hired prostitutes. His wife contracted a STD from him and confronted him with this irrefutable proof. His secret life had taken a toll on him and he was ready to confess and get help. He admitted that he had a problem with both drugs and women, that he was putting his wife and himself at risk, and did not want to continue living a secret life.

Age and opportunity are other determinants of the number of sexual partners. Professional athletes are often followed by "groupies" who intend to have sex with the person. In some sports, these women greet athletes at private entrances to sporting arenas and solicit sex by exposing their breasts and throwing underclothing and room keys. The adrenaline rush of the game, celebration parties with drugs and alcohol, and expectation of sexual promiscuity can promote hypersexual behavior in such groups. The important challenge is to establish whether the sexual acting out is part of a pattern or an isolated event.

We are finding an increasing incidence of sex addiction in our practices. Sometimes the couple is referred as a part of the treatment of the sex addiction. More often, we have noted that a discovered affair is sometimes just the tip of the iceberg. The disclosure begins a process of unveiling problematic sexual behaviors that can include Internet pornography, one-night stands, multiple incidents of EMS, the solicitation of prostitutes, and other offending sexual behaviors. Although there is disagreement in the psychiatric community about whether or not such hypersexuality constitutes the clinical diagnosis of sex addiction, we use the term for many reasons. First, if a sex addiction is at issue, the treatment is vastly more inclusive than what is required for infidelity. This regimen includes individual, group, and couples formats and provides ongoing support for the spouse as well as the addict. It encompasses psychoeducation, relapse prevention strategies, and often pharmacotherapy. In addition, the systemic component of treatment addresses the needs of the intimate partner and the issue of coaddiction. Often, the damage created by the web of secrecy and betrayal of trust is immense and damages the marriage irreconcilably.

The term *sexual addiction* was popularized by Carnes (1992, 1991). Currently, diagnostic criteria are proposed for inclusion of sex addiction in the next revision of the *Diagnostic and Statistical Manual* of the American Psychiatric Association, the *DSM-V*. For more information about sex addiction—a syndrome of driven sexual behavior with harmful consequences—we recommend the following articles: Goodman (2001), Leedes (2001), Finlayson, Sealy, and Martin (2001), and Manley and Koehler (2001).

When the affair is part of a chemical and or sex addiction or another mental illness (e.g., a bipolar disorder), the spouse can be educated about the relationship between these problems. Sometimes the betrayed partner views the infidelity from a moral perspective and ends the marriage. In other instances, the betrayed partner may accept the view that it is part of a psychological problem for the spouse that requires specialized treatment.

GENDER OF THE AFFAIR PARTNER

We generally suppose that if a married heterosexual individual is unfaithful, it will involve a person of the opposite gender. In most of our cases, this assumption holds true. However, we have seen some exceptions, and this issue has also been discussed in the clinical literature (Lusterman, 1995). In fact, the therapist should not overlook the dimension of the gender of the affair partner due to personal discomfort or assumptions about the person having the affair.

We have worked with a few married women in the age range of mid 40s to late 50s who developed close emotional connections with other women. In some of these relationships, sexual intimacy occurred. Typically, the marriages were stable, albeit unexciting, and had lasted for more than 20 years. The husbands spent many hours each week working or traveling for their jobs, and the children had been launched from the family. Often the husbands enjoyed leisure activities that consumed many hours on the weekends and involved occasional trips without their spouses. Without realizing it, these women yearned for an intense meaningful connection and had the opportunity to develop a relationship that provided companionship as well as sexual intimacy.

In one case, the relationship occurred between a female spouse and her female personal trainer. In another instance, the two women were business associates who spent many hours together each day working from the home. Typically, women in this type of affair report that they were never conflicted about their heterosexual orientation. They simply developed deep intimate and loving feelings toward a close friend and the relationship gradually became sexual. It is useful to remember that infidelity may be emotional, sexual, or a mixture of both. In these examples, an emotional bond developed into a sexual attachment.

Some people who are heterosexually married eventually question if they are gay or bisexual. In the cases where gender orientation is at issue, the individual might begin to experiment by exploring homosexuality while in a heterosexual marriage. Of this group, some will eventually enter into affairs with persons of the same gender. In one couple, a married man who had always been conflicted about his sexual orientation began to explore homosexual friendships by going to gay nightclubs where he shared drinks and danced with other men. He was not ready to start a sexual relationship, but he was beginning to explore his feelings in this context. His wife wondered why he had so many new male friends and why they called his home to make dates to do things together. In another example, a recently married woman discovered that her husband had been having an affair with a man. He subsequently left the marriage and established a live-in relationship with his affair partner.

In many of these couples, the issue of homosexual infidelity generates additional emotional concerns for the betrayed partners, including doubting their own sexual confidence and wondering how they could have been in love with someone who is homosexual. They often report feeling confused, ignorant, and flawed. Furthermore, homosexual affairs cause heterosexual spouses to feel hopeless about reconciliation, because they believe they cannot compete for their partner's affections and they often assume that the spouse does not care for their gender.

In one example, a woman sought therapy with her fiancé because she wanted to be sure that she was not "making the same mistake" as she had done in a previous marriage in which her husband left her for a man. Her perplexed fiancé agreed to attend the sessions. He supported her through the process of accepting that her former husband's sexual orientation was not related to a weakness or deficiency in her.

A fascination and compulsion toward certain fetishistic behavior drives some extramarital affairs. A few cases stand out. In each of these cases, the men had been married for a number of years and by all appearances were heterosexual. Terry, a 28-year-old man, reported that he was fascinated with men who were in the process of transsexual transition to become women. Incidentally, many of these men still had intact penises in addition to hormonally induced breasts. Terry met a so-called "she-male" at a bar during a business trip and decided he wanted to delve into his sexual curiosity. He spent the night with this person, engaging in a variety of sexual activities. When he came to his next therapy session following this encounter, he reported what had happened and said that the fantasy was much better than the reality. Terry did not enjoy the experience and even felt self-revulsion over it. He decided not to tell his wife, because he never intended to engage in such infidelity again.

Another case is somewhat similar. Joe, 43, was a professional man married to a professional woman. He had been secretly cross-dressing for years without his wife's knowledge. He cross-dressed at home while his wife was at work, and had his feminine clothing hidden in the house. On a few occasions, he had asked his wife if they could make love while he wore some article of her clothing, but she looked disgusted and told him no. During the course of therapy, Joe revealed to his wife that he was a transvestite. She reacted by acknowledging that his "problem" was untreatable and asked that he cross-dress when she was not present. Joe agreed, but a few weeks later he pressed her to try having sex once with him while he was wearing some of his favorite clothing. She agreed to try it once under the condition that she be blindfolded. As soon as she felt his undergarments, she jumped out of bed and said she would never participate in this experience again. Joe appeared resigned that this was not an option in his marriage. Several months later, he called for an emergency session without his wife. He reported that he had met a man at work and as they got to know each other started to talk about cross-dressing. They discovered that they were both "closet transvestites" and wanted to experiment sexually. Joe immediately realized this experience did not meet his fantasies and he would not want to repeat it again. He was also worried about diseases and saw a physician immediately to rule out any medical problems. After that incident, the couple continued the original agreement that he may cross-dress only in her absence but not be sexually unfaithful.

In another example, the couple sought treatment because of the husband's lack of desire. The husband complained that he was not interested in sex because his wife did not seem interested. She disagreed, asserting that she was the one who usually requested sexual intimacy. Traditional sex therapy for hyposexual desire disorder (HSD) failed and the couple began to argue frequently, each blaming the other for the lack of sex in their lives. One day, the wife discovered an unfamiliar gym bag in the trunk of his car and looked inside it. She unearthed female clothing, stockings, cosmetics, and a wig. Finally, the husband admitted that he had been cross-dressing outside the home and that he had several sexual encounters with men while he had been dressed as a woman. She divorced him, remarried, had children, and 15 years later reports having a harmonious relationship with her second husband.

It should be mentioned that we have also worked with couples in which the male partner was a transvestite. These marriages were stable, and any cross-dressing occurred with the partner or the partner's knowledge. In these cases, the men were able to draw the line between fantasy and acting out extramaritally.

TYPE OF INFIDELITY

The degree of actual involvement with the affair partner is another dimension used to describe extramarital affairs. Typically, we see three nondiscrete categories of participation in infidelity: primarily sexual, primarily emotional, or mixed. Although embodied in most typologies, we include this dimension because we believe that the level of emotional attachment to the affair partner is negatively correlated with marital viability. When strong emotional and physical connections exist, there is less likelihood of cessation of the infidelity. Often, persons having an affair will state that they are in love with two people, the affair partner and the spouse. Thus, terminating the infidelity and / or commencing treatment may be considerably more difficult than if the attachment were purely recreational or sexual.

Glass and Wright (1985) conducted a series of studies revealing some gender differences with respect to this dimension. Typically, men have predominantly sexual affairs with a lower degree of emotional attachment to the affair partner than women do. Women's affairs frequently grow from friendships to emotional attachments and then may graduate to the mixed emotional and sexual variety. Of course, there can be considerable overlap, and gender differences may blur. Nonetheless, we find that men are better able to compartmentalize or believe that they need to have affairs even if their marriages are happy. In our experience, when women have affairs they are usually much less satisfied with their marriages; hence, the affair can be more likely to lead to marital dissolution.

A sexual affair is difficult to dispute. On the other hand, emotional infidelity is easier to deny under the guise of a close friendship. It may take longer to establish that the spouse is in fact having an inappropriate emotional relationship. Thus, emotional affairs can be slippery and difficult for the couple to clearly identify, ostensibly because of the lack of obvious sexual intimacy. One such case involved a fundamentalist Christian woman who assisted a man in her church who was blind. She spent every day with him. Eventually, she developed a close attachment that was made possible by her husband's frequent travel. She initially denied any wrongdoing, but finally saw that she was using this other man as a substitute for her husband. She denied ever having sex, but admitted to romantic feelings.

The impact of any type of infidelity can be devastating; however, in our experience, a primarily emotional affair can have far-reaching damaging effects on the marriage. It is often easier to accept a strictly sexual relationship, especially if it is short term, than emotional infidelity that is covert and insidious. It is assumed that a marriage or committed relationship is ultimately and most importantly an emotional bond. This assumption is shattered upon the discovery of emotional infidelity. Often, this type of infidelity occurs over a protracted time period during which the unfaithful person repeatedly chooses to invest time and emotional energy in someone other than the spouse. Invariably, persistent lying to the spouse exacerbates the damage to the marriage by creating a gradual emotional distance and reduction of intimacy between the spouses. There is an undeniable likelihood that the intensely close union between the affair partners will become sexual. Furthermore, the treatment is often complicated by an intense and protracted rage response once this type of infidelity is discovered (Lusterman, 1995). This is addressed in greater detail later in the text, when accusatory suffering is discussed in Chapter 10.

The type of involvement can also be used to assess and treat cyberinfidelity. Frequent emotional communications can fuel the consummation of an Internet relationship. The couple may involve themselves in ongoing nonphysical contact that can include sharing emotionally sensitive and sexual material. This sort of relationship can fulfill our criteria for infidelity because emotional and sexual energy is secretly diverted from the primary relationship and channeled into the virtual relationship. We have seen cases in which partners have terminated long-standing marriages after months of online communication and occasional meetings with the affair partner. Again, the most damaging condition is the degree of emotional involvement with the affair partner.

Unilateral and Bilateral Infidelity

This dimension examines the extent to which each partner is unfaithful or enables infidelity in the other. Most couples present with one spouse having had an affair. Sometimes, the other partner may have been unfaithful at some distant point in the past. Obviously, when one is betraying the other, it produces inequity in the marriage in terms of commitment. The unilateral affair enables an avoidance of emotional and / or sexual intimacy through triangulating a third person. However, when infidelity is bilateral, the clinician should question the ability of each partner to form and maintain an emotionally close relationship. In one example, both spouses were involved in Internet affairs; the marriage dissolved when the husband moved to a distant location in order to consummate his affair. The wife remained in the marital home and became physically involved with her Internet partner.

Although uncommon in our experience, some spouses have multiple bilateral affairs in the absence of an explicit agreement to have an open marriage. In some cases, the infidelity is retaliatory. In others, the partners implicitly agreed to have a distant or parallel marriage in which they assume it is acceptable to have other relationships. We have also noted this phenomenon in dating couples, including older dating couples who are ambivalent about becoming married. Sandy, 38, and Mark, 40, attractive professionals living in a large urban area, are an example. They were in a long-term dating relationship and sought treatment about the decision to becoming engaged. As the therapy proceeded, it became clear neither partner wanted to lose their independence. Through the course of therapy, both Sandy and Mark admitted to maintaining sexual relationships with former lovers although those relationships would never lead to marriage.

For this couple, the discovery of bilateral infidelity helped them to better understand the problems each had in forming an enduring relationship. For many other couples, however, this form of behavior signifies that they "are not right for each other." Thus, the affairs offer them an easy exit from the relationship and a quick "resolution" of their ambivalence about being committed.

RELATIONSHIP OF THE AFFAIR PARTNER TO THE SPOUSE

During treatment, the betrayed spouse always inquires about the identity and other characteristics of the affair partner. Once rendered, however, this information rarely satisfies inconsolable betrayed partners. Typically, they are searching for a reason for the betrayal. Often, they obsessively compare themselves to the affair partner, looking within themselves for shortcomings or other factors that could explain the infidelity. In one case, the wife compulsively asked about the affair partner's identity until the husband relented. She did not feel any relief in knowing the woman's name so the tormented wife called the affair partner just to hear her voice. Still, there was no relief. The therapist reframed this dynamic as the wife's need to know the significance of the infidelity to the husband. This intervention served to interrupt the wife's threats to visit the affair partner and facilitated discussion about the meaning of the affair.

This identity dimension can be conceptualized in two ways. How well did the unfaithful spouse know the person? How well did the betrayed spouse know the affair partner? A prostitute or a perfect stranger constitutes one sort of threat, whereas an affair with a close friend or family member is significantly more damaging to the relationship. The degree of knowledge of the affair partner is a major determinant of the levels of threat and betrayal felt by the spouse. Invariably, if the affair partner is a close friend, neighbor, or relative, two people who were assumed to be trustworthy have violated the betrayed spouse. Sometimes, the transgressed spouse feels stupid about not knowing and proceeds to blame him- or herself for not being more vigilant. In addition, the betrayed spouse may have lost an important source of social support if the affair partner was a close friend. The betrayal is compounded by embarrassment that others might have known about the affair and fear of ridicule for not detecting the infidelity.

In many cases, the betrayed spouse knows the affair partner because that person was the partners' friend or colleague. After the disclosure, the unfaithful spouse is forced to interact with someone from whom he or she is attempting to disengage. Furthermore, the hurt spouse must endure the thought that the two will continue to be in daily contact with each other. The level of threat imposed by such a situation is massive. In Chapter 6, we discuss what to do about this common occurrence.

We could mention any number of examples involving infidelity with a coworker. Charlie, 50, was a manager in a large business. He had an affair with an associate. They saw each other every day and frequently took business trips together. Because of his age and salary, he felt he could not leave the company, divulge the infidelity, or fire his affair partner. Fortunately, the company was large enough that his coworker applied for a different position, was transferred to another building, and there was no need for further contact. Because we have a disproportionate number of physicians in our practices, we have also found that many doctors have affairs with nurses or other physicians. Their schedules are so erratic that it is easy to conceal the infidelity, and they spend an inordinate amount of time outside of the home. Often, they invest so much emotional energy in their work that their marriages suffer from lack of intimacy. The workplace becomes the living space replete with many meaningful relationships. Without an enormous degree of effort, infidelity can arise from opportunity and need for closeness.

PERCEIVED ATTRACTIVENESS OF THE AFFAIR PARTNER

Another question related to the identity of the affair partner involves physical appearance, age, education, socioeconomic status, and overall level of attractiveness to the spouse. Sometimes, the betrayed spouse will go to great lengths for even a momentary view of the physical appearance of the affair partner. The presupposition is that the affair partner must be more desirable than the spouse. Typically, such an assumption is more related to projections of the betrayed spouse rather than the actual motivations of the person having the affair. Often, in an effort to come across an explanation for the infidelity, the injured spouse finds perceived weaknesses in the self. Of course, the reasons are multidetermined, and are only partially related to the physical attractiveness of the affair partner. Nonetheless, discussion of the perceived attractiveness of the affair partner can help the therapist and couple to consider dimensions of the infidelity such as individual vulnerabilities, fears of commitment, and so on.

The research on EMS in the American population demonstrates that affairs occur most often when there is opportunity to meet partners, when the unfaithful partner has a sexually permissive value system, and when marital dissatisfaction exists (Treas & Giesen, 2000). Our own clinical experience supports that given the opportunity and inclination, men often choose affair partners with whom they feel they have good sexual chemistry; they care less about compatibility. They often select women younger than their spouses and are drawn to the most attractive females. On the other hand, women are looking for an emotional connection, one that is more satisfying than the one they share with their spouse. For them, compatibility is more important than the physical appearance and age of the affair partner.

Moreover, the age and attractiveness of the affair partner may be a reflection of the need to prove virility and recapture youth by means of a relationship with someone much younger. For example, in a few couples with whom we have worked, the unfaithful men were wealthy, intelligent, charming, overweight, and concerned with aging. When they spoke of their affair partners, they would stress physical beauty even though they would also lament that the women were "high maintenance." Thus, the attractiveness of the affair partner was more related to their own perceived inadequacies than actual dissatisfaction with their spouses.

Nonetheless, physical attractiveness and other personal characteristics can have a great impact on the betrayed spouse, particularly if the affair partner is perceived to be preferred in some way. Often, these spouses become preoccupied with the dilemma of how to compete with such a person should the spouses elect to work on or stay in the marriage. In one of the cases mentioned earlier, the husband had an affair with a wealthy woman who worked as a professional model. The wife felt threatened because she was of average attractiveness, somewhat overweight, and financially dependent on her husband. On the other hand, affair partners may be much less attractive than the betrayed spouses and have personal characteristics that are perceived to be far below what the spouses have to offer. This is the situation with Martin and Wendy. He selected a woman who was less attractive, less intelligent, less educated, and less socially presentable than his wife. Wendy wondered why Martin preferred a woman whom he described as "beneath" her in every way imaginable. She asked herself whether she was such a horrible spouse that almost anyone else was perceived as more desirable. Was he attempting to punish or embarrass her? Did Martin actually choose someone at his true level of self-comfort? Was the marriage to Wendy a "stretch" in terms of his sense of entitlement? Regardless of the answer, when the affair partner is viewed as being more or less attractive along a variety of dimensions, the outcome is often perceived as a "no-win" situation for the betrayed spouse. This condition can promote skepticism about ever resolving the painful issues surrounding the infidelity.

THE SOCIAL CONTEXT OF INFIDELITY

Infidelity never occurs in a vacuum. Many factors contribute to what is perceived to be either acceptable of shameful about any presentation of infidelity. Is the behavior sanctioned within a specific social context, as in the example of a man working in the entertainment industry? Is it clearly forbidden by the couple's intimacy contract? The assessment and treatment of infidelity includes context variables such as ever-changing societal norms, patterns, and vicissitudes within a period of time. Other salient characteristics include the individual's socioeconomic group, geographic community, and ethnic, cultural, and religious affiliation. The therapist must be sensitive to how each spouse views the affair within the many contexts of daily living. In addition, whenever possible the clinician should become familiar with research dealing with the various social norms. We discuss the existing research on culture, race, and ethnicity in Chapter 2.

Infidelity is better tolerated in some groups or eras than others, and is even accepted in some societies. One author can remember working with couples in the early 1970s who described themselves as members of the "swinging" movement in America. This phenomenon involves conventionally married couples who choose to exchange partners for sexual purposes only. Although swinging is no longer socially promoted, the movement is still alive, although less visible and subversive. In Las Vegas, there are currently four well-known swinging establishments. Nationally, there is a movement known as "the lifestyle" that holds national conventions designed to bring together members of this group and to promote swinging as a viable alternative lifestyle. However, in our culture there is open condemnation of infidelity in virtually every conceivable group.

The clinician must also consider the religious aspects of infidelity and various meanings connected to it. Clearly, couples who profess to be religious or spiritual have strong values about fidelity. The more conservative religious groups, such as the Fundamentalists, take the firmest stance against infidelity, equating the act with sin and shunning the sinner. Regardless of the religious orientation of the couple, the therapist must make every effort to understand the meaning and significance of infidelity to each partner. The reader may also find the work of Penn and colleagues (1997) helpful—these authors attempted to understand infidelity from the spiritual perspective, because members of each culture are strongly influenced by religious teachings. They investigated religious and cultural perspectives on infidelity of three ethnic minorities in the United States: African Americans, Hispanic Americans, and Asian Americans. They also focused on the more fundamental aspects of Catholicism, Eastern philosophy, Islam, and Protestantism.

One couple we treated had recently emigrated to the United States from the Middle East. The husband had been discovered having an affair. In the session, he justified his actions by stating that in his town and community in the Middle East, EMS is a common and accepted behavior. His wife firmly disagreed, stating that affairs were never a part of the culture or religious norms. The clinician was not familiar with the particular Middle Eastern country, so he consulted with the couple's clergyperson for guidance in this matter. In addition, the therapist recommended that the couple meet with their clergyperson for a religious consultation and to report the results in the next session. The husband could not disagree with the therapist's recommendation, as he was adamant that he was right and would be supported by their clergyperson. When the religious doctrine concerning his behavior and the norms of his former community were explained, the husband's infidelity was clearly deemed improper; thus, he acquiesced that his behavior could not be socially justified. This admission opened the door for a psychological exploration of his behavior.

CONCLUSION

The purpose of this chapter has been to show that infidelity is a complex phenomenon that must be viewed or understood from multiple perspectives. The dimensions mentioned were selected from the many presentations of affairs and other forms of infidelity that we have treated throughout the years. The list is not inclusive, nor is it intended to be. In addition, some of the dimensions might overlap with the typologies described in this and other texts. Nonetheless, typologies reflect motivational factors for infidelity whereas dimensions provide a broader examination of the more common characteristics. In addition, the multidimensional perspective subsumes a systemic viewpoint and includes the important role of the spouse in understanding the couple's vulnerability to infidelity. Thus, the clinician gains a more complete picture of the motivations, attitudes, values, behaviors, social contexts, and contributions of each partner to the development, maintenance, interruption, and recovery from the crisis.

4

❀ ❀ ❀

Consequences of Infidelity

THE DISCOVERY OF INFIDELITY IS OFTEN THE PRESENTING PROBLEM for initiating marital therapy (Glass & Wright, 1997; Humphrey, 1982; Penn et al., 1997; Sprenkle & Weis, 1978). Furthermore, infidelity is a leading cause of separation and divorce (Betzig, 1989; Daly & Wilson, 1988). In nearly all instances, there is concern about the tremendous potential for damage to or dissolution of the marriage, even for couples who report positive personal or relational outcomes of affairs and other forms of infidelity (Boekhout, Hendrick, & Hendrick, 1999; Charny & Parnass, 1995). This chapter combines empirical research with our combined clinical experience about the impact of infidelity on marriage or other committed relationships.

In a research study by Whisman and colleagues (1997), therapists classified marital problems in terms of frequency, difficulty, and severity. Infidelity, specifically extramarital affairs, ranked second (after physical abuse) in negative impact on the marriage. Most experienced couples therapists acknowledge that cases involving infidelity are difficult to treat and emotionally depleting to all parties involved. Fundamental beliefs regarding relational commitment, attachment, trust, and exclusivity are exposed and questioned, often for the first time (Charny, 1992; Drigotas & Barta, 2001). Typically, the couple begins treatment in crisis and remains uncertain about continuation of the marriage. Consequently, the sessions are often emotionally charged and the course of therapy is precarious. Even the most experienced therapists report that managing the emotional sequelae of infidelity is a daunting assignment.

Numerous empirical investigations attest to the negative effects of infidelity on marital adjustment and longevity. Charny and Parnass (1995) administered surveys to 62 therapists, who each described the details of a closely followed marital therapy case involving an affair. In the opinion of the therapist respondents, couples impacted by infidelity struggled more than did other clinical pairs who did not have affairs. Only 43.5% of marriages reported in this study continued after the affair, and the overall atmosphere of these marriages was described as dysphoric or negative. An additional 6% of couples affected by infidelity reported a sense of emptiness in their marriages and pessimism about the future of their relationships. Only 9% of the therapists surveyed by Charny and Parnass (1995) felt infidelity had improved the marriage or produced growth, particularly in couples who experienced only one affair. Charny and Parnass (1995) also mentioned that many marriages continue to suffer for years after the discovery of infidelity, and some eventually end in divorce.

COMMON THEMES

Ambivalence and Depression

Using a clinical sample, Beach, Jouriles, and O'Leary (1985) investigated the prevalence of ambivalence and depression in couples seeking marital psychotherapy. They compared two samples of couples, those with and those without infidelity as an issue. The spouses in this study who had experienced EMS had higher levels of depression and / or lower levels of commitment to the marriage. Further analysis revealed that the unfaithful partner was the one with the higher scores in both areas. In this study, infidelity was considered an expression of ambivalence about commitment to the marriage. Depression is another consequence of infidelity; it is related to the many losses resulting from the realization that assumptions about trust and loyalty were faulty. Our clinical experience supports these findings and, in fact, we often see high levels of depression in both partners.

Turmoil

Thompson (1984) found that after an affair is discovered and acknowledged, the partners frequently undergo a period of disorienting thoughts and emotions. The couple's contract regarding intimacy and exclusivity has been violated; thus, confusion results from shattered expectations and assumptions about the marriage. Moreover, there is often a resurgence of unresolved relational issues in the areas of emotional intimacy, sexual relating, and communication. Commonly, both partners utilize idiosyncratic strategies to defend against the painful emotions stimulated by the affair. These defense mechanisms further exacerbate the cognitive and emotional disequilibrium for the couple. For instance, intellectualization is often employed temporarily to help insulate the individual from unpleasant feelings. In addition, minimizing or dismissing the significance of the infidelity temporarily circumvents painful feelings.

Jealousy

Jealousy adds to the confusion. The betrayed partner may insist on protracted discussions about the intimate details of the infidelity. This partner is attempting to make sense of or look for reasons for the betrayal. The therapist should warn the couple that such discussions only intensify other agonizing emotions related to the breach of trust. Furthermore, the unfaithful partner often feels compelled to defend or justify the infidelity or to lie about the details.

Brian and Ann entered treatment after she disclosed infidelity. In the initial sessions, he was often agitated but silent. Brian struggled because the only emotions that he was able to access were jealousy, frustration, and confusion. He acknowledged that the therapy was necessary and helpful, yet he had to force himself to attend because the sessions were so difficult for him. The turmoil he experienced was staggering, particularly because he could not circumvent and only inconsistently defend against the pain of the betrayal. In order to reflect on his emotions and gain perspective, Brian sometimes sent e-mail messages to the therapist. This information was used in subsequent sessions with his permission. In the following e-mail correspondence, Brian reported feeling overwhelmed by jealousy, rage, shock, and hopelessness:

> I don't have a good handle on my feelings and when asked to put them into words I get frustrated. That turns into resentment rather quickly towards Ann for putting me in the situation [of having to deal with an affair]. Add to that the fact that walking in there [the therapist's office] reminds me that she gave some dude movie-quality head on many occasions while she was married to me. Forget it.

Therapists must explain that emotional intensity, confusion, and jealousy are expected consequences of the disclosure of the infidelity (Cano & O'Leary, 1997). In fact, couples often feel relieved if they are given a "map" to help them understand the emotions they can expect to experience (Olson, Russell, Higgins-Kessler, & Miller, 2002). Commonly, the partners will undergo feelings of turbulence, chaos, and disorientation, especially in the beginning phases of the recovery process. The couple can expect these feelings to subside, with other intense but less confusing emotions replacing them over time. Often, the future is discussed with varying degrees of rationality and uncertainty. Therapists can remind the couple that any decision made during a time of confusion is premature. According to Spanier and Margolis (1983), the course of recovery from infidelity can take months or years. Eventually the couple will begin to examine the reasons for the infidelity, although fierce outbursts or defenses against overwhelming emotions (affect) often interrupt this process.

Reactions to infidelity depend on numerous factors, such as the method of discovery, preexisting marital circumstances, and personality characteristics of the partners. There has been a considerable effort in the research and clinical literature to provide a framework of "normalcy" when dealing with the tumultuous phase of treatment. The therapist must anticipate that the couple will be pessimistic and skeptical, especially in the beginning of treatment, and that reassurance and normalization of the expected consequences can serve to defuse the crisis and keep the couple in treatment.

Olson and colleagues (2002) proposed a stage model for understanding the course of events following the disclosure of an affair. This information helps couples to realize some of the factors that made their relationship vulnerable to an affair and make sense of the chaotic emotions they are encountering. The authors identified three stages, beginning with the emotional turmoil of the disclosure. In the second stage, the partners disengage somewhat in an attempt to understand what has happened and why. In this stage, hypervigilance and acts of revenge are common. In the final stage, the partners work on building trust, offering apologies, and giving forgiveness.

In the next section, we discuss the impact of discovery on the couple. We illustrate reactions commonly encountered by each partner in the postdiscovery phase. In later chapters, we concentrate on the final stage of recovery from infidelity and the necessity of remorse and forgiveness.

THE IMPACT OF DISCOVERY

After months and sometimes years of insidious betrayal of trust, the partner discovers the infidelity, the spouse admits to being involved, or both. The marriage will never be the same from this point forward. In addition to crisis of disclosure, the couple must deal with the numerous problems that may have contributed to and surely will follow the infidelity. The issues are numerous and surface with overwhelming intensity. The revelation or discovery of an affair or any other form of infidelity can be reframed as an opportunity to reassess the relationship and establish a more workable contract. Yet, for many, unearthing of the intimacy betrayal is a lethal turning point for the fragile, ailing marriage.

Shock, Anger, and Denial

The emotions subsequent to the discovery of infidelity are often as challenging for the partner who has transgressed the loyalty bonds as they are for the betrayed spouse. It is understandable that the couple cannot see beyond this dilemma because the experience is so confounding. According to Humphrey (1987), the most common feelings of the early disclosure are usually shock, anger, and denial. The order of these emotions occurs differently among couples and if often influenced by the gender of the betrayed partner. If the husband is disloyal, the wife is likely to experience shock, then anger. When the wife is unfaithful, husbands usually report feeling anger first, followed by shock (Atwood & Seifer, 1997; Humphrey, 1987).

Grief

After a period of unwavering shock and anger, the next emotional reaction to emerge in the immediate postdiscovery phase is grief (Rhodes, 1984; Rosenau, 1998). The partners begin to acknowledge the damage to their assumptions about exclusivity, commitment, and trust. They can no longer expect honesty, intimacy, and protection against intrusion in the relationship. The shock of reality occurs when the partners comprehend that the marriage is no longer unique and special in ways that were presumed. The partners lose a sense of confidence in the relationship, which affects their individual levels of security. We have found that feelings of skepticism and pessimism often obscure the other immediate feelings of denial, anger, and grief.

Another excerpt from Brian portrays the immediate reactions of the betrayed husband. Despite his discomfort in the face of exquisitely painful discussions, he endured the sessions and often reflected his feelings afterward while sitting at his computer. Clearly, he struggled to contain his anger by attempting to understand his wife's justifications for the EMS. Nonetheless, his pessimism is apparent, as he doubted if he could withstand the processes necessary to rebuild the marriage:

> It is hard for me to understand this behavior [her infidelity] and deal with such vagueness [her partial concealment of some of the details]. The only way I am able to tolerate it is to imagine that Ann is under

the influence of some narcotic and not in full command of her brain. Still, that makes me doubt her intelligence and strength of character, and this doubt grows every time she opens her mouth and frustrates me more. I'm reaching the end of my rope but I'm still hanging on. I'll let you know if I feel myself slipping.

Traumatization

Another way of viewing the impact of infidelity is to reframe it as a trauma or injury to the relationship, using the analogy of a posttraumatic stress disorder (PTSD) (Glass & Wright 1997; Janoff-Bulman, 1992; Lusterman, 1995). The traumatic event is the disclosure of infidelity and the betrayed partner often suffers from PTSD symptoms, even if he or she was previously stable. The signs include, but are not limited to, hypervigilance, difficulty concentrating, anger, irritability, numbness, depression, anxiety, sleep disturbances, and eating disturbances. Typically, the betrayed partner imagines scenarios of the spouse in sexual situations with the affair partner. In addition, there may be obsessive ruminations about various social activities enjoyed by the couple having the affair. Situational stimuli can trigger flashbacks of the actual event or fantasized versions. Suicidal ideation and homicidal threats can occur during this unstable time, and the research literature attests to the fact that infidelity is a leading cause of spousal abuse and homicide (Daly & Wilson, 1988).

Humphrey (1982) offered a limited number of outcomes to the therapist working with the couple in the early postdiscovery phase of infidelity. He suggested that the resolution of the the betrayal can take three possible forms:

- The affair will end and the marriage will continue.
- Both the affair and the marriage will continue.
- The marriage will end.

The therapist can encourage the couple to accept, allow, and articulate the feelings of shock, anger, and denial, while controlling for pessimism and skepticism. Core beliefs about the marriage will be excavated and the relationship will be reassessed in light of the continually emerging information. The couple will discuss the future of the marriage; however, no decisions should be attempted during this time. The therapist should remind the couple that instability surrounding the infidelity will diminish eventually and, when the emotional climate is calmer, the future of the marriage can be considered.

The Postdiscovery Phase

The reactions of the betrayed and unfaithful partners are often very dissimilar. Customarily, each has little tolerance for and comprehension of the experiences of the other. The individual spouse is absorbed with the task of understanding and managing his or her emotions and there is little opportunity for empathy or support of the other partner. The resulting feelings of isolation and disconnection can additionally polarize the couple. We next discuss the reactions of the betrayed and unfaithful partners separately, because of their disparity.

Reactions of the Betrayed Partner

The reactions of the betrayed partner have been the subject of numerous empirical and clinical investigations. Researchers share a prevailing view that infidelity violates the committed relationship and is extremely damaging to the spouse (Balswick & Balswick, 1999; Boekhout et al., 1999; Buunk, 1995; Charny & Parnass, 1995). We review some of the empirical research in an attempt to categorize the kinds of reactions the clinician is likely to encounter in the betrayed partner.

Loss of Illusions About the Marriage

Boekhout, and colleagues (1999) and Janoff-Bulman and Frantz (1996) found extremely detrimental outcomes of infidelity. These include the destruction of presumptions and core beliefs about the marriage, the universe, and the self. The betrayed partner suffers from the traumatic loss of the following pivotal illusions:

- My partner is benevolent.
- My world is meaningful.
- I am worthy.

Loss of the trust and confidence that existed in the marriage before the betrayal produces an extreme grief reaction. The bewildered couple faces the task of rebuilding or ending the marriage. In an extremely helpful book dealing with the sequelae of EMS, Spring (1996) discussed the role of loss in the early reactions of the betrayed partner to the disclosure of infidelity. She explained that the assumptions about one's self-identity, sense of "specialness," self-respect, control over thoughts and actions, sense of order and justice in the world, and sense of purpose are destroyed. Although it would be unwise to place an arbitrary time span on this process, according to Rhodes (1984) it takes roughly 6 months for many couples to grieve the losses from infidelity.

Loss of Belonging

A sense of uniqueness or specialness distinguishes one marital relationship or partnership from another. Moreover, the support, love, and trust between partners provide a sense of "us against the world" that essentially protects the couple's union. The feeling of being a member of a unique couple is lost immediately after disclosure of infidelity. The betrayed partner experiences the privation of trust through betrayal, disappointment, loss of belonging, and feelings of abandonment (Boekhout et al., 1999).

Feeling of Rejection

Betrayed partners realize that they have been excluded from the loop of intimacy. They feel abandoned and alone, and experience an intense loss of belonging to a partnership. A 35-year-old mother of three children under six years of age was shocked and grief-stricken when her spouse announced that he did not "feel anything" for her anymore and that he would probably leave the marriage. She explained that they used to act as a team and made all decisions together. They determined that she would stay at home to care for the children and that he would be the major provider. They selected a home and an economic plan giving them a sense of togetherness. Suddenly, he was uninvolved with the family and she felt compelled to act alone. She shed bitter tears with each realization that she was forced out of the partnership: "We wanted these children and this house. Now I care for all of it by myself. He doesn't want me. What am I supposed to do? How am I supposed to act?"

Self-Doubt

Infidelity has profound negative effects on the sense of adequacy of the betrayed partner (Balswick & Balswick, 1999; Buunk, 1995; Charny & Parnass, 1995). Typical feelings include intense self-doubt, lowered self-esteem, lowered confidence, inadequacy, and insecurity. Concomitantly, there are always concerns about physical attractiveness, sexual confidence, and normalcy. The common question is "What is wrong with me?" The 35-year-old wife asked, "What is it about me that you cannot tolerate? What did I do wrong? Why don't you love me anymore? How can I accept that there isn't something terribly wrong with me?"

Anger and Rage

The experience of anger or rage is a by-product of the emotional makeup of the betrayed partner, level of marital discord, events surrounding the infidelity, and the degree of betrayal that occurred. There is no universal pattern. Anger often continues in varying degrees throughout the duration of the postdiscovery and recovery periods. It is often combined with other concentrated emotions, such as sadness and shock. The betrayed partner often tries to save face and regain power in the relationship through a variety of anger-based behaviors (Balswick & Balswick, 1999). These may include possessing a superior or self-righteous attitude or taking the moral high road toward the unfaithful partner (Humphrey, 1982). Other faces of anger may involve hurtful, depriving, blaming, or "browbeating" behaviors. Sometimes, power is reclaimed through an increased urge to leave the marriage rather than resolving the discord. Regardless of its varied manifestations, anger can be understood as a reaction to the trauma of the betrayal.

In another session, the betrayed wife mentioned earlier raged at her husband, stating: "Why didn't you tell me you were so unhappy? Why did you wait until it was too late? We all get unhappy and you need to grow up and face the music. *You* are unhappy so now you want to leave me."

Jealousy

A potent emotion, jealousy, is associated with the threat or actual loss of a valued partnership to a rival (Cano & O'Leary, 1997). Jealousy is often described as a blending of emotions or as involving elements of anger, sadness, fear, anxiety about what will happen next, and depression about the loss of the benefits of the relationship. Because of jealousy, the betrayed partner often engages in behaviors of hypervigilance, such as monitoring, stalking, and interrogating. In some situations, betrayed spouses may become so consumed by morbid suspicion that they physically assault or even murder their unfaithful partners in a jealous rage. Francis (1977) examined several aspects of jealousy, and determined that there is great variability in the ways in which it is experienced, defended against, and expressed. For instance, men use denial and rationalization of infidelity more than women do, whereas women are more apt to experience jealousy in such a situation.

Gender Differences

In the beginning of the chapter, we discussed a few gender differences with respect to infidelity, noting that the order of emotions experienced by the betrayed partner is often different for men and women. In earlier chapters, we also discussed some of the gender-based justifications for infidelity, specifically the love justification for women and the absence of this explanation for men. Individuals do not necessarily react in gender-prescribed ways to infidelity or any life circumstance; nonetheless, knowing some of the general clinical and empirical findings can prepare the therapist and couple for the reactions to come.

In the immediate postdisclosure period, according to Atwood and Seifer (1997), betrayed men often report anger whereas betrayed women frequently react with shock. Boekhout and colleagues (1999) found that aggressive responses to infidelity are more typical of men than of women. Perhaps the male's reaction is an effort to gain control of the situation or to deny the humiliating feelings resulting from the realization that his wife chose to be with someone else (Spring, 1996). Betrayed women are more likely to respond with disappointment, self-doubt, and forgiveness. In fact, women attempt to restore the marital relationship more often than men do (Botwin, 1994). Men are more likely to search for another partner than to forgive (Spring, 1996).

Another interesting gender difference is that betrayed women tend to obsess and ruminate about the details of infidelity, dwelling on and reliving the unpleasant memories of the partner's betrayal. Men are more able to isolate their feelings of sadness and pain and sublimate their emotional energy into esteem-building activities (Spring, 1996).

A well-designed study by Cano and O'Leary (2000) showed a dramatic effect between affairs and depression in women. Women whose husbands had an affair were six times more likely than the women in the control group to experience a major depressive episode. This group of women often reported feelings of betrayal and humiliation. In addition to major depression, they were also significantly more likely to report nonspecific symptoms of dysthymia and anxiety than were women in the control group. Spring (1996) noted that women are almost twice as likely to become depressed after the disclosure of infidelity. She cited the tendency for women to blame themselves for the partner's affair and to suffer from depression because they equate their self-worth with being in a relationship.

Regardless of gender issues, continued lack of trust, anger, grief, and jealousy in the betrayed spouse can complicate the recovery phase and therapy, particularly if the clinician is unfamiliar with these reactions. The therapist can prepare the couple for the work ahead by knowing what to expect, when to expect it, and the typical duration of emotional reactions. The couple has the arduous task of evaluating the rules of the relationship, and particularly considering those that created problems in the marriage (Rhodes, 1984). In reality, the old contract is rendered null and void by the disclosure of infidelity and a new one will be reconstructed in the months and years to come (Sager, 1976; Sager & Hunt, 1979).

REACTIONS OF THE UNFAITHFUL PARTNER

The emotional reactions of the unfaithful partner are often considerably less understandable to most observers. Nonetheless, many conditions within the individual, the families of origin, and the relationship create vulnerability to infidelity in this partner. Empathy for the betrayer is a necessary condition for the assessment of and ultimately for treatment of the couple. The therapist cannot ignore or circumvent, but must anticipate and deal with this partner's real feelings. The spouse who violated the trust must also partake in rebuilding the relationship. Alienating this partner through negative judgments or failure to empathize will only serve as another barrier to intimacy for the couple.

Relief

The partner may fear that revealing the affair will further deteriorate or end the marriage, or cause emotional harm to the spouse. In addition, revelation could potentially identify or endanger the extramarital partner (Cottone & Mannis, 1996). Spring (1996, 1999) displayed a poignant sensitivity to the reactions of the unfaithful partner after the disclosure or discovery of infidelity. Typically, this spouse has violated his or her own values system by engaging in a web of deception; thus, disclosure leads to relief, even at the cost of creating a marital crisis.

Nonetheless, it is appropriate to expect a period of grief and loss over the termination of infidelity. In fact, if the unfaithful partner does not become at least mildly depressed, the therapist can assume that he or she has relapsed back into the affair. In most cases, guilt and self-loathing will also be experienced (Spanier & Margolis, 1983).

Mourning the Ended Affair

The normal channels of support are not available to the partner who has cherished and ended an affair. Friends are unavailable for assistance because the infidelity was usually a secret. It would be inappropriate to expect help from children. Understandably, the betrayed spouse cannot offer comfort and the affair partner is, hopefully, out of the picture. The spouse who was unfaithful often suffers in silence, attempting to address the crisis in the marriage during an interval of mourning (Humphrey, 1982). Feelings of isolation, hopelessness, paralysis, and self-loathing are common in this depleted partner.

Lack of Guilt

In some instances, there is an unexplained lack of guilt for having been unfaithful. Occasionally, infidelity actually enhances the self-worth in this partner through experiencing new and different activities, developing a greater frame of reference, and receiving adulation from another person. These positive features also promote ambivalence toward the spouse and interfere with resolution of conflict.

We return to the case of Ann and Brian. Ann was not overwhelmed by guilt feelings about being unfaithful. In fact, the affair enabled her to reclaim parts of herself that were inaccessible for years because she evidently withheld them from Brian. In her affair, she enjoyed music, artistic endeavors, athletics, sex, and a view of the world that was very different from hers. She cherished and grew from the adventures provided through repeated contact with her affair partner. Moreover, Ann stated that even if given the opportunity, she would have made the same choice. Nonetheless, she was eager to share the journey with Brian with renewed vigor. Thus, the affair served as a "wake-up call" for the dying marriage. In essence, Ann sought a greater level of intimacy with her husband.

She was unprepared for other emotions she often experienced during the period subsequent to the admission. For instance, Ann was surprised to feel jealous when she discovered that her affair partner had resumed life without her. She was particularly angered when she heard that his wife became pregnant in the immediate postdisclosure period, perceiving this event as a direct assault on what was most sacred in their affair. Her reactions dampened her enthusiasm about rebuilding the marriage: How could she feel things so deeply toward her affair partner even after she gave up the relationship? How could she love Brian so much and still be so affected by events that should not matter anymore?

Lack of Patience

The person who had the affair often lacks patience with the betrayed spouse for the resulting intense, protracted, and painful reactions to the betrayal. These partners cannot tolerate seeing the affair's damaging effects and have little reserve to comfort and support a rageful, traumatized, and mistrustful spouse. They often lack the amount of empathy necessary to help mend the injured partner and appear to be cold and uncaring when they are often paralyzed with reactions of their own. This apparent lack of concern for the spouse can continue beyond the disclosure phase, after all communication with the affair partner has ceased for some time.

A case example occurred with a bright, attractive, professional couple in their late 30s who had two young children. The husband met a woman at work and had an affair lasting several months, with one relapse after the initial disclosure. The couple attended conjoint sessions every 2 weeks for a year, and was doing well in the rebuilding phase. Although many of their sessions were extremely somber, one was especially light and hopeful after they had purchased a new home. The wife expressed that even in good times, it was difficult for her to completely forget the affair and details associated with it. The husband appeared impatient and asked if his wife would ever "get over it." The therapist responded to his lack of understanding by stating that the wife's feelings were completely "normal" and had in fact subsided greatly in the last 6 months. The therapist calmly reiterated the PTSD information and predicted that they could expect her to experience intense memories from time to time and that they should discuss rather than avert her feelings when this occurred. The therapist's explanation helped to defuse the emotional reactions of the misunderstood wife and provided reassurance for the perplexed husband. Couples need this kind of explanation, even after the immediate postdiscovery phase, because the range, intensity, and duration of emotions after an affair surpass the typical experiences of most individuals.

Gender Differences

The foremost gender difference regarding the personal feelings of the unfaithful spouse involves guilt. Women tend to experience more guilt over infidelity than men do (Lawson, 1988; Spanier & Margolis, 1983). They feel remorseful for putting their needs first, and for the negative impact of the affair on their husbands and children. Furthermore, because women cannot compartmentalize their feelings as well as men can, they become unhappy with their marriages (Botwin, 1994). Spring (1996) warned that men can deny the impact of infidelity because it is not a core component of their self-esteem. Thus, they are better able to keep an affair separate from the marriage, because its effect on the self and the intimate primary relationship is undervalued.

CONCLUSION

The consequences of infidelity in the immediate and postdiscovery phases were reviewed, with particular emphasis on gender differences. We selected themes that we have seen most commonly in our clinical practices. The empirical literature and our clinical experience support that reactions to infidelity are intense and varied, yet they often fall within a range of predictable behaviors for the unfaithful person as well as the betrayed partner. It is essential that the therapist working with affairs and other forms of infidelity is familiar with the consequences for the marriage or primary relationship. This information, when appropriate, should be imparted to the couple in order to promote the best therapeutic outcome. The chapters that follow continue to discuss treatment strategies and modalities for infidelity.

5

❀ ❀ ❀

Therapeutic Dilemmas

IN COUPLES THERAPY, WE TREAT MANY EMOTIONALLY CHARGED relationship themes, such as abuse, rage, pain, envy, love, lust, and jealousy. However, when treating infidelity, the therapist faces particular challenges, such as the raw, intense, emotional reactions to a betrayal, and the couple's struggle to make sense of the situation. In addition, the therapist needs to maintain a therapeutic balance in the face of material that may suggest that one partner is more responsible than the other for the damage to the relationship. Ultimately, the therapist must examine his or her own values system and ensure that interventions represent unbiased efforts to assist the couple in making the difficult decisions resulting from the crisis.

Most therapists intuitively comprehend the difficulty in treating infidelity, yet there is little professional literature devoted to understanding why this might be the case. In two studies (Geiss & O'Leary, 1981; Whisman et al., 1997), practicing psychotherapists reported that working with infidelity is among the most perplexing problem areas encountered in couples therapy. Therapists universally perceive affairs and other betrayals of intimacy as extremely difficult and challenging, because they generate tremendous emotional turmoil in the couple, threaten the continuity of the couple's relationship, impact the therapeutic relationship, and carry powerful societal prohibitions. Our own experience with hundreds of couples who have come to grips with infidelity and in supervising student interns confirms the results of the two previously cited studies.

During a weeklong intensive workshop on couples therapy, the senior author of this volume noticed on the fourth day that participants began to show an unusual amount of interest for the next day's topic: treating affairs. Clearly, everyone was anxious about the subject matter and concerned that there might not be enough conference time to adequately address the issue. When asked about their anxiety concerning the next day, the attending therapists mentioned a number of different concerns, summarized as follows:

- Countertransference issues.
- The ethical issue of confidentiality.
- How and if affairs should be revealed.
- How much should be revealed.

It appears that therapists want directions and formulas when encountering the perplexing issues that surround an affair. We believe that countertransference dilemmas must be dealt with before addressing therapeutic strategies, and thus discuss them next.

COUNTERTRANSFERENCE ISSUES

In general, the term *countertransference* refers to the positive or negative feelings that a therapist develops toward the client throughout the course of therapy (Gelso & Carter, 1985; Kernberg, 1990; Stevens, 1986). For our purposes, countertransference involves the therapist's affective and cognitive reactions to the material presented by the client or the couple. These responses may be conscious or beyond the awareness of the therapist. Obviously, conscious reactions are the most productive, because they are within the direct control of the therapist. Unconscious countertransference feelings and responses are potentially destructive to the therapeutic process, because the individual partners or the interactions of the couple restimulate the unresolved conflicts of the therapist. Accordingly, the resulting interventions may be more related to the therapist's sensitivities than to the problems presented by the couple.

Very little attention in the family therapy literature has been devoted to countertransference issues, including writings on the treatment of extramarital affairs. Family systems thinkers abandoned this concept because it represented the old, individualistic, psychoanalytic, psychodynamic model of therapy. Some consider countertransference less of a factor in working with couples and families for two reasons: The intensity of the relationship between the therapist and client is diluted because there are more people in the treatment room; and the primary relationship is between the couple. No researcher has empirically tested this speculation. In our clinical experience, countertransference presents differently when working with couples. Specifically, therapists are vulnerable to the influences of their unresolved sensitivities, which are likely to be stimulated because of the intensity and precariousness of the situations involved in treating infidelity.

Silverstein (1998) is the only clinician to have written an entire journal article about the subject of countertransference in treating affairs. Her thinking was similar to our own on this topic: The primary countertransference reactions are overidentifying with either the unfaithful or the betrayed partner, blaming one partner, or defending the other partner. She agreed with our conclusion that such responses result from the therapist's fantasies about having an affair, temptation, dalliance, or other unresolved conflicts, which could produce inappropriate countertransference reactions. Additionally, the therapist may even collude with the couple or partner to conceal the infidelity because of an inability to handle the ensuing disillusionment, rage, and fury that might occur in the session. Moreover, the underlying and often hidden difficulties and events that have brought the couple to therapy are glossed over or go unrecognized.

Silverstein (1998) described two general categories of countertransference responses—objective and subjective. The former refers to a more common or universal set of countertransference reactions, such as identification with the betrayed partner. Subjective responses, however, are uniquely related to the idiosyncratic conflicts of the particular therapist. In addition, Silverstein cautioned therapists about the innumerable dangers of unrecognized countertransference reactions.

Some identification is desirable and may fall within the category of objective countertransference described by Silverstein (1998). It helps us connect and understand our clients better. In couples work, especially with infidelity, there is the potential danger that we underidentify with one partner and overidentify with the other. The therapist's polarized way of viewing the situation can create more distance for couples who are hoping for recovery. Often, this "all-or-nothing" perspective categorizes one partner as good and the other as bad or one as the victim and the other as the victimizer. It is antithetical to the systems perspective to ascribe such restricted roles to each partner. The greater issue, of course, is in determining if the systems perspective does apply when treating affairs. We explore this idea in a Chapter 7.

In an edited text on countertransference in couples therapy, Solomon and Siegel (1997) acknowledged that countertransference feelings are inevitable and often helpful to the therapeutic process, provided they are within the conscious awareness of the therapist. Taibbi included one short section in a paper on extramarital affairs about the therapist's values. He simply pointed out that therapists need to be clear about their principles because "the topic is one that can easily rub into the therapist's own skin" (1983, p. 204).

Emily Brown's (1991b) popular book on affairs included only a few pages on countertransference. Like other writers, she illustrated the relationship between unconscious countertransference feelings and the personal history of the therapist. She warned of the more common therapeutic errors in judgment that can result from a therapist's unrecognized conflicts regarding affairs. These include the tendency to:

- Collude with one partner in secrecy and avoidance.
- Attempt to keep a failing marriage together despite the partners' wish to end it.
- Be intolerant or judgmental of the partner having the affair.
- Fear and avoid the intense feelings unleashed by discussing an affair.

In rare cases, Brown mentioned that therapists could be impaired to the point that they will cross the line to have an affair with a client.

Moultrup's (1990) textbook about affairs examined the many ramifications of infidelity on the intimate relationship as well as on the psychotherapy. He integrated individual, relational, and family systems theory in his approach to assessment and treatment. Throughout the text, he discussed the need for the therapist to remain neutral and unbiased when dealing with the complicated layers of treating affairs. As with the previously cited writers, Moultrup agreed that the therapist's values and experiences play a key role in the management of infidelity.

We assert that therapists must make every effort to understand their countertransference feelings and personal positions toward infidelity. This is a prerequisite to avoid hiding behind techniques and formulas and to learn how to approach the problem and the couple from a human perspective. Therapists live in the same world as their clients do. Many of the same strong social forces that influence their clients affect them, and they too must deal with issues related to their own relationships' fidelity. The attitudes that therapists have toward infidelity are strongly representative of their moral, ethical, and religious value systems.

The professional literature does not prescribe an attitude that therapists should have, nor should it. In reading various texts on this subject, therapist attitudes are generally conservative, viewing affairs as an expression of individual psychopathology or marital dysfunction. In more extreme cases, therapists take a strong moralistic or religiously based stance against the affair partner. Rarely do therapists advocate for or view affairs or other forms of infidelity as healthy expressions, nor do they support a clandestine affair in one partner. In this culture, attitudes are often formed or influenced by religious beliefs that emphasize honesty and fidelity rather than adultery. However, personal experience may also play a key role. Each therapist has a unique outlook based on personal experience and socialization. It is probably safe to assume that a number of therapists have had affairs or have been personally affected by affairs in their families or among their friends. The impact of these experiences is not clearly known. For some, the encounter may have created a more permissive stance or greater understanding and empathy. Conversely, it may have taught the therapists that infidelity is damaging. In trying to reconcile breaches of their own value systems, therapists' reactions fall along a continuum from extremely liberal to extremely moralistic.

The following case illustrates the powerful impact that a therapist's personal attitude toward an affair can have on a client. A woman called for an appointment, asking how the therapist worked with couples when an affair had occurred. She mentioned in the initial telephone call that she had been in individual therapy, but did not want to go back to her therapist. The couple had been having marital problems for years. Evidently, the wife had decided to see an individual therapist about what she should do. During the course of therapy, she mentioned that she had been thinking of having an affair with a man that she knew. The therapist, who was by no means a novice, told her that her husband was a good provider and father, but she would never be able to get what she wanted from him. The therapist suggested that the client act on her desire to have an affair with her friend and keep it a secret. Although hesitant, she decided the therapist must be right and initiated an affair. Her guilt over the affair grew and the client decided this was not the right course of action for her. She had the courage to end the affair and the therapy, deciding that she wanted to work on the marriage. The client could no longer live a dual life and decided to address the long-standing marital problems, knowing there was a chance that the marriage could end.

The individual therapist's own history and experiences contributed to her therapeutic approach to infidelity. She was in her second marriage, having ended the first marriage to an alcoholic husband through an affair. In addition, she believed that women should have the right to conduct affairs as men do. Clearly, her unresolved conflicts provoked a projective countertransferential stance. Fortunately, the client was able to extricate herself from a situation that was becoming personally and relationally destructive.

Conversely, we have heard from therapists who have been personally affected in affairs who project a punitive judgmental therapeutic attitude.

They believe that affairs cause irreparable damage and that losing the marital relationship should serve as just punishment for having an affair. They suggest leaving the marriage as moral restitution for the damage caused to the partner and family. There is little or no consideration given to the chance of repairing the damage caused by the affair and reworking the marital contract.

Another possibility is that many people, including therapists, are occasionally tempted to have an affair as a way to escape a difficult marital situation, but resist such an urge. Social psychologists have known for years that when people resist temptation they generally "harden" their attitude against the enticement, believing that if they were strong enough to resist it then everyone else should also be strong enough. In such a situation, it is understandable that a therapist may have little patience or understanding when confronted with an affair. Conversely, other therapists may never have experienced the temptation to nor actually engaged in an affair. How would it be possible for them to understand or empathize with those who have entertained thoughts of an affair or actually had one or more? These are among the many questions unanswered in the research literature that therapists must consider overtly or covertly before imposing their own feelings, beliefs, or values onto their clients.

The previously mentioned examples are rather extreme and obvious instances of the personal issues of the therapist having a negative impact on a couple's therapy. We offer two more examples in which the therapist's unrecognized countertransference issues complicated the course of treatment. The first involved a psychiatrist who had strong ethical and religious beliefs against infidelity. He accepted a referral of a 35-year-old female client for treatment of situational depression. During the course of therapy, she revealed that she had had an affair that precipitated the termination of her marriage. Throughout the course of 8 months of weekly psychotherapy, the therapist failed to show up for a scheduled weekly appointment with his client on three occasions! For this therapist, forgetting a scheduled appointment had rarely occurred, and never more than once with the same client; thus, he suspected that the behavior might have a greater meaning. The therapist presented the situation to his supervisor, and they uncovered his discomfort with the client's issues related to the affair and his ambivalence about working with her. Another example involved a therapist in training for marital and family psychotherapy who inadvertently left the couple's file opened on her desk and the suspicious spouse noted that her husband had revealed an affair in a prior individual session. In each example, the therapist's unconscious behaviors "acted out" an inability to handle the conflict generated by the issues of the therapy. Ultimately, the therapist caused a breach in the working alliance in each example. This is truly unfortunate, considering the stress levels of the clients who were seeking assistance with their problems.

Having defined countertransference and reviewed the literature about countertransference in marital and family therapy, Weeks's (1989) Intersystems Model can be used to summarize the broad categories of sources of countertransference:

- Family-of-origin issues.
- Current intimate relationship with a spouse or significant other, and past relationships.
- Personal strengths or psychological vulnerabilities.

TROUBLING TACTICAL PREDICAMENTS

Therapists deal with at least two common presentations of infidelity, and these presentations can stimulate strong feelings in the therapist. The first is one in which an affair is ongoing yet is adamantly denied by the unfaithful partner. The second is when the unfaithful partner and / or the couple want to minimize the impact of the infidelity on the intimate relationship. In each case, the tactical issue involves an extramarital affair. The same reactions apply to additional forms of infidelity that utilize the Internet, strip clubs, and other betrayals of intimacy.

When a Partner Denies Infidelity

We generally assume that when couples seek therapy they are interested in being open and honest. However, infidelity may initially be concealed, and revealed or discovered at a much later time. One way to suspect the presence of undisclosed infidelity is to realize that the progress of therapy is extremely slow or lacking, with no apparent reason. Over the years, the authors have learned to trust our therapeutic intuition that the cause for halted or "stuck" couples therapy is usually a secret, and that secret is often an affair. In some cases, we may like the couple and, because of our positive countertransferential feelings, we may want to believe that they are being honest. Furthermore, we may reason that their work situation and responsibilities would make an affair impossible. One such case involved an elevator mechanic who appeared to be either working or at home virtually every minute of the day. He worked 12- to 14-hour days and was usually dispatched from one job to another. Every minute of his day was recorded for billing purposes. The couple had been in treatment for several months and was not making the expected progress. Eventually, his wife discovered that he was having an affair with his dispatcher, with whom he had found creative ways to meet secretly.

The point is that infidelity is usually insidious, leaving no discernable sign (at least in the beginning). Therapists have no foolproof way of ascertaining the truth when a client wants to deceive us. One way of anticipating and preparing for the possibility of concealed infidelity is for the therapist to adopt a default assumption that virtually everyone having an affair will in fact lie about it initially, whether the deception is directed toward the spouse or the therapist. Therapists must comprehend that affairs involve two levels of deception or violation. First, there is the affair itself, which is an incredible violation to the couple's intimate relationship. Second, there is the intricate and complicated web of deception around the affair, which can leave the betrayed partner feeling crazy. In some cases, the deception is more damaging than the act itself. We must always be prepared for this deception, and understand that it is considerable part of the problem. Once the therapist has internalized this concept, it is easier to intervene in a therapeutic rather than narcissistic manner when deceived.

When infidelity has been concealed and the therapist has been deceived, the therapist's experience is isomorphic with that of the betrayed spouse. Feelings of betrayal, anger, disbelief, and foolishness are common. The therapist may even consciously or unconsciously wish to retaliate against the deceiver, risking the loss of neutrality. Such countertransferential feelings will need to be discussed and processed with the client in the conjoint context, in supervision, or through peer support.

The unfaithful partner is so mired in the emotional intensity that there typically is a great degree of denial and an ostensible lack of guilt. The underlying logic involved is the individual's need to conceal what is unacceptable. Therapist competence or partner acceptance is not the issue. Because unfaithful partners often fail to comprehend the consequences of their deception, therapists can serve as an "observing ego." Frank discussion during couples therapy of the therapist's feelings of betrayal can serve as both a model for the partner and a reality check for the deceiver. The conversation the therapist has with the betrayer affords an opportunity to model how to deal with the affair's discovery or revelation. Furthermore, the therapist can defuse the negative feelings about the deception, thereby making the situation more manageable.

Infidelity can also place the therapist in an emotional bind. Once an affair is revealed or discovered, it requires an immediate response. The therapist might fear that confronting the affair directly or spending too much time on it would only make matters worse. In fact, some therapists are afraid to step in immediately because of the of the countertransference issues mentioned earlier, lack of skill in handling such matters, discomfort with the anticipated emotional intensity, or fear of precipitating a premature ending of the relationship. When the therapist delays or avoids addressing the affair for any of these or other reasons, the couple will remain stuck. Moreover, the unknowing partner is doubly betrayed and left unprotected by the therapist.

We have seen situations in which the couple wants to talk about the affair, but the therapist finds ways to block the discussion or minimize it. For instance, many beginning therapists acknowledge that an affair was or is occurring and then quickly move on to a topic that is more "comfortable" for them. An astute supervising therapist can intervene to ensure that the trainee addresses the affair more effectively.

When a Partner Minimizes Infidelity

In an effort to diminish the impact of infidelity on the intimate relationship, a number of partners proclaim that it represents an isolated indiscretion and argue that it could not possibly interfere with the continuity of the relationship. Typically, they will downgrade the encounter to the status of a "one night stand" or "just sex." They oppose any therapeutic interventions that will promote discussion of the meaning of the indiscretion or reveal additional information that might suggest more than they have admitted. Sometimes, the unfaithful partner will try to make a deal with the therapist to work on the marriage while the affair continues, noting that if the marriage improves the affair will end.

In one case, the couple was aware that the woman had been sexually involved with a caretaker of their home. The wife was unconvinced that continuing "nonsexual" contact with the known affair partner would compromise the marriage. The apprehensive husband inadvertently colluded with his wife in denying the detrimental impact of the affair on their marriage by stating: "She will decide when to stop talking to and seeing him [her affair partner]. She needs to do this for herself, not for me." He went on to say, "It does not bother me as long as she is not having sex with him." The therapist imposed reality by refusing to continue with conjoint sessions unless the wife terminated communication with the affair partner. Concurrent individual therapy with both spouses was conducted until the wife was able to commit herself exclusively to the marriage. When she discontinued telephone and other contact with her affair partner, conjoint sessions resumed. During her individual sessions, she realized that the ongoing affair indeed affected her husband. Later in the therapy, she revealed that the continuing conversations served to stimulate her passion toward her affair partner. The husband confessed how frightened and betrayed he felt with each meeting she had with the affair partner.

When the Couple Tries to Minimize Infidelity

In other cases, the couple may want to deny the infidelity or its importance. They collude to circumvent the topic because they realize that confronting it may be too stressful for an already weakened marriage. One couple sought treatment because the wife became emotionally and physically removed from her husband. She had stopped socializing, no longer worked on joint projects, and ceased having sex with her spouse. They argued constantly about finances and their lack of togetherness. He confided that he suspected she had been having an affair for some time, yet he did not dare mention his fears. Although the warning signs were apparent, she denied having an affair but admitted that she liked to socialize with men from her workplace. Both partners agreed that despite their continuous discord they would not consider separating on account of their children. The therapy was not progressing, because the obvious issues related to her suspected infidelity were not being addressed. The therapist attempted to intervene through a change in format to concurrent individual sessions, hoping that each would be more willing to work while not in the presence of the other. He attended a few; she refused.

In other instances, the couple may attempt to get the therapist to collude with them in minimizing infidelity. Some couples can be quite convincing. They will talk about how an affair has improved their sex life, opened up their communication, and even gotten them into therapy. This is the perfect presentation for the therapist who is unable to deal with all the distasteful associations that accompany confronting, exploring, and understanding infidelity. Further exploration usually reveals that the couple has not processed the infidelity nor understood the reasons why it happened. The therapist and couple collude, proceeding on the basis that "the past is the past." They convince themselves that improving the marriage is the task at hand. Sadly, in our experience, the success of such a course of psychotherapy is limited.

The therapist must learn to be comfortable with or at least be ready to confront infidelity immediately. If the couple resists, the therapist must employ strategies designed to interrupt any attempts by the partners to divert, circumvent, or minimize the process of confronting the violation of the couple's agreement regarding intimate exclusivity. The therapist must explain that a serious event has occurred that can have far-reaching consequences on the couple's relationship; failure to address the precipitating factors as well as the consequences will keep the couple stuck. Such a statement is nothing more than informed consent. Most clients will appreciate the therapist's clear explanation of the reason why immediate confrontation of infidelity is necessary. Once the rationale is understood, compliance is more likely even if the work is expected to be difficult and painful. As mentioned in an earlier case, sometimes the person who had the affair will refuse to engage in this process and terminate therapy. Therapist of such couples may have no alternative but to refer the remaining spouse for individual therapy or retain that partner in individual therapy, knowing that they cannot be such couples' therapist in the future because of the imbalance created in working with only one spouse.

ETHICAL CONCERNS: CONFIDENTIALITY

The most ethically problematic and anxiety-provoking aspect of dealing with infidelity is the dilemma of confidentiality. This important issue has received little attention in the literature on affairs or other forms of infidelity. Furthermore, an ethical violation may result in legal consequences for the therapist, particularly when dealing with situations in which there is a secret. Information about affairs may be revealed in a myriad of ways. The ideal situation is when the affair has already been disclosed and is clearly identified as the presenting problem. Any situation short of the ideal means that the therapist must confront the predicament of having to manage information that one partner may want to reveal secretly. In some cases, a partner will request an individual session and then reveal one or more secrets or provide information such that the therapist strongly suspects infidelity of one kind or another. In other cases, the therapist may learn about an affair through other sources, such as the community grapevine, an adult child, other family member, an "interested" party, or another client. Therapists are often caught offguard with this information.

We cannot assume that therapists know what to do by following their particular code of ethics. When confronted with a complicated situation involving a secret about one partner, many therapists go to the default position of maintaining confidentiality due to their own discomfort and inexperience. In some instances, therapists may find a way to end treatment without an explanation due to their personal discomfort over having secret information.

Unless rules of confidentiality have been specified and agreed to by all parties in the first session, therapists will find themselves in an ethical bind of one form or another. For instance, should the therapist insist that the secret is revealed, or should the therapist proceed knowing that withholding information from the unsuspecting partner is counterproductive and damaging? In order to avoid this predicament, therapists must decide which rule of confidentiality they wish to use, explain this to the couple in the first session, and obtain their agreement. This precaution is necessary when dealing with any presenting problem, because secret relationships may not be apparent in the initial session or early phases of therapy. An added level of protection involves writing the rules of confidentiality and having the clients sign the form, acknowledging that they understand the rule and accept it.

The following discussion provides information designed to assist therapists in developing their confidentiality rules. We use Karpel's (1980) classic paper on this subject, which suggested three ways of handling confidentiality, and then add our own ideas to his suggestions.

All Information Is Confidential

One position the therapist may take is to maintain that all information received from any source is confidential. Thus, if a partner requests an individual session and reveals an affair, the therapist will maintain this information in confidence. This is a simple position to take, but it raises a number of dilemmas for the therapist—for example, how should the therapist proceed with treatment knowing that there is a significant secret with far-reaching consequences? The fear of violating confidentiality aligns the therapist and the partner with the secret, excluding the other partner. When this happens, therapeutic progress halts and the therapist is ineffective. Moreover, there is collusion with the betraying partner to keep the secret information from the unknowing partner. This represents a situation in which therapists must question if they can ethically proceed with treatment.

Our experience has demonstrated that when there is an active affair or other acts of infidelity, conjoint treatment is ineffective. The unfaithful partner is not invested in improving the primary relationship and will justify continuing the infidelity because of unhappiness in the primary relationship. This individual is unable to work on the primary relationship because of the emotional expenditure on the affair. The therapist may be protected ethically and legally, but the betrayed spouse may discover the affair and suffer more emotional trauma due to being deceived by the partner and the therapist. The risk is that the betrayed partner will leave therapy angry, disappointed, and unprotected.

All Information Must Be Shared

A second option for the therapist is to consider any information received through any source as public information as far as the couple is concerned. The therapist's position is that he or she does not keep secrets and that anything said to the therapist in private is the same as saying it in a conjoint session. This position appears to simplify the therapist's task regarding confidentiality. The major pitfall is that the partner who is actively engaging in an affair will not wish to reveal this information. Everyone then proceeds on the assumption that an affair is not taking place, even if the betrayed spouse or therapist suspects an affair. The partner having the affair lies in order to conceal the infidelity and is not given the opportunity to choose between the affair and the primary relationship. In effect, this partner tries to choose both relationships. This approach will have the same disastrous consequences as the previously mentioned rule that protects secrets.

Although the two opposite positions appear to be simple and easy to assimilate into the value system of the therapist, their initial appeal begins to fade once the implications or consequences are realized. Unfortunately, there is no simple answer. Our aim is not to dictate that a therapist should choose one position over another, but instead to offer what we believe to be the most effective and useful principle. We have used the third rule of confidentiality for many years and with great success, although it is more complicated and anxiety provoking for the therapist. It allows us to avoid the pitfalls mentioned here, and gives us the most flexibility and maneuverability.

Accountability With Discretion

In this approach, therapists may choose to keep the secret information confidential for a specific time period while unfaithful partners are encouraged to accept responsibility for their behavior by revealing the information (Karpel, 1980). In effect, this stance puts pressure on the unfaithful partner to end the affair or reveal the secret. If the client refuses to be accountable, the therapist may unilaterally choose to terminate conjoint treatment without giving a specific reason. This termination is certain to raise suspicion in the betrayed partner. Nonetheless, the therapist is enforcing an ethical stance by refusing to collude with the partner who is involved in infidelity.

We implement this rule through the following steps:

- The therapist does not divulge the secret information received in individual sessions, and in return expects accountability for behavior.
- Accountability means taking responsibility for any conduct, such as secrets or affairs, that violate the couple's agreement about intimacy and exclusivity.
- The individual is told that an active affair or other forms of infidelity will make doing couples therapy impossible and will keep the couple stuck.
- The unfaithful partner must choose between the primary partnership or the infidelity. The infidelity must stop if the partner chooses the primary relationship. This means that an active breach of intimacy must be terminated in order to work on the primary relationship.
- The therapist gives the partner a deadline for stopping the infidelity. If he

or she is unable or unwilling to end the affair in a month, the conjoint sessions will have to cease.

- The therapist requires individual sessions with the partners, in order to understand why the infidelity started, what is being gained from it, and how to end it.

- If the partner confesses a refusal or inability to end the affair or other breach of intimacy, accountability for this behavior is encouraged. The betrayed spouse or partner must be told about the infidelity or the eventual consequence is the demise of the marriage. If the client refuses to be accountable despite the original agreement, the therapist must unilaterally end conjoint treatment. We recommend saying in the conjoint session that an individual issue has been discussed in a private session that makes doing couple therapy and change in the couple impossible. We sometimes reframe the breach of intimacy by stating that the partner is unable to decide about being in or out of the marriage or partnership.

- The therapist statement creates an isomorphic relationship with the couple. One partner has a secret that makes conjoint therapy impossible, and the therapist has the responsibility to report the secret. The unfaithful partner will be forced to become accountable. This technique also enables the betrayed partner to come forth with suspicions and fears about the presence of infidelity. Many times this partner had been unconsciously colluding by failing to confront the unfaithful partner despite suspicions and evidence. In all but one case we can remember, the betrayed partner immediately knew and understood why the therapist needed to interrupt the conjoint sessions. In other cases, the unfaithful partner is in denial of the infidelity, and this strategy is sufficient to break the denial. Although we do not know the rule of confidentiality used, Humphrey (1987) found that 24% of husbands and 23% of wives were still involved in their affairs at the end of a course of brief therapy. The accountability with discretion approach to confidentiality would not allow therapy to continue beyond a few sessions if an active affair was known.

- If the partner agrees to cease to be unfaithful, the couple's therapist should have a few to several sessions of concurrent individual therapy with that partner to learn about the motivations for beginning the affair or other breach of intimacy, to examine why it continued, and to process the feelings of loss that are certain to occur upon termination. The therapist must feel comfortable that this partner has acquired enough insight that another affair will not occur. It is also useful to periodically assess that the initial affair has not restarted. Affairs are difficult to stop and even more difficult to keep stopped. Continued monitoring and processing of feelings is necessary. Even after the affair is terminated, this partner may require some individual sessions to discuss feelings that would be unnecessarily hurtful to the spouse.

- Concurrent sessions with the betrayed partner might be necessary in order to process feelings about the partner's struggles.

- For couples in which one partner is not willing to be accountable, the final recommendation is that they must consider their options as individuals. They should each be referred to an individual therapist in the hope that some individual movement can be made that will enable them to resume couple therapy. Sometimes the betrayed partner states that the relationship is dead or stuck. The couple's therapist could then shift roles and help the partners to separate and divorce.

The major pitfall with this rule is not what the reader might anticipate— that is, therapists often worry that the betrayed partner will be angry with the therapist for concealing information, even for a short period of time. In our experience, this phenomenon has never occurred. In fact, this partner has, on occasion, felt badly that the therapist was caught temporarily in the middle. The trick is being able to explain and implement this complex ethical intervention. Experience with this approach should bring about comfort with the ethical strategy and proficiency in carrying out the other various steps as needed. We can also remain cognizant of the fact that couples who come to therapy are usually motivated to improve the relationship, even though an affair might be taking place. In our experience, the vast majority of partners who admit to infidelity in an individual session are able to stop the affair within the time constraints mentioned. We discuss the content of the individual sessions in Chapter 6.

ETHICAL ISSUES: DISCLOSING THE TERMINATED AFFAIR

The final ethical issue is also the most perplexing. How does the therapist handle the unrevealed terminated affair ethically and responsibly? This category includes undisclosed affairs that have occurred in the past history of the current primary relationship or those that have concluded recently. Should the terminated affair be revealed to the partner? No empirical research has been done on this difficult issue, although many authors discuss it from a clinical standpoint. Moreover, there is a striking lack of consensus in the clinical literature regarding how to approach undisclosed affairs. This is understandable, because the issue is so complex. Interestingly, those who take a position of revealing an affair also find special circumstances for not doing so.

Brown (1991) offered some ideas about when and when not to expose a terminated affair. She was clear about her bias that all affairs, whether current or "ancient" should be revealed. She contended that if couples want to improve their relationship through therapy, then they must be honest about past and present behavior. In theory, this argument makes sense, yet infidelity is generally more precarious than most relational problems. Brown (1991a, 1991b) mentioned several special circumstances that should cause the therapist to pause and consider the destruction that might occur if an affair is revealed. In these cases, she argued that more harm than good could occur if the affair is disclosed. These include the threat of potential harm from physical violence, potential legal ramifications, or when the betrayed spouse is permanently incapacitated.

Others have also taken positions on this question. Pittman (1989, 1995) is often viewed as having taken a moralistic stance toward infidelity. He equated infidelity with lying, and believed lying can only lead to distrust and distance. Thus, he strongly supported being honest about all past affairs. Glass and Wright (1997) asserted that current affairs must be disclosed, but they proceed with couple therapy if the unrevealed affair has already ended. Moultrup (1990) also believed that ongoing affairs should be disclosed; a one-time occurrence in the past or an ended affair need not be revealed. Westfall (1989) suggested that affairs not be revealed if they are over and no longer appear to be affecting the marriage, or if the affair was an isolated instance with no emotional attachment. Finally, Humphrey (1987) took a position of ethical neutrality, stating that it is the client's decision to reveal or not to reveal the affair.

The decision to reveal a terminated affair is a perplexing one, requiring clinical judgment that considers the long-term consequences. This is why we offer the therapist three ethical alternatives from which to choose. Our position is based on the fact that the revelation of an affair can and usually does have a devastating effect on a relationship that can persist for many years. There are two general assaults to the primary relationship when an affair occurs. First, there is the betrayal of trust that erodes the core of the alliance. Then, the protracted, intense reaction of the betrayed partner to the knowledge about an ended affair can take on proportions of the highest magnitude. This reaction can be as devastating as the initial violation of the affair. We discuss this issue in greater detail in Chapter 10.

With respect to ethical issues, we clearly believe that there is damage to the fabric of the relationship any time infidelity occurs, whether the partner knows about the affair or not. Optimally, we believe that partners should never hold back secrets, because the act of withholding information saps energy from the relationship. Furthermore, honesty is the foundation for intimacy. Unfortunately, in our clinical experience, many marriages and relationships have ended unnecessarily because the betrayed partner could not recover from the knowledge of an undisclosed terminated affair. In the best of circumstances, revealing a past or recently terminated affair sidetracks the couple from dealing with the presenting problem and lead to months of repairing the damage resulting from the revelation of the infidelity.

We do not condone infidelity; however, the only circumstances in which we insist on the revelation of an affair is when it is ongoing or if the past affair is getting in the way of the current relationship. If a partner is having an affair at the beginning of treatment and is able to end it, we assert our stance about secrets but do not make revealing the affair a condition of continuing treatment. This is a discretionary judgment, however, involving only partners who have learned about why the affair occurred, feel genuinely remorseful about it, and wish to work on problems that made the relationship vulnerable to infidelity. Furthermore, we must believe that these clients will not be predisposed toward another affair or acts of infidelity. Of course, we can never predict what will happen in the future. We base our decision on a cost / benefit analysis of all factors that exact a heavy toll on the relationship. The rule of accountability with discretion would apply. The affair does not have to be ongoing to impede progress.

We believe that self-disclosure is a fundamental component of establishing and maintaining intimacy in a relationship (Weeks & Treat, 2001). However, we also accept that we can never share every thought or fantasy, nor should we. For instance, in another text on the treatment of sexual dysfunctions, we suggested that not all sexual fantasies need to be revealed to the partner, particularly those that might involve other persons (Weeks & Gambescia, 2000). In healthy relationships, partners share information about their thoughts, wishes, and fantasies that can lead to increased intimacy, but also use good judgment about some disclosures that may damage a relationship. Revealing an ended affair can be specifically reframed as follows: Do the client and the therapist believe that self-disclosure serves any useful and or therapeutic purpose? Our view is ultimately pragmatic; does it help or hurt to know? We are well aware how much harm results from revealing this information, and can only speculate about the potential benefit.

CONCLUSION

This chapter addressed some of the more difficult and perplexing issues encountered when treating infidelity. The very nature of this work is replete with quandaries, predicaments, and other complexities that can challenge the competence and ethical position of the therapist. The rewards usually outweigh the dilemmas, especially when the couple is able to survive the crisis of infidelity and reach new levels of strength in the relationship.

6

✹ ✹ ✹

Initial Phase of Treatment: Issues and Strategies

Very few events in the life of a marriage or committed relationship stir up as much emotional turmoil as infidelity. In this chapter, we discuss common presentations of infidelity as well as strategies to help the couple recover from the resulting emotional trauma. The most important therapeutic challenge in the initial phase of treatment is the method of discovery of the infidelity. This factor significantly impacts the way treatment is conducted. Typically, a married couple seeks treatment after an extramarital affair has been discovered. Another common clinical presentation is when infidelity of any type is concealed from an intimate partner. Frequently, the secret betrayal is revealed to the therapist in an individual session, although this is not always the case. In each presentation, the revelation or discovery of infidelity prompts immediate action by the therapist.

In the case of the disclosed affair, the therapist contends with intense emotions in the betrayed partner, such as shock, hurt, betrayal, anger, and fear about the viability of the relationship. Often, the unfaithful partner is not fully convinced about working on the marriage and is ambivalent about giving up the affair partner. Sometimes, a couple is in treatment for another problem, a spouse becomes suspicious of infidelity, and is able to confirm it during therapy. Less frequently, an affair is suspected yet the betrayed partner does not press the issue for reasons having to do with dependency, finances, status, children, and so on. In some cases, the infidelity involves virtual adultery or perhaps an inappropriately intimate friendship rather than EMS. The therapist must be prepared to deal with every possible contingency regarding how an affair is revealed, discovered, hidden, denied, minimized and even projected onto the partner.

We believe the therapist will have the skills required to deal with many factors involved in treating infidelity by learning to tackle these common manifestations. The following discussion provides anchors to assist the therapist in navigating the unsettled territory of infidelity, particularly in the immediate postdisclosure phase. The foundations of treatment include challenges such as understanding the level of commitment to both therapy and the relationship, the judicious use of therapeutic separation, dealing with feelings of the betrayed and unfaithful partners, using individual sessions, and issues of accountability and trust.

COMMITMENT

Commitment is a core issue in the treatment of infidelity. Two interrelated aspects of commitment involve engagement in therapy and responsibility to the intimate relationship. Therapists often assume that if the couple is attending sessions, they must have some level of dedication. This is not necessarily the case. Sometimes, the therapist is surprised that the couple has dropped out after just one or a few treatment sessions. The couple who decides to separate often terminates therapy. Although it is true that the conjoint therapy will not proceed more than a few sessions after separation, it should not terminate abruptly. The couple will need to discuss issues of living apart, such as housing and legal, financial, and childcare concerns. In addition, the partners can continue to work with the therapist individually, or one or both may obtain referrals to another therapist for individual therapy.

A great deal of emotional reactivity may stand in the way of being able to maintain commitment to the relationship. The partners are likely to make unsound decisions in an effort to avoid pain, only to reverse themselves within the next day or hour. We have witnessed couples struggling for months and even years trying to decide whether to stay together or separate. Such a pattern can go on endlessly until one partner is exhausted from the indecision. Making the issue of commitment explicit from the beginning of treatment reduces the dropout rate and gives each partner some idea about the other's level of responsibility to therapy and the relationship.

The therapist must communicate to the clients that there are only two acceptable outcomes to treatment: working through the infidelity and rebuilding the relationship, or dissolution with some understanding of how they ended up in the present situation. Not all relationships affected by infidelity can be saved. In such cases, the couples can learn from their mistakes. The therapist begins by discussing the importance of the commitment to therapy. This involves continuing treatment to a rational conclusion that provides the couple with closure. The therapist must illustrate that the alternative to commitment is the indecision described earlier. Ask the partners directly if vacillation is a desired outcome. We have never had a couple accept this alternative when it has been put to them so bluntly. For those who decide to separate or divorce, the therapist must suggest that partners often repeat their patterns in new relationships without the benefit of insight and behavioral change. Thus, another reason to commit to therapy is to interrupt the pattern of destructive relationships.

Next, the therapist must mention that there will be times when the couple will want to exit therapy prematurely because of feeling anger, hurt, disappointment, emotional pain, betrayal, and demoralization. It is important to normalize such feelings and to explain to the couple that these emotions do not constitute a reason to terminate therapy. The therapist's goal is to extract as much public commitment to the process of therapy as possible. Often, couples do not know how to respond to the question "What do you want from therapy?" because they do not understand what they want, need, or are capable of achieving in therapy. The therapist can assist the couple by stating as an expectation the goal for the states of closure mentioned previously. Pursuing a complete course of therapy or remaining committed to the therapeutic process also means that the couple makes their best effort. Unless partners believe they have given the treatment their total commitment, they may have lingering regrets about remaining in or ending the marriage.

Commitment to therapy and commitment to the relationship are interrelated but separate issues. The next task of the therapist is to assess each partner's level of commitment to the relationship. For instance, couples often proclaim that they are committed to the marriage despite being involved in an affair. However, this statement should be examined closely, because one or both parties may be committed, uncommitted, ambivalent, or unequally committed. Often, the partners do not understand that the affair is the behavioral equivalent of ambivalence or lack of engagement in the partnership. Those who state they are committed can be congratulated for putting faith in the injured relationship. Asking them to talk more about the strengths of their relationship can emphasize the resiliency of their partnership.

For other couples entering therapy for treatment of infidelity, there is a rapid transition to discussing preexisting relationship problems. After 1 or 2 weeks of knowing about the affair or other forms of infidelity, they will attempt to avoid the pain by minimizing its importance. An example of this is a female client who proclaimed that the terminated affair was a "wakeup call" for the marriage and did wish to discuss it in greater detail. For most, however, the level of commitment to the relationship is unequal, and this must be recognized and discussed. Circumventing this discussion only adds to the confusion and turmoil of the crisis.

Issues of Commitment

With the exception of Weeks and Treat (2001), the marital therapy literature is bereft of concrete ideas about helping couples improve their commitment to each other. The assumption appears to be that bettering the quality of the relationship will somehow improve the level of commitment. For instance, Sternberg (1986) mentioned the need for commitment in a loving relationship, but limited the character of commitment to a cognitive process. Thus, the therapist must extrapolate from the social-psychological literature in order to acquire clinically useful ideas about commitment. Using an intrapsychic and interpersonal perspective, Kelley (1983) identified several major principles that can be used as therapeutic strategies for improving commitment to the relationship. The first principle is increasing the reward–cost ratio in the relationship. There are two ways of accomplishing this task therapeutically. One method is to ask the couple to recall the period of time they felt their relationship was working or satisfying, and to identify what they liked about each other, themselves, and the relationship. Most couples are able to recall more positive than negative features, particularly when remembering the beginning of the relationship. The therapist can ask the couple about reinstating these attributes again. The other method is to ask the couple to identify what is currently enjoyable about the relationship and what they would like to add in the future to make the relationship even better.

The second principle identified by Kelley (1983) is future oriented. Do the partners believe that they can meet each other's needs in the future? The clinician must help the couple identify what they need, whether they believe the partner can provide it, and ask the partner to comment on his or her ability and interest in satisfying the other's need. When partners believe they can get their needs met, eventually they are much more optimistic, happy, and likely to stay in the relationship.

The third principle deals with the irretrievable investments made in the relationship. The degree of investment in the relationship and fear of losing this investment should the relationship end determine whether couples stay (Kelley, 1983). The therapist asks the couple to talk about what they have already invested in the relationship and what they will lose if they decide to end it. Some couples may talk about the sense of family if they have children, a lifestyle, home, finances, relationships with extended family and in-laws, and so on. A more subtle investment is the sense of couple identity—such as comfort in their respective roles, expectations, and shared history—which cannot be replaced. The therapist may ask the couple what makes them special or unique as a couple, how well they have complemented each other, or to discuss the unique history they share.

The last principle for improving commitment to the relationship comprises a consideration of the attractiveness of the alternatives (Kelley, 1983). Some partners develop a fantasy that if they can rid themselves of the current relationship they will quickly and effortlessly find another alliance that works almost perfectly. The therapist explores what partners believe will happen in their lives next if they end the relationship. As they describe their future, the therapist can infuse some reality-based thinking into their idealized fantasies. As we stated earlier, the therapist discusses how partners frequently leave one relationship only to recreate the same or similar problems in a future relationship. This statement is intended to prompt the couple to stay in therapy, learn more about themselves, understand how they created the current situation, and avoid similar patterns in the future.

Commitment should not be underestimated or undervalued in the therapeutic process. Many of the couples coming in for treatment of infidelity are at best ambivalent about whether they can and will stay in the relationship. They are uncertain if the damage to the relationship can be repaired or if trust can be reestablished. Working through infidelity is a long and difficult process. Unless the couple begins the process with as much commitment as the therapist can facilitate, the prognosis is less favorable. In our experience, a high degree of commitment to therapy and to each other is correlated with a successful outcome.

THERAPEUTIC SEPARATION

One outcome of therapy following the revelation or discovery of infidelity is the decision to separate as a precursor to divorce. If the couple has been through a therapeutic process of self-examination leading to the irrevocable conclusion that they can no longer be married, this is certainly an acceptable outcome. It is one form of closure. In other instances, couples may desire a separation because living together is too painful but they are not certain about divorcing. In addition, they require time alone to contemplate their feelings without the ongoing distractions of living with the partner. In these cases, we recommend a therapeutic separation, in order to allow the couple more time to explore their relationship or themselves, make a rational and fully informed decision, and reduce the pain of daily contact with each other. The concept of a therapeutic separation is missing in the clinical literature that we reviewed. In our conceptualization, several ground rules need to be followed. These include:

- Marital or relational fidelity.
- Minimal contact initially, with the exception of therapy sessions.
- Accepting responsibility to gain the insight or clarity needed to make a decision about commitment to the relationship.
- Accepting responsibility to work toward restoring the marriage or partnership, but understanding that goal may not be achieved.
- Limiting discussion of the separation with friends, family, and other invested parties while saving this content for therapy sessions.
- Putting children's interests first.

The couple will need to discuss such issues as who will move out of the home, and how children and finances will be handled. Decisions must be made about how children are to be managed and where they will live, including explaining the separation to the children. It is imperative that the partners do not blame or demean each other in the presence of the children. Sadly, this occurs, even in the most well-intentioned parents, as a by-product of justifying one's position in the infidelity. Sometimes the betrayed partner is in so much anguish that he or she complains about the spouse in the presence of the children or even inappropriately discloses intimate details of the infidelity to them. Explain firmly that demeaning the other parent is injurious to the children's psychological development and interferes with their right to love one parent without feeling disloyal to the other.

Children need to be told repeatedly that they are loved and the parents will always be there for them. They should expect access to each parent by telephone and consistency of rules. For longer separations, children need a place to stay with the parent who leaves the family home. We often recommend bibliotherapy dealing with separation, divorce, and effective parenting (Athrons, 1995; Farmer, 1989). Clients are encouraged to read books or articles related to a specific topic. Then, they discuss the material with the therapist in order to clarify the information.

The couple is asked to estimate the length of the separation. The therapist may also have some sense about how long it might take to work out some of the individual issues and suggest a minimal time period. The separations we have facilitated usually last from a few weeks to a year. We do not have conjoint sessions for the first few weeks of the separation. Instead, we see each partner individually, with the rule of confidentiality described earlier as accountability with discretion. The hope is that the individual therapy will help both partners become clearer about their involvement in the partnership, factors that might have made the individual and couple vulnerable to infidelity, and the impact of the infidelity on the relationship. This time allows some emotional healing to take place, so that the couple can resume their conjoint therapy. In the vast majority of cases we have treated, the couples resumed their conjoint treatment and often ended the separation earlier than expected. The therapy can then proceed until the couple has addressed and worked through their problems.

The therapist should explain that therapeutic separation is not a legal disunion and that the partners should consult an attorney regarding legal implications. We view a referral to an attorney as providing the couple with information that will increase their knowledge base, reduce anxiety about the unknown, dispel fantasized notions about divorce, and add reality to the picture.

Therapeutic separations can and often do help the partners reunite. However, some couples will divorce or end their partnership. When one partner is ready to end the relationship, the therapist calls for a conjoint session in which that partner must take responsibility for sharing the reasons for the decision. If this occurs, the therapeutic separation is over and the couple is now moving toward divorce or termination of the relationship.

DEALING WITH FEELINGS

In earlier chapters, we elucidated that disclosure or discovery of infidelity produces a boundless array of feelings in the partner who had the affair as well as in the betrayed partner. The depth and intensity of these feeling, coupled with the fact they can change so quickly and dramatically, may be very frightening. The therapist's foremost task is to listen actively, accept, and moderate these feelings while encouraging the partners to remain on task. Neutrality and balance must be maintained in order to encourage commitment to the process of therapy in the face of such arduous work.

Significant parts of the first few sessions are devoted to managing feelings of intense pain due to the infidelity. Both partners can easily become absorbed with their own individual pain, believing that they are the "most hurt" party. The betrayed partner intuitively knows that the unfaithful partner undergos feelings such as guilt and sadness over the loss of the affair partner. However, the betrayed partner may be so wounded that there is little room for empathy or understanding. To reduce this polarization, we use two techniques. The first is to ask the partner who had the affair to be willing to listen to the feelings of the betrayed partner and to acknowledge them whenever they arise. This technique is practiced in session and encouraged at home. Next, we suggest that the couple set aside a few minutes each day to check in with each other about their feelings in general. The couple should reserve issues about the infidelity for discussion during the initial hours of therapy and should not discuss them outside of the session.

The therapy session provides a safe place for the couple to discuss many aspects of the infidelity within the guidelines provided by the therapist. Initially, the therapist anticipates and allows some time for appropriate fact-finding about the affair; for example, the identity and appearance of the affair partner, length and frequency of meetings, and what happened sexually. Searching for explicit and graphic sexual details is of little value and may complicate recovery because of the memories and images that linger from what the partner has reported. However, it is appropriate to know the kind of sexual activity that took place, particularly if the betrayed partner is at risk for contracting sexually transmitted diseases. If this is the case, abstinence is recommended, and a medical examination scheduled.

The therapist carefully monitors and controls the discussion. Too many fact-findings preclude the important process of expressing feelings about the infidelity. If betrayed partners persist in seeking factual information, the therapist redirects them to ask themselves "What am I feeling?" and "What do I need?" Then, the therapist helps them to express their needs and feelings to their partners. The partners' job is to listen closely and nondefensively. Unfaithful partners need to reassure their spouses / partners that the affair is over, that they want to rebuild the relationship, and that their partner is considered attractive and lovable. The unfaithful partner must also acknowledge the pain and damage caused to the relationship.

The feelings of the betrayed partner should gradually diminish, although the duration varies among individuals. In some cases, however, infidelity restimulates a deeper, preexisting issue in the betrayed partner that interferes with the resolution of intense, painful reactions to the affair. One example is a woman whose mother had abandoned her after her father died. She selected a dependent, socially awkward spouse because she assessed that he would never be disloyal, but he later left the marriage without an explanation. Knowing her mother's abandonment helped the therapist to put her reactions to the marriage betrayal in context. Another example involved a woman who knew from childhood that her father was a philanderer. He took her to bars, picked up women, went to their homes, had sex with them, and told her to keep the secret or she would destroy the family. As an adult, her greatest fear was that her husband would have an affair. She chose a man she thought she could trust only to be devastated when her worst fear was realized. She could not separate the affair in her marriage from the affairs in her family of origin. In another example, a man was married three times. In the first two marriages, his wives had an affair and then divorced him. He feared the same outcome in his present marriage and, in fact, discovered his wife having an affair. Understandably, it was difficult to contain his fear that he was going to lose another marriage.

Personality disorders may also exacerbate the intense expression of feelings. The histrionic personality may overreact, the schizoid underreacts, the psychopath uses feelings to manipulate the other, the obsessive-compulsive may never let go, and so on. If the feelings do not abate within a reasonable period, or if the individual cannot follow our guidelines (discussed previously), additional individual sessions will be required to address the underlying issues. The intense feelings usually subside in a few months, and the emotional roller coaster is over. However, if they continue beyond a reasonable time frame for appropriately incorporating the trauma and dealing with it, a referral to an individual therapist will be needed.

Grief is another predictable reaction to the many losses that result from infidelity. The couple realizes that previously held assumptions about the relationship (e.g., loyalty and specialness) are invalid. In addition, presumptions about trust and the dreams for the future are abandoned, leaving the partners with a sense of unreality or emptiness. Sometimes, feelings of hopelessness and pessimism preclude anticipation of the rebuilding stage. Some people are more prone to these reactions than others. Again, premorbid functioning needs to be assessed and the infidelity placed in context. A psychiatric referral may help with some of these problems. Psychopharmacology may be indicated, and sometimes antidepressants are useful in lifting depression as well as reducing anxiety and obsessional thinking.

INDIVIDUAL SESSIONS

We have mentioned many instances when individual sessions are required during conjoint therapy for infidelity. Skilled couples therapists generally have a sense that the treatment for infidelity should unfold in one of three directions: toward resolution of the betrayal, toward therapeutic separation, or toward divorce. Sometimes, the therapy never seems to get beyond the initial information-gathering stage or stalls after a few sessions. When the therapist cannot find a reason for the delay in progress, it is useful to talk with both partners individually in order to confirm hypotheses and discuss information that each would not want to mention with the partner present. This is the most common reason for individual sessions. Before these sessions, the therapist should review the rules of accountability with discretion. The individual sessions begin with a review of the problem and the course of treatment. The therapist expresses puzzlement about the lack of progress in therapy, asking the partner to provide a theory regarding why change is not taking place. If the conversation does not produce any ideas about the lack of progress, the therapist suggests that being stuck often means that one person has a secret, such as an addiction or an affair. Furthermore, if this is the case, the therapy will remain stalled, and continuing with the couple's treatment will be nonproductive.

The Secret Affair

In the case of an undisclosed affair or other form of intimate betrayal, the strategy of discussing the lack of progress exerts pressure on unfaithful partners to take responsibility for acknowledging it, if only to the therapist. These partners might dread that they have been caught, or perhaps they have wanted to talk about the affair but feared the consequences of sharing the secret. If the therapist is successful in extracting this concealment, a nonjudgmental attitude is essential. In our experience, the vast majority of clients will admit to a secret in an individual session. For those who do not, the therapy will remain stuck and will probably end within the next few weeks despite best efforts to effect change.

Earlier we discussed that a secret betrayal of intimacy poses ethical quandaries for the therapist. In cases such as an affair, the infidelity is a secret from the beginning of therapy. The uninvolved partner may express suspicions, a lack of progress may be observed as described previously, or the unfaithful partner may request an individual session. In the instance of a clandestine affair, several scenarios may unfold. The first is that the partner has been unfaithful in the past and the spouse does not know. In many cases, the affairs were single encounters, are not current relationships, and happened many years ago. These types of affairs do not generally impede the progress of therapy, because they are not ongoing. Nonetheless, their occurrence should be explored and understood in individual sessions. The insight gained will help to decide if and how they should be revealed to the partner and how to prevent reoccurrences.

In other situations, a recently ended concealed affair will be disclosed to the therapist in a private session. The therapist should know that even if the physical contact has ceased, an emotional connection could endure for some time. In the case of a married couple, the spouse can still be suffering from the grief of ending the affair, missing the affair partner, wishing to restart the affair, and dealing with an affair partner who wishes to restart the affair. In short, at this time this spouse does not have the emotional energy to put into the marriage. The first priority is to ensure that the affair has stopped. Individual sessions will focus on three outcomes: the affair will end and marital therapy will commence, the affair will be disclosed to the betrayed spouse with unknown results, or the marriage will end.

Fortunately, most partners coming to therapy want to work on the relationship. In this instance, the therapist reiterates the point that undisclosed infidelity blocks progress and suggests a time-limited period in which to sever the affair, usually within a few weeks. Stopping the affair means no contact whatsoever. A practical discussion of how to stop the affair needs to be held. In many cases, the affair partner is aware of the intention to seek couple therapy and anticipates an end to the relationship.

Partners who are ambivalent about stopping their affairs will spend several individual sessions understanding their motivations. Often, these spouses are unhappy in their marriages and feel a desire to leave the marriages for their affair partners. Nonetheless, stopping these affairs is the first priority. The concept of commitment and its relationship to outcome is reviewed. We explain that we do not know the outcome of the couple's therapy. However, full investment in the marriage is the only true test of its viability. If the marriage does not work after a genuine effort is made, the partner with the affair can exit with a clear conscience. It must also be emphasized that a positive future for the affair relationship is not a certainty, given that currently it is largely based on fantasy, idealization, and intermittent moments of being together.

Uncovering the Secret

When therapists suspect secret infidelity, they can produce mistrust in the uninvolved partner by explaining the possible reasons for the lack of progress in conjoint marital therapy. This is not a negative outcome. We often hear that this partner has been suspicious for some time but is afraid to discover the truth, fearing a crisis in the marriage. The therapist helps such partners to see their role in maintaining the secret and thereby colluding in the infidelity. Explain that a confrontation can end the therapeutic impasse and enable the couple to work openly on the real issues. Reframe the anticipated crisis as a period of opportunity or a turning point, which will bring about one of two outcomes: The couple can begin a process of rebuilding the marriage, or the marriage will end. Emphasize that continuing with a relationship based on deception is unacceptable.

If the unfaithful partner is confronted in the conjoint session and denies an affair, recommend that the couple continue having discussions at home. Usually, this strategy will yield an admission of the infidelity. However, continued denials and increased suspiciousness will usually lead to an impasse in the conjoint therapy. The betrayed spouse is helped to decide on a plan of action, given that the partner is lying.

Duration of Individual Sessions

The therapist is available to help each of the partners to work concurrently on the marital issues that have been raised in the conjoint marital therapy sessions. Individual sessions can be used to gather history, provide an opportunity to express emotions that could interfere with the progress of couples therapy, or enable discussion of factors that the partner is not ready to address conjointly. These sessions can occur intermittently, but should not exceed 5 to 10 sequentially. If a factor such as a secret precludes conjoint sessions for a greater time frame, continuing to work with either partner will effectively rule out future conjoint sessions. The therapist may elect to refer each partner to another therapist for individual sessions in order to be the designated couples therapist should the individual issues resolve. Couples with good boundaries can sometimes transition back to the same therapist after a prolonged period of concurrent sessions. However, it should be clear at the outset that the effort will initially be experimental and that one of the spouses or the therapist may decide that is not a workable situation within the first few conjoint meetings.

AFTER THE DISCLOSURE

Once the unfaithful partner agrees to stop the infidelity, there are three basic beginning therapeutic issues:

- How to prevent relapse.
- Understanding motivations for the infidelity.
- Dealing with feelings about the affair partner.

In cases of EMS, our default assumption is that most are difficult to end. Unfaithful partners may be ambivalent about stopping, or they may know that it is time to end the affair but have grown emotionally or physically attached to the affair partner. The therapist can normalize the difficulty in stopping an affair by suggesting that it is often an ongoing struggle. The affair partner may attempt a phone call or to have some contact. Help the unfaithful spouse to devise ways to prevent falling back into the relationship. The final measure is to ask unfaithful partners to call the therapist when the urge is motivating them to act.

Relapse Prevention

In order to prevent infidelity from starting again or to prevent future infidelity, the therapist will need to spend considerable time helping the client to understand the meaning and motivations for having the affair or engaging in other breaches of intimacy. A rather long list of questions needs to be explored in gaining this understanding, such as:

- How did you meet this person?
- What was the attraction? Was it an immediate or gradual attraction?
- At what point did the attraction become emotional?
- When and how did it become sexual?
- Who initiated the relationship?
- How were you feeling about yourself when this relationship started?
- How were you feeling about the primary relationship when the unfaithful relationship started?
- How attached have you become to this person?
- Do you think you love this person?
- How much do you like, respect, and admire this person?
- What was going on in your life in general around the time that this relationship started?
- What has this relationship meant to you and to the person with whom you are having the unfaithful relationship?
- What were your motivations for this affair?
- How has the infidelity helped / hurt your marriage / partnership?
- How has the infidelity helped / hurt you?
- Do you feel that you are or have been living a double life?
- Did you ever imagine that you would be unfaithful?
- Were you actively seeking the relationship or did it "just happen"?
- How has the unfaithful relationship challenged your ethical, moral, or value system?
- What do you like most about this person / relationship?
- What do you like least about this person / relationship?
- How do you feel about ending this relationship?
- How do you feel about your partner ending this relationship?
- How do you feel about your primary partner finding out / being told about it?
- Do you think your affair partner will be able to let go of this relationship?
- Have you tried to end it unsuccessfully, or had thoughts of ending it?
- How much of your mental energy does it take to keep both of these relationships going?
- How do you think you will feel when it is over?
- Do you think you might resent your primary partner for having to end this relationship?

- What has it been like when relationships have ended for you in the past?
- Are you prepared to grieve over the loss of the relationship?
- What have I not asked you that might be important to understanding the reasons for this relationship?

Understanding Motivations

The motivations for infidelity are often complex, involving a confluence of factors. We recommend using the tools suggested in earlier chapters to help understand the conditions surrounding the affair, such as its duration, frequency of contacts, type of involvement, social dimensions, and so on. The therapist should discuss each factor until satisfied that the clients have resolved the issue and are able to maintain their commitment to the partnership / marriage.

John, a 55-year-old physician, married for 30 years, is an example of the multidimensionality of affairs. He came to treatment at the end of a 2-year affair that was unknown to his wife. He met his affair partner almost daily, telling his wife that he had emergencies, additional patients, and extended hospital hours. He felt a tremendous amount of stress due to leading a double life. Ultimately, the affair partner ended the relationship. Several factors contributed to John having an affair. First, he was beginning to think about his own mortality and pondered whether he had enjoyed all that life had to offer him. In addition, John felt he had devoted his life to medicine, to the exclusion of having hobbies and pursuing other interests. He expressed a need for adventure, excitement, and courage in order to test himself. The affair was a way to examine whether he could veer from the prescribed path that he had so well internalized. Moreover, he assumed that the devitalization of marriage was a normal part of growing older. Finally, John held the unconscious assumption that affairs were expected of the husband. He reported knowing that his father had had an affair, because he heard his parents arguing about it when he was a young boy. He believed that if a moral and proper man such as his father, a very distinguished physician, could have an affair, then it must somehow be acceptable.

Feelings About the Affair Partner

The third issue that requires attention in the individual sessions is the need for the unfaithful spouse to deal with feelings about the affair partner. This material would be inappropriate for discussion in the conjoint sessions. Explain to the couple that grieving for the affair must take place, so that the spouse can fully invest in the marriage. Suggest that it would be hurtful for the betrayed spouse to hear these feelings. The typical experiences of the unfaithful partner were included in Chapter 4, in the discussion of consequences of infidelity. These feelings are intense, yet rarely discussed in conjoint therapy because partners who have had an affair believe they have done enough damage already without inflicting these feelings onto their partners. The therapist is the person who can now help partners who have had an affair to face and understand these feelings. This process may take more than a few sessions, and is largely dependent on the unfaithful spouse's degree of involvement with the affair partner. Clients are surprised that they experience feelings of such duration and intensity. In addition, these emotions are often triggered because of seeing the affair partner somewhere, hearing a song, coming upon a card or gift, and so on. In one couple, the partner who had the affair required an individual session every few months. He reflected on emotions of loss and guilt for misleading his affair partner. These topics would have been unbearable for the wife.

In our culture, marriage is essentially a vow to only love one person at a time. Our clients often express that they love two people, in different ways, and that each love relationship is incomplete. Sometimes they will talk about their wish to magically combine the two love partners. The feelings are quite real. Furthermore, the affair may be a highly idealized relationship that embodies a good deal of projection. As this partner becomes more aware of idealized and projected fantasies, it becomes possible to accept that the relationship is over and to put the feelings in perspective.

ACCOUNTABILITY AND TRUST

Honesty—one of the most salient aspects of any intimate relationship—is inexorably tied to trust. An affair is a betrayal in two senses: The unfaithful partner violates the solidarity of the relationship, and then lies about it. In many cases, the lying is more striking to the betrayed partner than the affair is. Trust is conceptualized in many ways, but it generally involves the following:

- A strong belief in the partner's integrity (Larzelere & Huston, 1980).
- An assumption that the partner's motives and intentions are positive (Franklin, Janoff-Bulman, & Roberts, 1990).
- The ability to predict another person's actions based on consistency of behavior over time (Rempel, Holmes, & Zanna, 1985).
- The expectation that another person's word can be believed and relied on (Rotter, 1967).

- Faith in the future intentions and motives of each partner, permitting the couple to predict and feel secure about the future of the relationship (Rempel et al., 1985).

The development of trust is a slow and precarious process, and is notoriously easy to break down. The unfaithful partner violates a basic trust in the relationship through dishonesty and deception, creating damage. Once trust has been betrayed, it is doubly difficult to reestablish. Therefore, trust must be rebuilt over time, slowly, through accountability and honest communication.

Rebuilding Trust

The partner who was unfaithful has lost all credibility and will have to earn back trust by being accountable. *Accountability* refers to accepting responsibility for having created rejection, sensitivity, hypervigilance, and suspicions in the partner. Betrayed partners cannot help but experience these feelings. They do not wish to be further hurt, betrayed, tricked, fooled, shamed, and so on. Thus, they want and deserve to know that the lies and deception have ceased. Being accountable entails developing a continuous method of communication between the partners, even when in different locations. This involves conferring frequently, being where one is supposed to be, and doing what is necessary to give the partner information about one's plans. It is especially important to have phone or physical contact at those times in the day when the affair occurred. For example, one man typically met his affair partner over his lunch break. As an act of good faith, he started going home for lunch (fortunately, he lived close to where he worked). Had he not lived so close to home he could have called his wife at lunch or she could have called him. In another situation, the affair partners often met after work and made excuses for coming home late. To rebuild trust, this couple decided that he would make a telephone call to let the partner know where he could be found when he would be late. One man, a sex addict, always had sex in a particular part of the city where prostitutes worked. His office was in this area. Rebuilding trust involved using a cell phone to call his wife whenever he approached this area and remain on it for about 5 minutes until he arrived at his office.

Another aspect of being accountable is what we call "absolute honesty" about any contact with the affair partner. Often, the former affair partner attempts to meet, call, e-mail, or otherwise contact the unfaithful spouse. Failure to report such contact only perpetuates more mistrust and pessimism, even if the interaction was innocent. We predict that former affair partners typically attempt to make contact even after the affair has ceased. We warn that it can and will happen, and we have the couple plan and rehearse a response. Disclosing such an event to betrayed spouses may be difficult for them to hear, but the consequences of not divulging this information could have more serious effects. We explain that trust needs to be reestablished over time, and reporting and checking in are necessary for some period. Some of our clients may feel guilty over the hurt they have caused the affair partner and attempt to provide some emotional support. We resolutely state that the spouse can no longer be emotionally involved with the affair partner and that all contact must cease.

In one case, the affair partner called the previously involved spouse at work. He did not report the phone call to his wife, fearing a bad reaction and further damage to the marriage. The withheld information eventually created guilt feelings and he began acting defensively. In an individual session, he confided the information about the telephone call and his anxiety about reporting it. He practiced ways to share this sort of information with his wife, and later revealed this and another occurrence in a conjoint session. They decided on a plan of action, he carried it out successfully, and 6 months later there was further contact from the affair partner. Without warning, after months of no contact, the affair partner sent an e-mail message to the husband. He immediately reported the occurrence to his wife and the therapist. The wife left her workplace, visited her husband at his job, and the couple went out to lunch together. The message was erased and never read. This occasion represented one of many turning points for a couple who struggled for more than 2 years. Initially, they had left another therapist because of the therapist's lack of knowledge about time parameters in resolving infidelity. Currently, the crisis of the affair is over and the couple is able to work successfully on other issues.

CONCLUSION

Infidelity is often the presenting problem that prompts the couple to seek therapy. Sometimes, however, an affair is concealed from the spouse and therapist, and thus creates an impediment to treatment. In this chapter, we explored the ways in which affairs and other forms of infidelity are disclosed or revealed, and the appropriate responses to each situation. There are many conditions necessary for the treatment of an infidelity, such as a commitment to the relationship as well as an investment in the treatment. These factors need to be carefully assessed—therapy cannot proceed with them. The major issues of accountability and trust are integral to repairing the damage created by infidelity. Treatment strategies such as the therapeutic separation and the judicious use of individual sessions were also reviewed. This chapter provided many of the tools needed for treatment, particularly in the initial phases of recovery from infidelity. In the following chapters, we discuss advanced techniques and factors necessary for rebuilding the relationship, such as forgiveness.

7

❈ ❈ ❈

Treatment: Systemic
Considerations

IN THE PREVIOUS CHAPTER, WE DISCUSSED STRATEGIES for dealing with the acute crisis phase that surrounds the discovery of infidelity. During this period, the therapist addresses the feelings of the betrayed and unfaithful partners while emphasizing the salient issues of commitment, accountability, and trust. As the couple begins the important work of rebuilding confidence in their relationship, other treatment regimens are necessary. In this chapter, the overreaching therapeutic approach and essential strategies are discussed in detail. The former is the intersystems approach that integrates multiple perspectives into the assessment and treatment of infidelity; the latter is the use of the therapeutic reframe, a systemic technique. These methods will effectively defuse many of the painful and intense emotions surrounding infidelity while circumventing the destructive effects of blame or moral righteousness. Use of these approaches enhances the effectiveness of the therapist and helps couples attain positive therapeutic outcomes more often than do traditional approaches to treating infidelity.

AN INTEGRATIVE TREATMENT APPROACH

Throughout this volume, we stress the importance of an *integrative* manner of treatment. This involves attending to the cognitive, affective, and behavioral aspects of the couple from a contextual or systemic perspective; that is, the partners are regarded as interacting members of a union that is governed by reciprocity or interdependence. Treatment concentrates on the working elements of a relationship, emphasizing its strengths rather than its weaknesses. This integrative perspective is also *intersystemic*: The etiological understanding and treatment include the individuals who comprise the system, the couple's relationship, and the influences of the family of origin (Weeks, 1994). Furthermore, the integrative approach is growth-oriented in that couples are helped not only to overcome their problems, but also to optimize their relationship (Weeks & Hof, 1995). Unfortunately, couples are rarely given this opportunity in traditional relationship therapy because of its emphasis on problem resolution or remediation. This is particularly apparent with the influence of managed care and the brief therapies that focus on rapid treatment with an eye on eliminating the problem. Sadly, in such brief therapies, the deeper and more human aspects of the couple are never touched.

THE INTERSYSTEMS APPROACH

The intersystems approach, developed by Weeks (1989, 1994), is a strategy used in couples treatment that integrates three perspectives: individual risk factors of each partner, relationship issues, and family-of-origin influences. This model was described in previous texts dealing with the treatment of erectile dysfunction and hypoactive sexual desire disorder (Weeks & Gambescia, 2000, 2002). It has become our unique contribution to the field of sex therapy, and we believe it also provides a tool for the comprehensive treatment of infidelity because the phenomenon is multidimensional.

Individual Risk Factors

Many individual risk factors can contribute to one's susceptibility to infidelity. We have found that these vulnerabilities can be situational, such as midlife issues, whereas others are more embedded within the individual's personality structure. Sometimes, undiagnosed depression and or anxiety can adversely affect the ways in which partners relate and work through problems in a relationship. A detailed psychological assessment of the intrapsychic components of each partner is undertaken when treating infidelity. The therapist evaluates for the use of cognitive distortions, irrational beliefs, and ego-defense mechanisms such as denial and projection. Likewise, biological conditions—such as the psychological effects of disease and aging—must be considered, because they sometimes contribute to low self-esteem, impulsivity, reactivity, and other emotional reactions at various stages of the life cycle.

In addition, infidelity can be a consequence of major psychiatric conditions defined using the Axis I and II diagnostic categories of the *DSM-IV* (American Psychiatric Association, 1994), or of addictions. In many of these cases, a combination of individual and couple therapy and psychiatric intervention is necessary. For example, partners suffering from depression and bipolar disorder sometimes engage in infidelity in order to distract themselves from their depression and to feel better. The bipolar individual may act out during the manic phase, when the personality is expansive and the behavior poorly controlled. Psychotherapy can be used to educate, treat, and help ensure compliance with the medical treatment. Unfortunately, clients with bipolar disorder are notorious for not taking their prescribed medications because they like the high feelings they experience during the manic phase. In such cases, a strong support system will include the psychiatrist, relationship therapist, and partner to ensure compliance with the treatment regimen.

Personality disorders may place the individual at risk for infidelity. For example, partners with dependent personalities may not be getting enough attention from their partners and subsequently seek affirmation through an affair. People with obsessive-compulsive characters may be searching for emotionally expressive partners who will supply their missing feelings. Sociopaths may have no regard for the usual rules and norms and thus engage in one or numerous affairs before being discovered. People with narcissistic personalities may feel a sense of entitlement to whatever they want, and need the adoration and attention of an affair. Personality disorders are known to be difficult to treat; again, a combination of couple and individual therapy is often necessary. The therapist can use texts by Millon (1999) and Beck and Freeman (1990) for help in educating clients about and treating these problems.

We have worked with many couples in whom individual factors placed the couple at risk for infidelity. In one example, the female spouse had been addicted to prescription and recreational drugs for half of their 20-year marriage. Although the couple had experienced long-standing marital problems, the process of recovery from addiction destabilized the homeostasis of the marriage. One year after recovery, she became involved in an affair and concluded that she could not remain in the marriage. In another case, the male spouse suffered from an undiagnosed depression. His affair offered a reprieve from dysthymia, boredom, agitation, and general unhappiness that he ascribed to the marriage. Again, the individual risk factor was not the only problem for this couple, yet it influenced the husband's beliefs about the marriage and his subsequent choice to have an affair.

Relational Issues

In our experience, infidelity is usually an outcome of relationship discord, even in cases in which individual risk factors are influential. Therefore, the therapist must examine the operating principles of the couple's relationship by investigating the expressed or assumed expectations of each partner, expectations of the spouse / committed partner role, emotional contracts, styles of communication, conflict resolution style, and ways of defining problems. Treatment also centers on each partner's capacity for intimacy and the rituals that enhance or preclude intimacy for the couple. Sometimes bibliotherapy, which concentrates on relational issues, helps the couple to develop a frame of reference and language for discussing their assumed roles and ways of acting in the relationship. We often recommend books such as *The Dance of Anger* and *The Dance of Intimacy* (Goldhor-Lerner, 1985, 1989) to help provide insight and promote discussion.

A couple sought treatment when the husband discovered that his wife of 10 years had been involved in an affair for over a year. Each had been married previously, had a boy from the first marriage, and lived together in the couple's marital home. They frequently disagreed about discipline for the boys, recreational activities, finances, and many other aspects of their lives together. They often averted discussions because their conflict-avoidant natures. The partners admitted that they had grown apart, spending very little time enjoying leisure or intimate activities together. They frequently occupied different parts of the house in the evenings, coexisting without the benefits of intimacy. The therapist was able to help the couple recognize that the relationship was vulnerable to infidelity due to the lack of intimacy. Although the female spouse was the partner who had the affair, the husband admitted that, if the opportunity had become available, he might have been the one to be unfaithful. After dealing with the crisis of the disclosure, this couple addressed the many underlying areas of discord within their marriage.

Ongoing and unresolved conflict and anger will eventually lead to deeply embedded resentment toward an intimate partner. The resentment serves to build emotional distance between them, which is a fertile ground for infidelity. Michael and Terri are an example of this phenomenon. They were married for 25 years and had three children in high school and college. Michael had a long history of depression and ADD, but did not take medications until just prior to seeking marital therapy. (In fact, his psychiatrist had referred them to marital therapy.) For years, Terri had been unhappy with Michael's emotional absence due to these two undiagnosed disorders. Michael knew that he had some problems, but did not see how they impacted his relationship. Terri was clearly the dominant partner in the relationship and, due to Michael's depression, had to take over many of the decisions and responsibilities of the family. This fact led to numerous conflicts. Michael avoided fights, saying that because Terri was more adept verbally he had never won a fight. During the later years of the marriage, he had come to the erroneous conclusion that she remained in the marriage for his money. While in conjoint therapy, Terri learned that Michael had been having an affair with one of his employees for many years. She confronted the employee, and her worst fear was confirmed. Subsequently, the couple made a brief attempt at reconciliation, and then separated. When Michael filed for divorce, he demanded a significant portion of Terri's considerable assets. In a final session with Michael, he admitted that he had been resentful and angry for years and would never be able to overcome it. He also felt his wife would never change. Given his ongoing affair, marital conflict, and the fact that his children were leaving for college or in college, Michael could not see any point in continuing the marriage. The situation might have been avoided had the couple sought help many years earlier and learned how to deal with anger and conflict.

It is impossible to be in a close relationship and not experience anger and conflict. Unfortunately, many couples go to great lengths to avoid and deny conflict because it is viewed as having destructive consequences. They may also believe that anger and conflict do not exist in a good marriage. This attitude is often based on early experiences in the family of origin and can be difficult to change.

The first step in working with couples is to normalize anger and conflict. The therapist will need to persistently suggest that dealing constructively with these normal emotions will produce a greater sense of intimacy and of mutuality. Bibliotherapy is also useful; the repetition in print of what the therapist says orally helps to drive the point home. In addition to the previously-mentioned books, we use *Your Perfect Right* (Alberti & Emmons, 1990), which contains a range of information related to conflict and anger, addressing topics such as assertiveness, communication, and negotiation. It offers a number of useful suggestions in each of these areas.

The literature on conflict resolution contains several major behavioral treatment programs (Kassinove, 1995; L'Abate & McHenry, 1983). All these programs are based on the development of specific skills. The assumption is that couples will want to learn the skills and be willing to use them. In our clinical experience, we have found that couples often resist using these skills because of their rigid attitudes toward anger and conflict. If they believe that the skills will be destructive or harmful, they will not use them. Thus, the first task is to change this kind of attitude and then further explore what anger and conflict mean to the couple. We have developed a set of questions designed to help the couple better understand the meaning and function of anger and their attitudes toward it, including:

- What thoughts does the word *anger* conjure up for you?
- What does it mean when you are angry?
- What does it mean when you are angry with your partner?
- What does it mean when your partner is angry?
- What does it mean when your partner is angry with you?
- How do you respond to your partner's anger?
- How do you let your partner know you are angry?
- What other feelings often underlie your anger?

These questions do not call for simple answers; they are points of departure for extended conversations or therapy. The first and the last questions are particularly important. The first is designed to get at the core issue of each partner's attitude toward anger. The therapist must ask a number of follow-up queries in order to uncover the attitudes. The last question addresses what we call the "anger iceberg." Anger is at the pinnacle of the iceberg; although a greater amount of emotional material lies beneath, anger is more easily accessible. Thus, anger is generally part of a feeling complex with many other feelings under it. Without the ability to access and express the unseen feelings, the partner will remain stuck at the top of the iceberg, embroiled in antagonism and resentment. The underlying feelings are often more important to discuss than the overt feelings are. The partners are asked to describe these emotions in the session, paying particular attention to underlying feelings. Some of the common fundamental feelings include fear, hurt, grief, depression, guilt, shame, resentment, and so on.

The intersystemic approach to conflict resolution and anger management deals with each individual's attitude toward anger, as well as the feelings, cognitions, and behaviors that are associated with anger. To summarize, the basic guidelines for dealing with anger include:

- Exploring the feelings, beliefs, and the underlying emotions first.
- Learning to recognize the interlocking nature of conflict and anger.
- Making a clear statement of complaint without blame.
- Taking responsibility for feelings, and understanding them historically or contextually.
- Learning to take timeouts when needed.
- Maintaining an attitude of negotiation and compromise.

Later in the text, we return to the topic of working with conflict and anger. In chapter 12, we discuss strategies for recognizing barriers to communication, facilitating intimate communication, and communicating conflict and anger.

Intergenerational Considerations

Infidelity is often a component of an intergenerational legacy. The individual has learned to be unfaithful in the family of origin, despite efforts to hide the infidelity. A helpful assessment device is the focused genogram (DeMaria et al., 1999), which examines various aspects of familial functioning. Specifically, this tool provides the general context of each partner's personal development as well as contexts relevant to the problem at hand. The clinician evaluates for secrets, incest, parentification, triangulation, enmeshment, and other dysfunctional patterns of familial relating that could have an impact on intimacy and sexuality.

We also use an anger genogram in order to facilitate an understanding of how each partner's attitudes toward conflict developed (DeMaria et al., 1999). These viewpoints toward anger did not evolve in a vacuum; they have a long history grounded in early familial experience, and have matured over time. The questions for the anger genogram are:

- How did your parents deal with anger / conflict?
- Did you see your parents work through anger / conflict?
- When a member of your family (name each one) got angry, how did others respond?
- What did you learn about anger from each of your parents?
- When your parents became angry with you, how did you feel and what did you do?
- How did members of your family respond when you got angry? For example, who listened / failed to listen?
- Who was allowed / not allowed to be angry in your family?
- Were other feelings expressed in addition to anger?
- What is your best / worst memory about anger in your family?
- Was anyone ever hurt because of someone's anger? Who? What were the circumstances?

Once the factors producing a problem have been identified, the therapist then links treatment techniques or strategies to each factor. Utilizing this theory is challenging, because the therapist must be well versed in several treatment modalities (individual, couple, and family therapy) and in the theories, techniques, and related research of these modalities. Although most therapists consider themselves eclectic in their approach to treatment, we have noted through years of practice and supervision that most operate within one modality at a time, using only a few models of treatment. We have seen many seasoned individual therapists in clinical programs seeking training in couples therapy who are wedded to a singular theory. Therefore, an individually oriented therapist will have more difficulty dissecting a couple's relationship or understanding the early impact of family dynamics on the dyadic problem. In addition, we have found that it is not easy for therapists to expand their repertoire to include several formulas for assessment and treatment, and to be flexible and integrative in their choice of approach.

We worked with another couple in which the husband believed that the role of the male partner included infidelity. For years, he had witnessed arguments between his parents about his father's philandering and his mother's resentment and helplessness. However, other cases are not so obvious. Discussions about family-of-origin influences will prompt one or both partners to investigate and discover well-concealed secrets that reveal family legacies of infidelity and betrayal. In one case, the female spouse finally realized that an affair was the reason for a separation between her parents when she was 9 years old. Her mother had an affair and left the family home. Her maternal grandparents assumed responsibility for helping with the children. After 6 months, the mother returned without an explanation, and somehow the children knew to avoid discussion of the separation. In an effort to understand her own infidelity, she addressed this and other family mysteries with her own parents.

By organizing the etiologic factors using the intersystems approach, we hope therapists will be able to perceive the various factors at work in contributing to couples' problems. The intersystems approach will help therapists increase their flexibility in choosing treatment options. The key to success in using this model is to be as adaptable as possible in selecting treatment options. If one strategy is not working, try another. It is often possible to address many levels of treatment at once; for instance, by illustrating how an intergenerational pattern is operating within the present marriage or relationship.

REFRAMING

The vast majority of affairs we have treated have primarily resulted from marital dysfunction or dissatisfaction. If the infidelity is viewed as a symptom of the couple's dysfunction, then it can be proposed that both parties share some responsibility for allowing the relationship to deteriorate. Thus, the affair is viewed as a symptom of problems in the marriage that both partners colluded in creating, maintaining, and avoiding. At the same time, the therapist must help the partner who had the affair to accept personal responsibility for it without being judgmental or blaming. The therapist must be very careful to articulate that infidelity is unacceptable in a committed relationship and there is no excuse for the behavior and deception surrounding it.

The exception to this concept is when the betrayal was motivated by reasons other than marital dysfunction. In both individual and conjoint sessions, the therapist needs to assess the motivation(s) for infidelity. Depending on the assessment of motivations, a reframe could help unfaithful individuals to see their part. For example, a therapist could frame an affair in such a way to help the individual understand his or her behavior within the context of a psychiatric illness.

Reframing Defined

Reframing is a concept that has been in the systems literature from the early days of its development (for a review see Weeks & Treat, 2001). It is the most generically used strategy in the systems therapies, including couple therapy. The purpose of a reframe is to help the couple see the problem in a different way or to attribute a different meaning to the dilemma.

Reframing is not the same as presenting a classical interpretation. Therapists with an analytical or dynamic perspective offer interpretations, believed to carry a high degree of objectivity, in order to help a client understand the problem. A reframe is based on the idea that there are many ways of looking at the same issue or difficulty. The therapist uses the reframe to help the couple understand the problem in a different way, one that moves the couple from being stuck. There are many ways to reframe a problem. However, each systemic reframe contains two basic elements. The first element is that the couple is helped to view the problem systemically; in other words, when most couples begin treatment they tend to have a linear view of their relationship in which one partner is good and the other bad, or one partner is right and the other wrong, or one partner is sane and the other is crazy. A systemic reframe helps to put the couple on the same level and to see that they are mutually responsible for a problem. The partners may begin to understand their relationship in circular terms and the reciprocal nature of their influence on each other. The systemic reframe often addresses the underlying dynamics rather than the symptomatic behavior of the relationship. For example, couples can fight about any number of issues. As soon as one fight is solved, another takes its place. The underlying issue may be that each partner fears becoming too intimate and, therefore, the couple uses conflict to maintain a comfortable degree of emotional distance. The reframe would address the underlying issue, not the hundreds of argument the couple has had.

The second element of most reframes is stressing the positive or good in the relationship. When committed partners enter therapy, they have a problem and tend to view the problem as all bad and each other as being bad in at least some ways. They fail to comprehend how the problem has positive aspects. (By *positive aspects*, we mean how the problem has been of service to them, helped them, protected them, and served other functions that have helped to maintain the relationship and fulfilled deeper psychological needs for each partner.)

Defining the concept of reframing and describing the most common type of reframe for a couple is a fairly easy, straightforward task. Unfortunately, the development and implementation of a reframe is anything but simple. In order to reframe a problem—including infidelity—the therapist must first develop a relationship with the couple. Reframing is not something that can be done *to* a couple, but rather is done *with* a couple. The therapist must have a good deal of information about the couple before beginning to develop a reframe that will make sense to them. If the reframe is too incongruent with the couple's ways of looking at the world and their values, they will simply reject it. Ideally, the therapist remains open to couples drawing their own conclusions and developing their own frames. Sometimes, the therapist may have to provide the reframing statement after sufficient cultivation of a particular reframe has taken place. The therapist needs to keep the goal of reframing in mind: to help the couple see the problem systemically and positively. The therapist asks a series of questions designed to elicit certain pieces of information. As each piece of information is metaphorically laid on the table, a mosaic begins to develop and eventually the partners see a picture emerge regarding their problem. From the couple's perspective, they have reached a natural conclusion based on looking at the facts in a different way.

Steps to Developing a Reframe

We have developed a six-step process to guide the clinician in constructing a reframe with a couple. These steps consist of six questions that the clinician considers:

1. *How does the couple frame their problem?* The clinician first obtains information from the couple about how they view their problem. Assess the contribution of each individual; then consider how the problem is maintained.

2. *How does the couple's frame help to create and / or perpetuate the problem?* As more information is gathered, the clinician helps the couple to see how their way of viewing the problem contributes to their being stuck. This information may also reveal to the couple that their view of a particular situation has caused them to label it as a problem.

3. *What new frame do you think will help the couple change?* The clinician begins to hypothesize possible new systemic and positive frames that are likely to help produce change.

4. *Why do you think this new frame will help the couple change?* The clinician considers the rationale for the reframe. What outcome do you predict from the couple making particular reframes, and why?

5. *What are the steps you will use to help change the couple's frame?* Imagine mini-transcripts of the ways you might intervene. Reframing is a strategic intervention that requires the clinician to anticipate how conversations can be directed and unfold with a particular intentionality.

6. *Evaluate the effect of the reframe and consider further reframes.* Consider the effect the reframe has on the couple. The clinician must test whether the reframe either produced change as a single intervention or whether it made the couple more amenable to change. The therapist may need to recycle through the six-step process several times.

An example of this process involves John, 35, and Marsha, 33, who were married for 10 years and had two children. John's affair was disclosed to Marsha by a coworker who also was a friend of Marsha's. Initially, he denied the infidelity, but in the face of overwhelming evidence admitted that he had been having an affair for the previous year. Several factors predated the affair. After the birth of their second child, the couple struggled with Marsha's depression, which required extended treatment. Marsha became overwhelmed with the children and the marriage, and no longer wanted to work. The couple's sexual relationship declined dramatically. John had anticipated Marsha's returning to work, because his income was modest. The couple did not discuss their problems and had never learned to resolve conflicts openly.

How is the couple framing their problem? They believe that the marriage can never be the way it was before the affair, they cannot afford a divorce, and do not want to break up the family. Marsha sees herself staying depressed, and John does not see any way to get what he wants from Marsha.

How did the couple's frame help to create and / or perpetuate the problem? Both partners are predisposed to see things as being hopeless. They have never been able to solve problems and they both view the world through a depressive lens.

What new frame do you think will help the couple to change? This couple needs an infusion of hopefulness or optimism. They have learned to think helplessly. Nonetheless, they have some skills and wish to be happier. The new frame should build on their skills and motivations to solve problems and form a better relationship.

Why do you think this frame would help the couple change? If the couple can empower themselves with optimism and new skills, they will not be so prone to give up before they start.

What are the steps you will use to help to help change the couple's frame? Several steps could be used with this couple. They could be asked about their strengths as a couple and what successes they have previously had in solving problems. Their motivations for treatment as well as their commitment to the relationship could be highlighted. Asking questions about the courtship and early phases of their relationship could revive the initial attraction they had for each other. John's continued sexual interest in Marsha is emphasized as a positive factor. Marsha could be asked whether she would be interested in him emotionally and sexually if she were free of the depression.

What are some possible reframes for the couple? The following are some examples of what might be said to summarize a reframe:

- "In spite of your mutual pessimism about the future, it took a lot of strength to ask for help. At some level, you must have hope that things between you can be better."

- "John's affair, although inexcusable, has led you to get help for a failing marriage. The two of you should be commended for willingness to work through a difficult situation."

- "John's affair, although inexcusable, is a symptom of a marital problem. The two of you have had some difficult years that would have lead many couple straight to divorce. John felt he had lost his wife, and was lonely and vulnerable. He, too, was depressed, but did not want you, Marsha, to worry, so he concealed it. Marsha, you had the misfortunate of a post-partum depression that became persistent. You could not help but think about this affair pessimistically, and feel more hurt than you would have if you weren't depressed. Depressed people have a tendency to withdraw and think that everything is hopeless. Neither of you understood the impact this depression had on your relationship. All this was compounded by the fact that, like many couples, you never learned to resolve conflicts, so the resentments built up. Everything you are presenting is common and can be effectively treated if you are willing to commit your time and energy to this process."

- "This will sound crazy to you, but you were in an emotionally and sexually dead relationship. John's affair has added another problem to your relationship that has caused both of you great pain. At the same time, it has created an opportunity for the two of you to overcome both this problem and the others that have plagued your relationship. Without this crisis, you probably would have spent most if not all of your adult life in a dead relationship."

Consider the effect of any of these reframes. They all serve the two main functions, mentioned earlier, of putting the couple on the same level and stressing the positive aspects of the problem. In our experience, a single reframe may not be powerful enough to help the couple modify their habitual patterns of interaction. Thus, multiple reframes that unfold over time more effectively promote the change process.

In another couple we treated, the situation was similar to the composite case described previously. The wife suffered from chronic depression and refused individual treatment. The husband felt powerless to effect any change because he had grown up with a mother who was also chronically depressed. Obviously, he had ended up marrying someone like his mother. He began to withdraw from his wife and instead overwork. She noted the distance between them, and felt more alone than before. She concluded that a relationship in which she received more attention would help her to feel better, and thus she began an affair. Each spouse suffered from dysthymia, although her symptoms were more obvious. He dealt with his depression through projective identification with her symptoms. Neither took a proactive stance to acknowledge or deal with their own depression. The underlying dynamic was that they did not want to have a relationship with too much emotional closeness because it would only stir up more feelings that were unpleasant. They had colluded in avoiding intimacy from early in the relationship. The reframe for this case illustrated how they both protected each other from getting too close.

Intersystemic Reframes

Reframing Intergenerational Risk Factors

We explained earlier in this chapter that intergenerational factors might also play a part in infidelity. The most common pattern we have observed is a partner having an affair in order to create distance in the marriage due to parental enmeshment. The adult child has learned to expect a trapped feeling from relationships because of the relationship experienced with one or both parents. Chris, for example, was 47 when he entered therapy. He and his wife had separated 12 years earlier. At the time he began therapy, Chris had been dating a woman, Jill, for 2 years. Jill expected him to divorce his wife and marry her. Chris visited his mother every day, ostensibly to help with housework. He also saw his wife periodically, and they often had sex during his visits. Chris's role in the problem and relationship dynamic became clear long before Jill's part did. Thus, a reframe of his behavior was possible before being able to reframe the couple's behavior. The reframe for Chris was as follows:

> We understand that you love Jill and wish to marry her. In spite of your good intentions, it is difficult for you to comprehend what it means to love someone, given your family history. In your family, being loved as a child meant being smothered, tied to your mother, and sacrificing yourself for your mother's needs. You must think the same thing will happen with Jill. Thus, you have found ways to distance from her that include the ongoing relationship with your mother and not divorcing your wife. In fact, having sex with your wife is another way to ensure that you will not get too close to Jill. For this relationship to move forward the way you both desire, you will have to face having a different kind loving relationship with your mother and Jill, and detach from you wife. Do you think you are strong enough to explore this new way of being in a loving relationship?

Reframing Individual Risk Factors

Although most affairs result from relationship unhappiness, we have found that, in many of our cases, psychological risk factors make the individual vulnerable to infidelity. We have mentioned a number of cases we have treated that involved sex addicts who have had multiple affairs. Most marriages of this type end, but some remain intact, although very shaky. Spouses of sex addicts rarely understand the nature of the addiction. They tend to view the addictive behaviors as morally wrong and their spouses as weak. An individual reframe that helps them is different from the typical reframe we have suggested for couples. It is not systemic or positive in the sense in which we normally think of things as being positive; the purpose of the reframe is to ultimately change the perspective so the couple can work together. First, the view of the behavior is moved from the moral to a psychiatric model of pathology. For instance, we might say:

> You have been suffering from a psychiatric condition for years and did not know it. You thought you were bad and weak, and now your partner thinks you are bad and weak. Sex addiction is a recently recognized illness. The person often uses such a powerful addiction to

escape unbearable emotional pain. For now, it is important for you to know that this addiction has been in control of you, rather than you controlling it. With a lot of commitment on your part and a good treatment program, you can get better. You must actively work on recovering from this addiction.

Second, the relationship implications are recognized:

This addiction makes having a real relationship impossible. The two of you are the rare couple that has managed to survive in the face of this addiction. After the addicted partner recovers from this illness, the two of you can begin to slowly work on the marriage. At some point, when the addiction is under control, your relationship will begin to change. You can then decide whether this relationship is meeting your needs.

The process of reframing infidelity promotes an understanding of the couple's dynamic that is central to the betrayal. The partners make a connection between their behavior as a couple and the affair, thereby viewing it in a systemic manner. Essentially, an effective reframe allows the couple to address the affair in a different light, defusing the negative patterns of anger and blame. As the therapist gains more information, other reframes may be made that address the intergenerational or individual risk factors.

Conclusion

The integrative model described in this chapter represents our particular contribution to the assessment and treatment of infidelity. The therapist must combine all three components of the clinical picture (psychological / biological, dyadic, and family of origin) in order to perform a comprehensive treatment plan. The focal point of treatment is the role of the couple in the development and maintenance of an affair or other forms of infidelity, because the most significant risk factors are often found in the relationship. From an intersystemic perspective, each partner plays a part in the betrayal. In fact, we are always vigilant for the less obvious yet equally important contributions to the clinical picture from the betrayed partner.

8

❋ ❋ ❋

Forgiveness

INFIDELITY PROFOUNDLY DAMAGES A MARRIAGE. Even with the best clinical help, many relationships fail to survive an affair or other betrayals of intimacy. Furthermore, traditional treatment can be protracted, laborious, and punctuated by impasses that create hopelessness and pessimism. In this chapter, we introduce a straightforward, systems-based approach to infidelity by incorporating forgiveness into the treatment process. We have found that forgiveness offers a solution to deadlocks and infuses therapy with a sense of optimism. Moreover, clinical approaches that include forgiveness have been found to be effective in the treatment of anger, depression, and interpersonal injury (Butler, Dahlin, & Fife, 2002). Finally, the discussion of forgiveness is a natural complement to the concepts presented elsewhere in this volume.

CURRENT VIEWS OF FORGIVENESS

A great degree of conceptual uncertainty and ambiguity exists regarding forgiveness. Often, it is confused with similar constructs such as accepting, excusing, reconciling, and pardoning. This misunderstanding leads to therapist ambivalence about the effectiveness of forgiveness as a treatment strategy for interpersonal healing and resistance by clients (Butler et al., 2002). Problems result from this notional confusion. Everyone has a strongly held personal definition of the forgiveness process, which may not be congruent with the research findings in the field. Therapists may be unaware of their preconceptions. Our clients also assume that they know what the act of forgiving will involve. Therefore, in every case, therapists must clarify their personal notion of forgiveness, help couples to define their own parameters, and construct common guidelines for use in treatment. Making sure that all participants in the therapeutic discussion are using the term *forgiveness* in the same way can dispel much of the resistance to the idea of it. Moreover, without this foundational effort, clinicians will frequently find themselves speaking at cross-purposes with clients.

Defining Forgiveness

For some partners, forgiveness seems too easy; therefore, they forge ahead prematurely. Others forgive incompletely, insincerely, or at great cost to personal safety or self-respect (Spring, 1996). Sometimes, the anticipated risks and personal costs to the injured individual are too great, creating resistance to this aspect of therapy (Coleman, 1998; North, 1998). The therapist must clarify that forgiveness does not imply exoneration, nor is it the same as pardon. It does not alter the justification for punishment, obviate the need for restitution, nor remove the need for behavior change. Forgiveness neither condones nor excuses. Clients are not asked to change their moral view of acts committed; what is seen as wrong remains wrong even following forgiveness. Forgiveness does not imply tolerating the unacceptable—partners can forgive and still protect themselves.

Forgiveness Is Not Acceptance

Fundamentally dissimilar from forgiveness, acceptance represents an attempt to understand the context of the injurious actions of a loved one (Fincham, 2000). Acceptance involves:

- Reconsidering assumptions about the partner's motivations.
- Excusing or condoning problematic actions.
- Exonerating the offending partner from guilt.
- Acknowledging that the harmful action was justified given all the relevant factors.
- Granting that the harmful behavior was inevitable because of the circumstances.

Acceptance as a strategy is commonly employed and often successful when couples are resolving minor difficulties. Partners use this approach to maintain relationship homeostasis, particularly in the face of offending behaviors (Jacobson & Christensen, 1996). Essentially, acceptance leaves one party injured but removes the necessity to acknowledge the injury and ascribe blame to the offending partner (Koerner, Jacobson, & Christensen, 1994).

Too often, the betrayed spouse wants to forget the betrayal and move on. Acceptance is insufficient to the problem of infidelity, because the partner who created the damage is not obligated to change the offending behaviors (Christensen, Jacobson, & Babcock, 1995). Moreover, forgiveness is only possible after the betrayed spouse ascribes blame to the unfaithful partner. Betrayed partners can only attempt forgiveness when they cannot under-stand, condone, or excuse the offending behaviors; they cannot actually *achieve* it at this point.

Forgiveness Is Not Accommodation

Accommodation is an individual's willingness to respond to questionable behaviors in a positive and helpful manner rather than by taking offense. Partners simply choose to ignore certain behaviors, judging them as the inev-itable price of the relationship (Rusbult, Bissonnette, Arriaga, & Cox, 1998). Although accommodation is often relationship-enhancing, particularly with benign responses, it is an inappropriate coping strategy in cases of sexual betrayal. In these instances, the damage to the relationship and negative effects are so widespread and persistent that even highly motivated partners find themselves unable to adapt. Indeed, the decision to resort to couple therapy is often precipitated by the failure of attempts by the betrayed part-ner to accommodate to sexual transgressions.

Acceptance and accommodation have important roles in the treatment of infidelity, but only as precursors to forgiveness. These strategies merely set the stage by narrowing the focus of forgiveness. That is, some aspects of the offense can be excused, tolerated, or justified, and therefore forgiveness is not necessary for them. The hardest work begins precisely when a particular portion of an offense remains unacceptable, inexcusable, and beyond tol-eration.

Forgiveness Is Not a Gift

The giftlike nature of forgiveness is much emphasized in the literature (Enright, Eastin, Golden, Sarinopoulos, & Freedman, 1992). In this view, through the commission of the offense the offender has lost any moral right to toleration, love, or acceptance. If the victim chooses to forgive, it is not for personal gain but because it is the right thing to do. The notion of forgiveness as a gift further exaggerates the relational imbalance created by infidelity. Some well-meaning clients are simply too eager to do either the right thing or what is seen as morally good. Such individuals may be highly religious, extremely sensitive, or easily influenced.

The notion of forgiveness as an unmerited gift emphasizes heroic, noble, or altruistic features, yet it often leads to unproductive therapy. Stressing selflessness rarely generates successful forgiveness. It is usually difficult for betrayed, angry, or vengeful spouses to imagine offending spouses benefiting from their benevolence. Betrayed spouses experience the forgiveness gift as risky, emotionally difficult, and sacrificial. If persuaded to engage in forgiveness, these clients may experience anger, resistance, or "psuedoforgiveness" (an outward attempt to act out forgiveness without any resolution of inner resentment). They are twice victimized, once by infidelity and again by therapy, which fails to meet their needs to reduce their anger and restore their well-being.

Real forgiveness promotes significant cognitive, affective, and behavioral changes on the parts of the offender and the offended (Coleman, 1998; Gordon, Baucom, & Snyder, 2000). Marriages and marriage partners suffer together, and must heal together in order to overcome interpersonal injury. We find that the most effective motivation for encouraging lasting forgiveness is a mutual desire to recover the relationship.

Forgiveness Is a Choice

Much of the empirical literature recognizes that forgiveness is a volitional act or a conscious decision on the part of the offended partner. It is an expression of altruism, which is not required of the victim but instead is freely given (Enright & Coyle, 1998; Fincham, 2000; McCullough, Hoyt, & Rachal, 2000; North, 1987; Worthington, 1998). It occurs in situations of interpersonal hurt or injury when the betrayed partner cannot understand, condone, or pardon the offending behaviors.

We do not see forgiveness as purely discretionary. Instead, both internal and external factors strongly influence the choice for forgiveness. Recent work suggests that certain individuals may have an innate disposition to forgive whereas others simply do not (Berry, Worthington, & Parrott, 2001; Emmons, 2000). Even in controlled studies, the willingness to forgive is extremely difficult to predict (Boon & Sulsky, 1997). It is becoming increasingly clear that the circumstances and social transactions surrounding infidelity can make forgiveness easier, more difficult, or perhaps nearly impossible. For example, forgiveness is more likely in situations where offenders show remorse, apologize, and attempt to make amends (Exline & Baumeister, 2000; Fitness, 2001). Essentially, forgiveness is a reaction in the wounded partner to the remorse expressed by the perpetuator of the interpersonal injury. In fact, some researchers even suggest that forgiveness can provoke subsequent behavior changes in the person forgiven (Exline & Baumeister, 2000; Kelln & Ellard, 1999).

The therapist must understand that all of the behaviors surrounding the offense (apology, remorse, accepting responsibility, and forgiveness) are recursive—they are interlinked systemic phenomena. The clinician who understands the transactional processes that promote or prevent forgiveness can help clients create circumstances in which the choice to forgive is more likely (McCullough, 2000; Worthington, 1998; Worthington & Wade, 1999). For instance, therapists must do more than simply ask individuals if they would like to forgive; therapists should promote conditions, such as the expression of genuine remorse, in which forgiveness is more likely to occur. For example, an unfaithful wife's shame-based defensiveness and anger prevented her husband from considering forgiveness. He stated, "How can I even think about forgiving her? I cannot trust her. She is so hostile that I fear she is still seeing him." For 2 months, the therapist varied the format from conjoint to individual sessions. Therapeutic interventions with the wife promoted insight about why the affair occurred and provided insight into her defensiveness. Additionally, she discussed feelings of shame, guilt, and sadness over the loss of the affair partner and ways to express genuine remorse. Eventually, the woman became able to conduct herself in a manner that was appropriate to the interpersonal injury created by the affair. During this time, the husband was supported and educated about possible explanations for his wife's defensive behavior. When she was more authentic in her apology and sincere in expressing remorse, the conjoint sessions resumed. Understandably, the husband became more accepting, less protective of himself, and increasingly willing to work on the marital problems.

The Phenomenology of Forgiveness

The Course of Forgiveness

The forgiveness process touches a wide array of emotions, behaviors, and cognitions, with each client exhibiting a unique response pattern. This is precisely why researchers have found it difficult to agree on a phenomenology of forgiveness. We have also found it challenging to predict either the clinical course of forgiveness or the particular changes that will result. Even among clinicians surveyed who favored forgiveness as a treatment option, they differed about the processes involved (Denton & Martin, 1998) and its effectiveness (Butler et al., 2002). Thus, it is unlikely that a formulaic approach to treatment will give good results, because the process of forgiving is so idiosyncratic (Coleman, 1998).

Likewise, a state of forgiveness is difficult to achieve due to the complexities involved. Our formulation of forgiveness embodies components formerly described by Sells and Hargrave (1998) and McCullough (2001). The person who forgives:

1. Releases anger toward the offender.
2. Abandons the perceived right to retaliate.
3. Is motivated to recover the relationship.

The therapist may find it extraordinarily difficult to determine whether this process has occurred. Many couples who experience infidelity had troubled relationships independent of the immediate effects of the betrayal (Brown, 1991a, 1991b). Often, the "preoffense" state of relatedness reflects a level of discord (Fincham, 2000; McCullough et al., 2000). Thus, assessing forgiveness can become particularly difficult in terms of judging whether anger or discord between spouses is the result of infidelity or of the relational problems that precipitated it.

Forgiveness necessitates giving up negative emotions and cognitions such as anger, rumination, and hopes for revenge (Fincham, 2000). A turning point in treatment occurs when the betrayed spouse is able to stop referring to the infidelity, or to begin to warm again emotionally. Such changes are often quite easily observed and readily reported by clients and their spouses. On the other hand, betrayed spouses may genuinely forgive the infidelity and still have problems acting in loving, compassionate, or tolerant ways. Moreover, forgiveness work in itself is rarely a sufficient therapeutic intervention to produce restructured marriages.

Forgiveness Takes Time

The time-intensive aspect of forgiveness is widely acknowledged in the clinical literature (Enright & Fitzgibbons, 2000; Fitzgibbons, 1986; Hargrave, 1994; Worthington, Sandage, & Berry, 2000). In fact, forgiveness is more a protracted struggle than a discrete choice. In our experience, forgiveness is a series of choices made by betrayed spouses in the face of daily-life events that remind them of the betrayal. These reminders and reenactment of associated behaviors can trigger a return of the feeling of unforgiveness. Betrayed spouses may be surprised that choosing to forgive has not permanently banished anger and obsessive rumination. They may perceive that they have forgiven unsuccessfully or that forgiveness only offers a false hope of healing. Likewise, the unfaithful partner may view the occasional return of anger, accusation, or rumination as proof that the forgiveness offered was never real. Both partners may become discouraged.

Therapists must frequently educate and remind partners about the natural course of forgiveness. Explaining that forgiveness occurs in small increments and that sporadic setbacks are typical serves to interrupt pessimism and skepticism. Also, partners require help with planning coping strategies should relapses occur. This approach was used with the husband in the previously mentioned example after the treatment progressed and forgiveness was contemplated. Each time he became pessimistic, the therapist reminded him of the path to forgiveness. Such reminders instantly infused him with new hope. In addition, the wife was encouraged to reassure her spouse that she wanted to work on the relationship with him to the point of forgiveness.

The quality of forgiveness relates directly to the time invested in treatment (Worthington et al., 2000). In our experience, forgiveness is not something that happens quickly or all at once. Our clients often report a waxing and waning of anger, ruminations, the desire for revenge, and so forth, with the general trend toward a lessening of these states. Typically, they are unable to determine the exact point of forgiveness, realizing only after the fact that the ability to connect with their spouse has returned.

Forgiveness Is a Systemic Phenomenon

Some models of forgiveness recommend therapeutic strategies that are tailored to the individual wishing to recover from interpersonal trauma (Gordon & Baucom, 1998). Symptoms that resulted from the injury, such as anger or depression, are addressed from the perspective of the individual using forgiveness as a therapeutic tool (Al-Mabuk, Enright, & Cardis, 1995; Berry & Worthington, 2001; Enright, 1996; Witvliet, vanOyen, Ludwig, & Vander Laan, 2001). With considerable effort, forgiveness can be enacted and maintained independent of the context of a relationship. However, models that acknowledge the fundamentally relational nature of forgiveness are believed to be more comprehensive and effective (Baumeister, Exline, & Sommer, 1998; Fincham, 2000; McCullough, Exline, & Baumeister, 1998; Worthington & Wade, 1999). Forgiveness occurs most readily when both partners are willing to work together. In general, the relational approach underscores the necessity of treating infidelity from a systemic perspective, which recognizes the following:

- Offenses arise within relationships,
- Offenses are causative factors in the degradation and / or dissolution of relationships.
- When the offenses are forgiven, repair and enhancement of the relationship can result.

The therapist must determine the following about the partner who was unfaithful. Did this partner:

- Apologize to the betrayed partner?
- Acknowledge fully the extent of the infidelity?
- Demonstrate remorse?
- Exhibit a willingness to change behaviors?
- Cooperate with efforts to build in relational safeguards to ensure behavior change?

In addition, the therapist assesses if the betrayed partner is:

- Willing to listen to the spouse who was unfaithful?
- Trying to understand the factors that influenced the infidelity?
- Able to acknowledge that some aspects of the marriage are still good and worth preserving?
- Recognizing other problems that may have contributed to the infidelity?

The best opportunity for forgiveness occurs when the therapist addresses and influences the transactions surrounding the infidelity—such as the apology and demonstrated remorse—and not just the transgression itself (Fitness, 2001; McCullough, 2000; Worthington & Wade, 1999). Thus, without concentrating on the systemic realities of the couple, therapists are left with little more than the option of inviting their partners to forgive one another.

Moreover, relational forgiveness is exquisitely sensitive to communication that surrounds the offense and its aftermath. Certainly, spousal interactions after the infidelity can make forgiveness more likely or conversely impede the process (Fitness, 2001; McCullough, Worthington, & Rachal, 1997). One couple comes to mind. The husband became involved in an Internet dating service, met a woman, and was unfaithful on several occasions. His wife and employer discovered the infidelity, and ultimately he was fired from his job. The interpersonal, social, and financial damage was substantial. Shaken by the crisis of discovery, the guilty husband vowed to terminate all contact with his affair partner and find another job as soon as possible. He expressed remorse and expected his wife to forgive him unconditionally. After he had apologized, he could not tolerate discussions about any aspect of the infidelity. Understandably, his wife reacted with anger, fear, and disbelief. The therapist influenced the transactions following the affair by insisting that the husband address his need for the affair, the damage to all involved, relapse concerns, and the negative consequences of trying to circumvent the relational issues. Fortunately, the couple belonged to a religious group that held the husband accountable for his actions and required religious and personal compensation. This religious perspective was also used in helping him to see the impact of his actions on his wife, the damage caused to the relationship, and the need for genuine apology and remorse.

Perception Shapes the Understanding of the Offense

Events must pass through the perceptual lens of the observer, and in so doing acquire subjective meaning. Therefore, understanding each partner's perception of the infidelity is critical to forgiveness work. What may seem an understandable and essentially minor transgression to one person may be perceived by another to be a heinous and unforgivable offense. The questions for both spouses become:

- What was the offense?
- What is being forgiven?
- In what ways was the couple's intimacy contract violated?

For example, the betrayed partner often wants to know if love was involved. The degree of emotional versus sexual involvement is another area of inquiry. Does the difference matter? If so, to whom? Is there a difference at all? Spouses frequently have difficulty finding common ground on these issues. Circumstances surrounding infidelity will take on great importance. For example, was the betrayed spouse publicly embarrassed? If so, was the embarrassment intentional? Do friends and family members know of the infidelity? Who publicized it, and to what end? Often, betrayed partners confide in family or close friends, finding the emotional support helpful. However, sometimes they share information about the infidelity in an attempt to win sympathy and turn friends and family against the betraying partner. In such situations, the unfaithful spouse may feel punished by public scorn. Does public embarrassment also require forgiveness in its turn? Similarly, involvement in infidelity is often hidden as long as possible, ostensibly in order to protect the spouse from hurt while disentangling from it. Does the betrayed spouse see this as a generous act of loving concern, crafty self-protection, or perhaps an act of cowardice? Subjective perceptions of these objective events are at the heart of forgiveness work. It is essential that both spouses understand and agree on the exact meaning of the offense and what is being forgiven.

The wife whose husband had engaged in Internet infidelity was overcome with rage. Subsequently, she expressed her resentment, anger, and other intense emotions in the presence of the couple's 8-year-old daughter. The wife felt justified in expressing her anger and did not consider the negative impact of her actions on the child. The husband was surprised and dismayed about his wife's lack of discretion. In fact, he felt betrayed that his wife transgressed the parent–child boundary in this manner. The spouses discussed this series of events from their own frames of reference when it became a focal point for some time in the therapy.

Sex Is Iconic

Sexual behavior is fraught with meaning far beyond the act itself. The clinician must appreciate that the iconic terrain of sex is unique to each individual. There is no shortcut for the laborious work of helping couples to discover for themselves and explain exactly what the sexual misbehavior means to them, and thus what needs to be forgiven. We are sometimes surprised at the array of responses to extradyadic sex. We treated a spouse who retained the opinion that her husband's visits to a topless club, which involved looking but not touching, qualified as infidelity. To this woman, viewing naked women, with sexual arousal as a goal, constituted an act of sexual betrayal. In addition, we have treated spouses who contended that oral-genital contact was not necessarily infidelity. In fact, one husband insisted, with complete seriousness, that receiving oral sex was an act of infidelity only if a condom was not used. In his view, infidelity was wrong because it risked transmission of disease and unwanted pregnancy. A marriage that routinely included group sex came close to divorce over a sexual encounter that occurred without the other spouse's involvement. The key offense was a violation of the tacit agreement regarding group sexual behavior through a secret encounter. Therapists cannot assume that they know what aspect of extradyadic sex is threatening to the relationship unless the couple provides the information. Sexual betrayal is never simple; thus, forgiveness work involves helping the couple to find the real motivations behind the affair, and the essence of the harm done.

The Work of Discovery

One essential part of the forgiveness process is the work of discovery, in which the couple "maps the offense" or elucidates aspects of the infidelity that are wrong, hurtful, and in need of forgiveness. This work is difficult, tedious, and time consuming. Both partners typically hold strong preconceptions about the betrayal and refuse to accept that there can be any view but their own individual perspective. The betrayed spouse often initially struggles with discovery, because this work can appear to exonerate or excuse the betrayer. Additionally, the unfaithful partner can resist discovery, seeing in it an effort to magnify the guilt surrounding the infidelity. Making up one's mind about the meaning of the betrayal serves a self-protective function, and clients sense the risk inherent in opening themselves up to a genuine understanding of the spouse's experience. Encouragement and support is necessary, because this aspect of forgiveness work is difficult and frustrating for each partner.

ATTENTION TO SYSTEMIC FACTORS

One of the benefits of fidelity is the sense of belonging to an intimate partnership. Infidelity fatally damages the shared identity or "we-ness" of the couple (Agnew, Van Lange, Rusbult, & Langston, 1998; Rusbult & Buunk, 1993). The loss of the couple's identity causes the betrayed spouse to feel alone rather than conjoined within the safety of the relationship. Thus, the unfaithful partner is perceived as being outside of the boundaries of the partnership or marriage. Keeping this partner out of the loop perpetuates a pernicious state of unforgiveness. The function of forgiveness is to deactivate the unforgiveness that is destroying the relationship. Forgiveness restores the partners to a state of we-ness by requiring that they work together to rebuild the marriage, thus returning the offending spouse to membership in the couple (Fitness, 2001; Tavuchis, 1991).

The intersystems approach protects the violated spouse and increases the likelihood of a restructured and strengthened relationship. It is unproductive to require that only the betrayed partner invest in the labor of recovering the marriage from the effects of infidelity. The unfaithful partner is seen as an equal coworker in the forgiveness process, sharing responsibility for improvement, and doing parallel work. Both partners need to take risks, experience pain, and struggle to change.

The result of true forgiveness is a change in the very nature of the relationship. Couples who have recovered from infidelity can often make the surprising assertion that the affair or other types of betrayal actually improved their marriage. They are not saying that infidelity was good; it cannot be accommodated, nor can it be reframed into something positive, acceptable, or benign. Instead, they recognize that their jointly created response to something very bad has resulted in a changed relationship, one that is large enough to encompass loving feelings and the inexcusable offense (Freedman, 2000; Mamalakis, 2001). This requires great courage and flexibility for both partners. The infidelity, its foundations within the marriage, and the damage it has caused must be looked at directly.

In one case, a woman who had an affair was in the process of being forgiven by her husband. She lamented that she almost lost the marital relationship and that she was happy to have it back again. The therapist offered the reframe that the old relationship was indeed over and that a new one was being rebuilt. This made sense to the couple, because they recognized the weaknesses in their preaffair relationship as well as their combined efforts to create a viable union.

Motivating the Couple

Certain aspects of infidelity can be understood, given that all persons can be vulnerable or weak at various times throughout the life cycle. Most adults can comprehend how another could do something vain, self-serving, immature, or foolish, especially if the act in question involves sex. In fact, we have noted that spouses who are recovering from infidelity can theoretically comprehend the conditions of human frailty and vulnerability to temptation. However, once the breach in trust occurs within their relationship, they are often unwilling to accept that such a common situation can happen to them! They do not ponder "How could you do this?" but rather "How could you do this *to me?*" Wounded partners have little empathy. Instead of working to understand infidelity, the betrayed spouse typically asks, "Why should I bother?" The we-ness of the marriage has been destroyed, and the partners are insufficiently motivated to address the difficult issues. In other words, wounded partners simply do not "care" enough about their betraying spouses spouse to try to forgive them. Thus, the first and most challenging task in therapy is to uncover the couple's motivation to become a couple again.

All aspects of forgiveness work, such as mapping the offense and discovering the meaning of the infidelity, are risky and painful. Many couples resist a frank exploration of the issues surrounding the infidelity by avoiding the subject altogether, or by stating that the betrayed spouse forgives the partner's unfaithful behavior. Forgetting has no role in forgiving. Others sabotage the discussion with accusations, ruminations, or extreme affect.

Essentially, each therapeutic task requires a strong motivation to recover the relationship, and most couples do not enter treatment with this level of inspiration. Typically, they need help from the therapist in generating momentum to do the difficult work ahead of them.

Maximizing Unifying Factors

From an intersystems perspective, motivating the couple involves helping them to understand and forgive one another because they once again want to view themselves as a couple. Thus, the first step focuses solely on the relationship, specifically helping the couple to find reasons to stay together. We do this by maximizing unifying factors that have the effect of drawing the couple together or promoting forgiveness directly. These factors are empathy, hope, humility, and relational commitment (McCullough, 2000; Worthington, 1998). The clinician also works to decrease or neutralize those factors that inhibit forgiveness or diminish a sense of we-ness. These are narcissism, shame, anger, and fear (Emmons, 2000; Worthington, 1998; Worthington & Wade, 1999). In most cases, these elements can be amplified or muted through therapist actions.

The couple is not simply invited to forgive. We know from our years of clinical experience that this approach to treating infidelity does not work. Instead, the central task for the therapist is to maximize the positive correlates of forgiveness and minimize the destructive forces. Each of these factors functions in an interconnected and reciprocal manner. The therapist can influence the system by addressing one element, thereby affecting all of the others. Moreover, these components need not be addressed in a stepwise fashion; the system can be entered productively at any point. By doing this, forgiveness itself is made easier. In the next two chapters, we discuss in greater detail the therapist's role in enhancing the couple's use of unifying factors and minimizing the barriers to forgiveness.

CONCLUSION

Existing treatment approaches to forgiveness are inadequate to the task of working with couples experiencing the trauma of infidelity. They fail to recognize that the major insult is to the couple's sense of belonging to a partnership. The betraying spouse acts outside of the relationship and the offended spouse suffers alone. The intersystems treatment of infidelity recognizes that relationship-enhancing forgiveness involves a conjoint effort to focus on the offense by discovering the aspects that are understandable and others that are reprehensible. In the next chapter, we elaborate on the unifying factors that increase the likelihood of forgiveness, such as empathy, commitment, hope, and humility. In addition, social transactions that have been shown to be highly productive of forgiveness, such as apology and expressed remorse, are addressed.

9

❋ ❋ ❋

Facilitating Forgiveness

IN THE PRECEDING CHAPTER, THE ROLE OF FORGIVENESS in the treatment of infidelity was introduced. Forgiveness does not simply occur—it is cultivated by a therapeutic focus on unifying factors such as empathy, hope, humility, and commitment (McCullough, 2000; Worthington, 1998). In addition, conditions that are divisive to the couple are discouraged (Worthington & Wade, 1999). A solid foundation of relational unity enables the unfaithful spouse to deliver a genuine apology, which in turn initiates a series of forgiveness transactions in the couple. In this chapter, we first consider the unifying factors that promote forgiveness, and then proceed to the role of apology.

UNIFYING FACTORS

The intersystems treatment of infidelity promotes the interdependence and interrupts polarization. The unifying factors are gradually shaped through a succession of judicious, indirect interventions over the duration of treatment. The expression of empathy, humility, commitment, and hope is progressively enhanced through rehearsal. Despite this shaping process, unfaithful partners often have a difficult time bringing themselves to the point of acknowledging and accepting culpability. This is the most precarious aspect of forgiveness work. If the guilty partner is guided too directly, a defensive response will occur. Likewise, openly requesting that betrayed partners express empathy may cause them to feel they are being asked to shoulder equal blame for the transgression (Coleman, 1998). Blame is at the very heart of many of such couples' transactions around infidelity, and clients are exquisitely sensitive to the possibility of shifting blame from the transgressor to the betrayed. Betrayed partners who conclude that the therapist is advocating shared blame for the infidelity may suspect a therapist alliance with the unfaithful partner. Although we are systemically oriented, we believe there is never a constellation of circumstances that make infidelity acceptable; it is always wrong.

Empathy

After the revelation of infidelity, both partners typically become absorbed by their own reactions. A protracted internal focus on the individual experience of pain or defensiveness only serves to further polarize the couple. Each partner benefits personally from an increased ability to understand the motivations and sufferings of the other. From the first moments of the therapeutic relationship, the therapist promotes the feeling of empathy in both partners in order to reconnect the fractured couple. More important, we believe that empathy will eventually enable the guilty party to express remorse and offer a genuine apology.

Empathy is a mainstay of couple counseling and an essential element of marital satisfaction. It is also recognized as a necessary condition for forgiveness (Coleman, 1998; Coyle & Enright, 1998; Denton & Martin, 1998; DiBlasio, 2000; Doyle, 1999; Enright & North, 1998; Fow, 1996; Freedman, 2000; Gordon et al., 2000; Griffin, 1999; Malcolm & Greenberg, 2000; Worthington, 1998).

In cases of infidelity, the couple is stuck in disparate positions due to the pain of the injury and the defensiveness of the guilty party. Thus, empathy is usually nonexistent and must be shaped through subtle means, particularly in the beginning stages of forgiveness work. Timing is important; therefore, we encourage empathy only when the emotions of the spouses are composed. We are cautious to avoid directly suggesting that the betrayed spouse identify with the unfaithful partner's situation. This is too great a leap and will only provoke rage and more suffering; victims of infidelity, in their pain and anger, simply cannot allow that, given similar circumstances, they too might have strayed. In fact, to suggest this sort of understanding is a recipe for disaster, because it returns the couple to an adversarial posture. Preferably, we might ask betrayed spouses to describe a time, either before or during their marriage, when they were attracted to another person. We often give considerable time to these recollections, because they have the salutary effect of normalizing the attraction process. The aggrieved spouse may slowly come to realize the common and enticing interpersonal aspects of attraction, a small step toward empathy.

For the first time, the unfaithful spouse realizes that the partner may be able to imagine that attraction is universal, but without exonerating this spouse for the betrayal. Moreover, the unfaithful spouse will react less defensively when there is a temporary reprieve in the intense expression of the partner's pain. Reducing defensiveness as early in treatment as possible is critical because of the destructive effect of attempting to justify a reprehensible deed. This step is also important because it increases the possibility of acknowledging guilt, accepting responsibility for the transgression, promoting engagement in treatment, and facilitating the eventual experience of empathy for the betrayed partner.

Humility

Aggrieved partners may understand some of the circumstances and forces involved in a spousal infidelity yet still find themselves unwilling or unable to forgive. Accordingly, empathy alone is an insufficient precondition for forgiveness—humility is of equal importance to empathy in paving the way for forgiveness (Worthington, 1998). Through humility, the unfaithful partner acknowledges responsibility for the damage to the relationship and personal injury to the spouse. A modest and respectful demeanor eventually replaces a defensive posture. This attitude is accomplished by subtly encouraging a series of small confessions for portions of the betrayal. Each confession serves as a rehearsal and strengthens this partner's ability to accommodate, appease, and accept responsibility. These elements are difficult in direct relation to the severity of the offense, yet are central to an effective apology. In cases of infidelity, lack of acceptance of responsibility creates a major therapeutic impasse. Rehearsal of minor confessions can make accepting responsibility more palatable. This clinical strategy is supported by numerous reports of the effectiveness of conciliatory behavior in forgiveness of a known offense (McLaughlin, Cody, & Rosenstein, 1983; Scher & Darley, 1997; Schlenker, 1980; Schneider, 2000).

A couple in their late 40s was in treatment because the woman disclosed that she had been involved in an affair for over a year. Conjoint sessions were conducted initially, and then concurrent sessions took place while she ended the affair. After the conjoint sessions were resumed, the woman continued to react defensively whenever her spouse discussed the infidelity. In fact, she was skeptical about continuing to meet conjointly even after the affair was terminated, because she could not tolerate seeing her husband's pain and anguish. He focused obsessively on her every action and did not trust her even though she provided credible evidence that the affair had ended. She agreed to continue conjoint therapy only after being reassured that her husband would not be punitive. Still, she appeared defensive, justifying the infidelity by claiming that she had been in love with the affair partner and that he had given her attention that she did not receive in the marriage. The therapist initiated work on humility by having the wife take responsibility for accepting telephone calls and lunch dates with her affair partner months before the relationship was sexualized. Her acceptance of culpability for those specific choices helped to incrementally foster humility. After a few months, the woman's defensiveness decreased enough to enable her to see the devastation she had created in her partner and the marriage.

The experience of humility for injured partners is somewhat different. The therapist must help such partners to see beyond their pessimism, so that they can work on the relationship. Humility is encouraged in a global way by discussing the frailness of human nature. For instance, we might suggest that anyone could weaken in times of vulnerability and behave in a manner that violates one's own value system. We ask betrayed partners to consider a time in their own lives when they felt fallible, vulnerable, or frail. This strategy is intended to interrupt the ongoing hurt and anger, and shape a more positive attitude that can support interdependent work. It is important to note that we do not ask the betrayed partner to simply understand or forgive what we believe to be an unacceptable breach of trust; we often return to the topic of human frailty throughout the course of treatment.

Commitment and Hope

Every relationship has a series of memories that punctuate the couple's time together, such as the first date, their engagement, their marriage, and the birth of their children. Infidelity is a marker event in the marriage that interrupts the memories of the happy past and halts dreams for the future. For the relationship to continue, the couple must bridge the gap created by the infidelity and restore the continuum between the past of the relationship and its future. The clinician must focus on increasing the couple's awareness of their commitment to each other and by intensifying their levels of hope for the future. The reason for focusing on commitment and hope is that they have a powerful positive influence on present behavior and decisions.

COMMITMENT

Increasing the couple's commitment to their relationship is a fundamental objective of intersystems work (Weeks & Treat, 2001). The topic of commitment has been the focus of much empirical research and, in general, it is positively associated to relational longevity and satisfaction (Arriaga & Agnew, 2001). More specifically, relational commitment is composed of several elements or factors that have been identified in empirical studies (Agnew, 2000; Agnew & Gephart, 2000; Agnew et al., 1998; Rusbult, Arriaga, & Agnew, 2001). These include:

- Psychological attachment.
- Long-term orientation.
- The intention to persist.
- Cognitive interdependence (sense of we-ness).

Rusbult and Buunk (1993) and Van Lange, Agnew, Harinck, and Steemers (1997) supported our intuitive understanding that the more committed a partner is, the more willing that partner is to relinquish self-interest in service of the relationship. We believe that the willingness to forgive in the face of infidelity is an act of sacrifice in the service of the relationship and, as such, it should be strongly influenced by levels of commitment.

The effects of commitment and cognitive interdependence are reciprocal and iterative (Agnew et al., 1998). Essentially, increases in commitment promote subsequent increases in cognitive interdependence, which in turn promote further increases in commitment, and so forth—a positive feedback loop. In fact, each of the previously mentioned components of commitment is interlinked and reciprocal, and they work together as a system to positively influence each other.

The research on commitment emphasizes that the therapist can enter the commitment system at any point and have broad salutary effects. For example, increasing couples' psychological attachment may subsequently increase their long-term orientation, their intention to persist, their sense of we-ness, their willingness to sacrifice, and so on. Ultimately, this positive feedback system should increase the likelihood of genuine apology and forgiveness. We suggest that the therapist focus on that aspect of the commitment process that is most amenable to influence in a particular couple, because intervention at any level in the system will affect all components. In fact, we recommend the therapist assess couples for their intentions at the start of treatment to persist in both the relationship and in therapy. The partners should be strongly encouraged to make a verbal commitment to each other and to the therapeutic process. This action is taken long before work to increase psychological closeness is begun (Weeks & Treat, 2001). Such a step can have a beneficial effect throughout the course of therapy. Every small investment the couple makes in therapy will increase their overall commitment and sense of we-ness.

In addition, the couple is asked to remember agreements, promises, bonds, memories, and other contributions they have made to their relationship. In moments of anger, couples often forget the emotional, financial, and personal investments they have made. Moreover, the strong negative affect surrounding infidelity overwhelms the couple and causes them to forget the positive affect of the past. For commitment to be increased, these investments and the strong feelings of love must be remembered and felt. Early in treatment, precisely when couples are most negative and hopeless, we often ask about the better times in their relationship, using questions such as:

- How did you meet?
- What attracted you to the other?
- How did your relationship begin?

These recollections cannot repair or restructure the marriage. However, a recollection of the salutary elements of the earlier phases of their history will positively affect the couple's commitment process.

One example involves a sullen young couple who entered counseling after only 4 years of marriage. During their short marriage, the wife had three affairs, all of which were discovered by the husband. Recently, the husband had begun a retaliatory affair, which he refused to break off. Apparently, infidelity was part of a larger pattern of immaturity, hostility, and emotional abuse. After taking a brief history, the therapist wondered what these two were doing in therapy; a divorce lawyer seemed a more logical choice! However, in response to questions about their courtship and first months of marriage, the couple softened their angry demeanor. It became clear that, for a brief time, they enjoyed a loving relationship and a very strong sexual attraction. The remainder of the first session was spent cataloging the emotional warfare of the subsequent years of marriage.

At the close of the session, the couple was asked about their commitment to the therapy and the relationship: "In light of all the pain and struggle you have shared, and considering all that you have lost in this relationship, how much more are you willing to invest to get back to the love you once shared?" They agreed to try to make sense of the pain they caused and resolved to embark on a long course of therapy.

In subsequent sessions, several things became clear. Both of these young people had lived very hard lives. They had grown up in unstable homes, and had each endured periods of incarceration in juvenile facilities. Nonetheless, both desperately wanted a happy marriage and expressed the desire to raise children in a stable home. In their families of origin, they had not learned how to bring about these goals. Nonetheless, their shared objectives were used to promote hope, which supported this couple through the hard work of therapy. Eventually, the combined forces of commitment and hope for the future gradually helped the partners to recover their love and sexuality. Each generated enough courage to make the leap of faith involved in forgiving the other for an entire catalog of infractions. The power of hope to elicit such forgiveness is explored in the next section.

HOPE

The empirical research on the concept of hope is in its infancy, and remains unconnected to the study of forgiveness. Nonetheless, based on our clinical experience with infidelity, we feel confident in linking hope with the greater willingness to invest in either apology or forgiveness. For this reason, we concentrate on increasing optimism and a future orientation with those couples facing the need to forgive. The scant research on the topic supports our observation that hope is a key element in promoting the forgiveness process (Worthington & Wade, 1999). Hope is conceptualized as having three interrelated components (Snyder, 2000):

1. Goals.
2. Self-directed motivation to achieve the goals.
3. The capacity to plan ways to accomplish the goals.

Initial clinical studies indicate that therapeutic interventions can influence each of these components, and increases in any of the components of hope result in a broad spectrum of psychological and health benefits (Irving & Cannon, 2000; Klausner, Snyder, & Cheavens, 2000; Lopez, Floyd, Ulven, & Snyder, 2000; Snyder, 2000). Furthermore, similar to commitment, the components of hope are additive and interactive (Snyder & Taylor, 2000). Thus, therapeutic efforts at any point in the hope system will likely have positive effects on the remaining components. All three components of should be addressed preparatory to forgiveness work.

An early clinical effort must be made to recover shared relational goals. However, after the crisis of infidelity, couples often forget the plans and dreams they had formulated at happier times. Nonetheless, in therapy they should be guided to salvage these dreams and decide which they want to continue to claim. Even highly conflicted couples will continue to share several common objectives, especially if they have children. Yet, often, before they are able to discuss these goals, the couple will reveal a common and fundamental problem: the perceived loss of their central goal—a happy marriage.

For many spouses, infidelity shatters the idea of marriage. In their experience, a good or happy marriage simply cannot include a history of infidelity, and thus they abandon future-oriented thinking altogether. Consequently, levels of hope sink substantially. The therapist's first task, then, is to help the couple to explore alternate shared goals. We discuss at length the idea of a good or happy marriage that contains a history of infidelity and recovery from infidelity. We share where appropriate, case histories of successfully recovered marriages, and we encourage the couple to search their own circle of acquaintances for evidence that marriage can survive infidelity. It is critical that the alternate goal becomes the central shared goal for the couple: a happy marriage that has not only survived an infidelity, but also is stronger.

Following this, the partners explore their capacity to achieve their goals. The therapist consistently supports motivation toward goal achievement, such as reminding partners of obstacles they have surmounted individually and jointly in the past. Moreover, the couple is encouraged to remember the special satisfaction of a jointly solved problem, or an obstacle overcome at an earlier time in the marriage. Recovery of the marriage is reframed as a similar challenge with a similar, eventual reward. We sometimes use a concept identified by Snyder (1994)—"You *can* get there from here"—in an attempt to repeatedly remind the couple that many other couples survive infidelity, recover, and build good, happy marriages.

The ability and willingness to strategize alternate routes to a goal should be encouraged (Snyder, 2000). Couples are often reassured of the many ways to achieve a solid marriage, and reminded that they are limited only by their own unwillingness to persevere. Again, appropriate case histories can have a powerfully encouraging effect, by modeling plans to accomplish goals that proved to be successful for other couples. Once the partners begin to experience significant increases in hope, there is a noticeable corollary effect on commitment and we-ness. Planning together increases both long-term orientation and cognitive interdependence. The imagined future and the remembered past begin to compete with the painful experiences of the present for the attention of the couple. Current pain, fear, and despair can eventually be displaced by feelings of commitment and hope. It is at this point that the couple is ready for the apology-forgiveness event.

The Role of the Apology

After a couple has experienced infidelity, offering a genuine apology and achieving forgiveness can be almost insurmountably difficult. Empathy can narrow the chasm somewhat, by providing a context and some understanding of why the offense might have occurred in the first place. Humility can help the unfaithful parter become less defensive and the betrayed partner to recognize that to err is human. Nonetheless, infidelity is an inexcusable transgression; it cannot be accommodated, accepted, or explained. It can only be forgiven.

Infidelity has led to a breach in the interdependence (we-ness) of the couple; the unfaithful spouse has been banished to intrapsychic exile. For the betrayed partner, who does not wish to be wounded again, forgiveness can seem risky and even foolish. Thus, for most people, relationship-restoring forgiveness involves a leap of faith, which takes incredible courage. Two crucial factors must be present if such a risky step is to be taken: The first is a high degree of relational commitment, and the second is a genuine apology (Couch, Jones, & Moore, 1999). These factors will return the unfaithful spouse to a position of being loved and valued despite the wrong committed, and thereby promote forgiveness (Fitness, 2001; Tavuchis, 1991).

Apology and Forgiveness

When the factors drawing the couple back together outweigh those pushing the partners apart, the individuals are ready for forgiveness work. That is, when the couple regains interdependence, the clinician facilitates communication that will produce forgiveness. The unfaithful partner must make obvious the following conditions (Couch 1999; Fincham, 2000; Fitness, 2001; Flanagan, 1992; Gold & Weiner, 2000; Worthington, 1998; Worthington & Wade, 1999):

- Sincere acknowledgment of the offense.
- Remorse.
- Commitment to change.
- A true apology.

Purpose of Apology

The purpose of the apology is to restore the fractured relationship. The unfaithful partner communicates genuine sorrow, regret, or remorse, primarily through the verbal formulation of an apology. Moreover, the intention of making atonement or reparation for the pain and damage caused is implicit in the apology. If correctly timed and genuinely delivered, the apology will provoke an empathic response from the betrayed partner (Couch et al., 1999; Fincham, 2000; Fitness, 2001; Flanagan, 1992; Gold & Weiner,

2000; Worthington, 1998; Worthington & Wade, 1999). In fact, Mc-Cullough and colleagues (1997) established that empathy that results from the apology positively affects the betrayed partner in three ways:

- Motivation toward retaliation decreases.
- Motivation to maintain estrangement from the unfaithful partner decreases.
- Motivation toward conciliatory behaviors increases.

Thus, empathy toward the unfaithful partner serves as a precursor to forgiveness (Tavuchis, 1991).

The available literature indicates that the apology serves additional functions, such as the mitigation of anger and aggression in the wounded party (Darby & Schlenker, 1982; Schwartz, Kane, Joseph, & Tedeschi, 1978). However, the method for accomplishing this remains in question. Additionally, the apology is hypothesized as a strategy that, when effective, alters the injured person's perception of the offender—the offender's responsibility in the injury or the degree of malice intended is perceived to be less after the apology has been made (Schlenker, 1980; Tedeschi & Norman, 1985; Tedeschi & Riess, 1981).

Fitness (2001) suggested that the apology partially repairs or redresses the extreme power imbalance that results from relational betrayal. The efficacy of the apology is related to the degree of submission exhibited by the offender (Miller, 1993). Demonstrated remorse, acknowledgment of culpability, and obvious emotional distress on the part of the unfaithful parter may reinstate the status of the betrayed partner by restoring balance or eliminating the one-up / one-down position. In this view, an effective apology must include demonstrated contrition; the unfaithful partner must be seen to be suffering emotionally.

We agree that the genuine apology accomplishes more than merely provoking empathy in the betrayed partner. Fundamentally, it results in emotional relief, particularly after guilt and remorse has been induced in the unfaithful partner (Baumeister, Stillwell, & Heatherton, 1995; Ohbuchi, Kameda, & Agarie, 1989). In other words, the evident emotional distress of the person rendering the apology has the effect of alleviating emotional distress in the betrayed partner.

Creating an Effective Apology

The apology offered must be proportionately related to the offense and the importance of the relationship (Tavuchis, 1991). However, the nature of infidelity makes it impossible for betraying partners to apologize effectively even when they are highly motivated to do so. In fact, as blameworthiness increases, the apology often becomes shorter and more aggravating rather than conciliatory; this is probably a function of anxiety (Gonzales, Pederson, Manning, & Wetter, 1990; Hodgins, Liebeskind, & Schwartz, 1996; Schlenker, 1980). Betrayed partners often find themselves in a comparable bind, unable to accept an apology and render forgiveness even though they want to preserve and improve the marital relationship. Helping clients to negotiate this impasse is one of the central therapeutic tasks in forgiveness work. Creating an effective apology is difficult and often risky. We find that both partners usually need guidance in creating and receiving the apology in a constructive way.

Mitchell (1989) offered some ideas to help couples with the apology process. We have found the strategies to be productive in cases of infidelity:

- The client must consider the purpose of the apology.
- Make sure that the prerequisite remorse and willingness to change offending behaviors are present.
- Make apologies simple and specific.
- Discuss only the unfaithful partner's behavior. The apology should not become a platform for critiques or complaints about the betrayed partner's role in the offense.
- In some circumstances, address the relational conflict or context in which the betrayal occurred. This is a risky strategy and must be pursued with caution. However, if carefully presented, a contextualization of the offense may help to expand the betrayed partner's perceptions of both the offense and the unfaithful partner. Advance preparation and rehearsal of apologies will help clients to avoid doing more harm than good. The reader may recall the discussion in Chapter 7 reframing in order to contextualize the infidelity.
- Use a straightforward presentational style. Pleading may amplify the betrayed partner's perception of the wrong done.
- Avoid complex, coercive, or manipulative accounts.
- Ensure that the timing of the apology is optimal. Premature apologies can seem superficial, insincere, or calculating. It may seem too easy, indicating that the offense in question is part of a larger pattern of offenses. It may also appear dismissive, and suggest a one-down position to the betrayed partner. A delayed apology allows the betrayed partner to ruminate over the offense and perhaps lose any motivation to recover the relationship.
- Anticipate the response of the betrayed spouse. Partners offering the apol-

ogy needs advance preparation that matters may appear worse initially, because the betrayed partners are reaffirmed in their views of the offense. Eventually, the intense reaction will subside.

- Consider the client's past pattern of apologies. If there is a history of insincere or manipulative apologies, the current apology will be less effective.

- Allow the couple's view of the future of the relationship to be central to the choice to pursue apology. If the relationship appears beyond repair, an apology may still serve a purpose, for instance, lessening the unfaithful partner's feelings of guilt.

Mitchell (1989) also offered suggestions for helping the betrayed partner receive the apology in a manner that is conducive to recovery of the relationship. The recipient of an apology has three options:

- Immediate acceptance of the apology.
- Delayed or conditional acceptance of the apology.
- Refusal of the apology.

A quickly accepted apology is likely to communicate a willingness to work toward restoration of the relationship. Unfortunately, the unfaithful spouse may be insufficiently motivated to change the offensive behavior if the betrayed spouse accepts the apology too rapidly. Conversely, too much delay can be counterproductive, leading the offender to disengage from the restoration process. Finally, rejection of the apology may have the perverse result of returning the offender to a position of power (Mitchell, 1989). Thus, the unfaithful partner might say, "I've tried to apologize and I've been rejected. I've done all that I can."

In a situation involving a breach of trust, an effective apology is both rare and exceedingly difficult (Schneider, 2000). Moreover, the response to the apology becomes less predictable as the seriousness of the offense increases (Darby & Schlenker, 1982; Schwartz et al., 1978). Sexual betrayal is the most profound and complicated offense to a relationship; thus, an apology for it must be carefully crafted to ensure that the unfaithful partner recognizes the impact of the offense on the relationship. This involves a twofold process: cognitively understanding the magnitude of the damage to the relationship, and affectively appreciating the betrayed partner's pain (Fitness, 2001; Steiner, 2000).

When sufficient genuine remorse is present, the apology can be given. However, our experience suggests that typically the unfaithful spouse either has not genuinely apologized for the infidelity or has atoned profusely and repeatedly without success. Indeed, this kind of "apology fatigue" is often the symptom that convinces the polarized couple to seek treatment. To break this deadlock, we employ paradox. Clients are asked to refrain from any more apologies concerning the infidelity until further therapeutic work has been done. The paradoxical injunction is given in such a way as to challenge the clients. For example, the therapist might say that they are not ready for a heartfelt apology. In other words, you would be trying to get the couple to resist your statement that they aren't ready. The resistance would appear in the form of a genuine apology. In many cases, both partners accept this injunction with relief. The course of treatment may continue for weeks or months while the therapist steadily lays the foundation for the successful apology-forgiveness event.

Problems With Apologies

The key therapeutic difficulty with apology is the same as that associated with forgiveness; clients will assume that they already understand the process. The first clinical challenge is convincing the unfaithful partner that previous apologies did not work for many reasons. Elicit the clients' cooperation in attempting to discover why the previous apologies were ineffective. Utilizing the therapeutic alliance, calmly explain that inneffective apologies are common. People offering apologies are often more protective of their own feelings than those of the betrayed partners. In this way, the apology is inadvertently more self-serving or manipulative than intended. In fact, many apologies are simply excuses, justifications, and disclaimers that contain some apology material (Gonzales et al., 1990). Ineffective apologies contain themes such as: "It wasn't my fault," "It only happened once," or "It didn't really mean anything." Indeed, unfaithful partners may think they have delivered an apology when in fact they have given a half-hearted, conflicted attempt to deflect blame or escape the consequences for their behavior (Baumeister, Stillwell, & Wotman, 1990; Hewitt & Stokes, 1975; Semin & Manstead, 1983; Tedeschi & Riess, 1981). Try as they might, many spouses are simply unable to formulate an apology that is free from defensive material. In such situations, recipients of such apologies are justifiably frustrated or confused. This is one of the reasons why apologies can provoke anger. Aggrieved spouses respond very poorly to such self-serving apologies.

This work is difficult and emotionally intense, yet this emotional intensity is precisely what makes forgiveness more likely. Explain that the effectiveness of a pure apology is dependent on the emotional distress of the unfaithful partner (Fitness, 2001). For this reason, we try to do as much of this work as possible in joint session. It is productive for the betrayed partner to see the unfaithful partner's distress. When it is finally formulated and delivered, a genuine apology has a much higher chance of helping to produce forgiveness.

The next clinical challenge is instructing the couple that apologies are often offered before the unfaithful partner has had a genuine emotional response to the betrayed partner's suffering (Blackman & Stubbs, 2001). Such apologies are half-hearted in that the betrayed partner's pain has been only partially felt and acknowledged. To be effective, the apology must not be a platform for self-defense. Rather, pure apology requires submission and self-abnegation. Moreover, it occurs after the painful work of acknowledging the damage that infidelity has caused. As such, it is a moment of profound vulnerability, and requires great courage.

CONCLUSION

The intersystems approach to infidelity strengthens the interdependence of the couple by promoting empathy, humility, commitment, and hope. This is the groundwork for the genuine apology and eventual forgiveness. The apology promotes empathy in the wounded partner and facilitates forgiveness. However, it is difficult to construct and requires direction and rehearsal in order to help produce forgiveness. Nevertheless, some couples prove resistant to forgiveness despite the clinician's best efforts. In the next chapter, we identify the most common blocks to forgiveness and some treatment methods that address such therapeutic dilemmas.

10

❀ ❀ ❀

Working with Refractory Cases

FOR MANY COUPLES, THE TECHNIQUES PROVIDED IN THE PREVIOUS CHAP-
ters will be sufficient to initiate the forgiveness process. However, emotional
barriers sometimes interfere with relational unity, prevent forgiveness, and
delay resolution of infidelity. The most common barriers include narcissism,
shame, accusatory suffering, anger, and fear in one or both partners
(Emmons, 2000; Worthington, 1998; Worthington & Wade, 1999). These
factors operate more in refractory cases, than in prototypical infidelity situations; thus, the usual treatment modalities might not be effective. In this
chapter, we discuss strategies for recognizing and removing the obstacles to
forgiveness when couples are refractory to the customary treatment for infidelity, and where forgiveness is difficult yet nevertheless possible. For couples
who are truly incapable of forgiveness, infidelity will become the reason for
the demise of the relationship, even if other problems coexisted; no amount
of treatment will repair the damage if the couple is unable to forgive.

BARRIERS TO FORGIVENESS

Narcissism

In Chapter 7 on systemic considerations, we discussed some of the individual
risk factors that complicate the treatment of infidelity. As a rule, narcissism

is the most likely of all personality characteristics to have a negative effect on achieving forgiveness. The narcissistic individual is distinguished by grandiosity, the need for admiration, a sense of entitlement, the lack of empathy, and the tendency to exploit others (American Psychiatric Association, 1994). Typically, this individual has difficulty doing the clinical work required for resolution of infidelity. The full-blown personality disorder is an absolute contraindication to forgiveness work. Likewise, individuals with a narcissistic personality style or traits present a significant obstacle to treatment because they have difficulty seeing and respecting another person's point of view. Because much of the intersystems approach to promoting forgiveness is predicated on increasing empathy in both partners, the presence of narcissism hinders the unfaithful partner's capacity to acknowledge guilt and accept responsibility for the damage done to the relationship. Consequently, sincere apology and subsequent forgiveness are prevented.

Fortunately, narcissistic personality traits are easily recognized through a pervasive pattern of identifiable behaviors. Central to the narcissistic style is difficulty with intimate relationships. Exploitativeness is typical; narcissistic individuals are concerned with meeting their own needs rather than investing psychological energy in another person. Commonly, they seek to "fix" one failing relationship by engaging in another, thereby taking advantage of both. Narcissists who are involved in one troubled relationship often seek refuge in an affair, only to find themselves involved in two problematic relationships.

In one case, a narcissistic man in his early 60s could not choose between his considerably younger affair partner and his wife of 8 years. The affair lasted for over 2 years, and he wanted to continue both relationships despite the pain and suffering each partner experienced. He often proclaimed his intention to make a decision, but each time he reached a deadline he could not give up either partner. There were several crisis points in the therapy, especially when each of the women discovered the identity of the other. Dramatic scenes occurred, replete with confrontations and threats by each woman to end the relationship, yet no one disengaged from the heated triangle. The attention, adulation, and passion simply fed this man's narcissistic appetite. Finally, the wife removed herself by moving to another state with the sons from her previous marriage; however, the couple did not divorce. The husband eventually cohabited with his affair partner. Roughly 1 year after treatment ended, the therapists discovered that the husband and wife sometimes met secretly and maintained a sexual relationship without the knowledge of the affair partner.

Other indicators of narcissism include a heightened sense of authority, superiority, vanity, and exhibitionism. Moreover, the narcissistic person often appears self-sufficient because of the inability to be intimate or to operate as part of a couple (Emmons, 2000). Another case involved an elderly man who had a history of extramarital affairs. He demonstrated many of the narcissistic symptoms mentioned previously, particularly the sense of superiority. Other capable therapists had been unable to help the man to halt his philandering and work on the preexisting marital problems. The couple offered a litany of complaints related to the incompetence of the therapists, and had prematurely terminated treatment with each one. The husband could not agree to stop the infidelity and would not leave the marital home. Nonetheless, he challenged the therapist to help reduce his wife's anger and resentment. She maintained that she was too old to divorce him and deserved to live an affluent lifestyle until she died because she had tolerated his philandering throughout the years. The therapist assessed that conjoint treatment was inappropriate because the couple colluded to maintain a polarized, hostile system. Individual sessions were recommended after an initial period of assessment. The husband became angry and attacked the therapist's suggestion and fee structure, and once again the couple did not continue treatment.

Narcissistic persons are particularly inept at accurate self-appraisal (John & Robins, 1994). Not only do they have difficulty admitting their mistakes, they also fail to accept that they have actually made any. In such instances, partners have great difficulty with the idea of forgiveness, because it is predicated on the admission of error. Forgiveness absolves one of an offense; however, the narcissist does not recognize the offense. Resolution of infidelity often stalls because the betrayed partner wisely hesitates to forgive a partner who has shown no signs of either guilt or remorse.

In addition, narcissistic people are unable to see beyond their singular points of view. In their convoluted logic, infidelity may seem to be a justifiable, even brilliant course of action. Often, they conceptualize infidelity as a good solution to an unhappy marriage and lie about it to shield their spouses from hurt. Typically, they cannot be helped to view these actions differently. Furthermore, we have worked with partners who have been perversely proud of their affairs, seeing them as proof of attractiveness and an innovative solution to stagnant marriages.

Narcissists have trouble understanding reciprocity. Their sense of entitlement blinds them to one of the foundational benefits of forgiveness, a salutary effect on the relationship. Understandably, betrayed partners often doubt that forgiving will be viewed as a selfless act that will bring about gratitude and humility in the unfaithful partner. Instead, they fear that narcissistic partners will expect forgiveness because they perceive themselves as unique and deserving of such a sacrifice.

Narcissism is the inverse of humility. As we stated earlier, our treatment approach requires empathy and humility in both partners. The unfaithful person is helped to understand infidelity from the betrayed partner's point of view—the pain, humiliation, fears of abandonment, and so forth. Empathy facilitates guilt and remorse in the unfaithful partner, both of which correlate well with forgiveness. Increases in humility are equally productive, sometimes representing the most critical advance toward apology and behavior change, both of which are highly productive precursors to forgiveness. Humility is a critical element of successful forgiveness work, and it is often blocked by narcissistic tendencies.

WORKING WITH THE NARCISSISTIC PARTNER

The preceding section presents a bleak picture of treating infidelity in a couple with a narcissistic partner. Moreover, the narcissistic personality disposition, not personality disorder, is one of the most common personality styles in the Western world (Emmons, 2000). Anecdotally, we have found that a large percentage of couples in treatment for infidelity contain a partner with narcissistic traits. However, not all cases involving narcissistic persons are refractory to treatment. A therapist can use specific clinical strategies to make progress with these couples. First, most narcissistic individuals have one or more of the previously mentioned traits but they do not necessarily have the personality disorder, which is considerably more pervasive. These traits reveal aspects of their personality that can often be counterbalanced by appealing to other, more positive coexisting traits. For example, a therapist anticipated therapeutic failure in a couple, both 60 years of age, in which the male partner had the affair. The husband exhibited several narcissistic characteristics. Fortunately, the assessment revealed that this partner was also extremely responsible and religious, and possessed a firm conviction about morality. In our experience, narcissists are not immune to the logic of forgiveness, nor are they incapable of understanding the importance of fidelity in marriage.

Second, characteristics that are typical of narcissism can nevertheless be used to advance productive forgiveness work. For example, the concept of self-sacrifice is surprisingly well developed in the narcissistic personality. Because these individuals possess an unrealistically high sense of entitlement, they believe that they have rarely, if ever, gotten all that they think they deserve. Thus, they have adapted to "getting less than their share." This is a critical point for dealing with narcissists. Despite their posturing, they have great experience adjusting to disappointment or settling for less.

Third, people with narcissistic style have an immense fear of rejection. Although they may try to exploit friends, lovers, and partners, they do not want to lose these relationships because they crave the attentions of others. By recognizing this fear of rejection, the therapist can convince the narcissistic partner to try to control the urge to be unfaithful for the sake of pre-serving the marriage. Such a suggestion is often accepted, because of the need to stay in relationship. With narcissistic persons, we do not talk very often about what is fair, right, or equitable; the narcissist may see these concepts as rules that other people live by. Instead, we seek to convince this partner of what is an inevitable consequence of unfaithfulness, because they understand the risks of rejection quite well.

Similarly, if the victim of infidelity has narcissistic traits, accepting and eventually forgiving the partner is difficult but possible. Again, this is accom-plished by reminding narcissistic partners of a truth they know well: One does not always get what one wants. Because narcissists respond poorly to public criticism, we schedule individual appointments and use this time to explain the ways that their insensitive behavior may have precipitated their partners' infidelity. We educate the narcissistic partner to some of the basic realities of intimate relationships by explaining that people need attention, praise, warmth, and so forth, and that when they cannot get what they need within the marriage they sometimes go elsewhere. As stated frequently in these chapters, we never suggest that infidelity is anything other than wrong, yet we help clients to understand what the betraying partner may have been thinking and feeling. In addition, we make specific suggestions regarding behavior changes and request that the marriage be given a second chance. Then, we offer a solution for the considerable pain that the narcissist is feeling. This solution is forgiveness of the unfaithful partner, followed by a new start in the marriage. Narcissistic clients are surprisingly amenable to this sort of approach because, despite their outward bluster, they are needy individuals. The therapeutic approach should be indirectly direct, because direct confrontation will provoke a defensive response such as rage. Defen-siveness will stall the treatment. Instead, appeal first to their self-interest, then gently to the need for change, and finally, return to their self-interest by addressing the pain they are feeling.

Some narcissists can also be moved by appeals to their own strongly held views about rightness, morality, or religion. This is a plea to their vanity and sense of superiority. If they are indeed superior, we imply that they can set a superior example in following these important rules. They can be faithful in their marriage, or they can forgive the unfaithful partner and work to rebuild the marriage because it is the "right" thing to do. This strategy works, of course, only with those partners who hold strong views on these issues. There is an attendant risk of pseudoforgiveness in such situations. Our advice is to move slowly, to use the idea of moral "rightness" only as a starting place, and then help the partner to achieve some level of empathy as well as self-understanding.

In one example, the husband was the partner with narcissistic traits and was also involved in a long-standing affair. At home, he demonstrated strong moral and religious beliefs. His children were educated in Christian schools, the family attended religious services regularly, and the couple was exceedingly generous with their time and money. When he traveled for business, the husband often met with his affair partner. In addition, he routinely attended strip clubs, viewed pornographic movies, and engaged in other behaviors that were clearly departures from his public persona. He had justified these behaviors because his wife was disinterested in sex and he did not wish to broach the issue with her. The therapist was able to convince the man that it was only a matter of time before the affair would be discovered. Numerous examples were given of partners who were caught and the public humiliation experienced in each situation. In addition, the man was educated about the strength of family legacies and the common situation of finding infidelity in the genograms of those who have affairs. He was asked what he would think if he knew that his son was at risk for the same sort of life. These strategies worked much better than suggesting that the infidelity was hurting his wife or creating stress in his marriage.

Shame

Shame is often confused with guilt. A person may feel both shame and guilt after doing something wrong, often with a sense of self-reprehension. Traditionally, shame is believed to be the outcome of public misbehavior, whereas guilt is seen as a result of private misdeeds. However, more current research suggests that both shame and guilt can occur in public or private contexts (Tangney, Miller, Flicker, & Barlow, 1996). There are several distinctions between guilt and shame, which carry ramifications for treatment of infidelity. The experience of guilt usually involves feeling bad about a behavior or misdeed. Frequently, internal comments such as "I made a mistake" or "I did something wrong" accompany guilt feelings. Moreover, guilt promotes regret for the misdeed and the wish to make amends.

The experience of shame is ubiquitous, resulting in attacks on the self, rather than mere contrition about behavior. Shame often causes individuals to lament their very existence. Negative cognitions such as "I am a loser" or "I don't deserve to live" often accompany the affective state of shame. The self-hatred that coexists with shame causes the individual to turn inward in an effort to hide from others (Tangney et al. 1996). This internal focus is so intense that it often manifests in behaviors that might suggest a clinical depression, such as slouching, sadness, and a reluctance to make eye contact. Nonetheless, the person suffering from shame is likely to act in different ways than is the depressed client. Most important, shame can predispose the sufferer to fits of rage because, more than anything else, this individual wants to hide. If therapy is too confrontational or if it leads too quickly to emotional exposure and further shaming, this client will terminate. Specifically, couples therapy can cause shameful partners to feel trapped; when denied escape, they may respond with fury directed not only to their partner but also to the therapist (Tangney, 1995). This can have predictably negative consequences for the course of therapy.

An interesting example involved a 40-year-old woman who was discovered having an affair with a man she met at the gym. Ostensibly, the affair had been terminated, yet she entered therapy in an extremely defensive and hostile state. Her husband was willing to stay in the marriage and work on the significant preexisting problems. Although the wife contended that she wished to restore the marital relationship, she was combative and uncooperative in session. The degree and intensity of her hostility alerted the therapist to underlying factors that needed exploration. The therapist realized that the woman was very sensitive to confrontation and proceeded judiciously. Nevertheless, the wife attacked the therapist and partner alternately. Individual sessions were suggested because the therapist suspected that she was so overcome with shame about the affair that she unwittingly attempted to destroy the possibility of forgiveness. This hypothesis was confirmed after a few individual sessions, and the couple returned to conjoint sessions when the wife was calmer and less driven by shame.

The empirical literature upholds another important difference between guilt and shame. In the presence of guilt, the partners are easily persuaded to engage in the work of forgiveness, whether their role requires seeking or granting pardon. Guilt motivates the unfaithful partner to express contrition, apologize, and make amends. The betrayed partner feels more inclined to forgive in the presence of genuine remorse. Furthermore, guilt promotes a range of relationship-enhancing behaviors, such as empathy, that can be productive of forgiveness and behavior change (Baumeister et al., 1995). Shame, on the other hand, is inversely related to interpersonal empathy (Tangney, 1991; 1995). In fact, the presence of shame in the unfaithful partner impedes the experience of empathy in the betrayed partner (Fitness, 2001). The shameful person is preoccupied with self-soothing, attempts to hide, and is unable to escape from the internal focus of pain. Often, they are belligerent with their partners or uncommunicative, choosing to withdraw from dialogue about the offense. All too often, the betrayed partner interprets such response as evidence of a lack of remorse. Intense shame-based feelings interfere with behaviors that could lead to forgiveness. Resolving the crisis requires the unfaithful person to express genuine remorse. Remorse triggers empathy and forgiveness. Thus, shame impedes joining with the betrayed partner to repair the damage caused by the affair.

Shame polarizes rather than unifies the couple. Moreover, the presence of this emotion in either partner is certain to interfere with resolution of infidelity and the rebuilding of the relationship (Fitness, 2001). In the betrayed partner, the damaging effects of deception and betrayal can provoke humiliation and thereby trigger shame. This partner is often embarrassed, disgraced, and feels foolish for not knowing about the affair. In the face of these experiences, self-protection precludes the expression of empathy. Thus, forgiving the unfaithful partner is much less likely.

DEALING WITH SHAME

Many of the clinical suggestions for working with shame are congruent with those we have made in the section on narcissism. Indeed, we are not the first clinicians to notice that shame and narcissism are closely linked (Broucek, 1997). In each instance, there is an exquisite sensitivity to rejection and resulting humiliation. Additionally, there are many clinical similarities between "narcissistic rage" and the "externally-directed, humiliated fury" associated with shame (Tangney, 1995, p. 123). Initially, however, it may be difficult to assess the source of the rage. Needless to say, shame is not limited to narcissistic persons; it occurs across a broad range of personality types. Regardless, the principal clinical suggestion is to proceed cautiously with individuals suspected of feeling shame. Therapeutic interventions should not be too direct. Shameful partners are highly sensitive to criticism, because they are experiencing so much self-reproach. Furthermore, empathy should be used to interrupt the raging and to help such partners to feel understood. The couple is already struggling with heightened affect such as anger, anxiety, guilt, embarrassment, frustration, and fear. Triggering more anger is unproductive to therapy.

Remember that both partners are equally likely to demonstrate and struggle with shame. Unfaithful partners feel shame for many reasons: being caught in an indiscretion, causing pain to their partners, or violating their own value systems. Additionally, these partners may feel embarrassed or humiliated about the necessity of attending marital counseling, particularly if their infidelity is perceived as a private failure that is open to public scrutiny. On a deeper level, the unfaithful partner may feel shame directly by having engaged in a sexual offense. Many individuals link sex and shame, ipso facto, because sex itself is shameful to them. Therefore, having to confront sexual material in therapy is often enough to provoke feelings of humiliation and vulnerability with consequent anger. Moreover, sexual shame is an underlying motivator for many affairs or other intimacy transgressions. When sexual shame interferes with establishing and maintaining rewarding sex within the primary relationship, infidelity is often a consequence. Such individuals hope to find outside their marriages what they have failed to establish inside. Finally, we stated earlier that some affairs are a manifestation of an undiagnosed sex addiction. Shame is an integral component of the cycle of sex addiction (as it is in many addictive behaviors). Individuals try to blunt the intense pain associated with shame by engaging in addictive behaviors, including sex.

It is also important to recognize the presence of shame-based emotions in the betrayed partner. Shame is an emotion associated with humiliation, vulnerability, and personal failure. Betrayed partners may blame themselves for the failure of their marriages. Each gender seems to have a script for shame resulting from infidelity. Men accuse themselves of not being "man enough" to keep their partners satisfied; women may berate themselves for being insufficiently attractive. In either case, the victim feels ashamed at a failure of the self. In addition, some partners may feel humiliated at having to seek outside help, which in their minds is further evidence of failure to solve their own problems. Even more troubling is the interpretation of infidelity as evidence that the betrayed partners have somehow deserved their current suffering. Individuals with this notion often blame themselves for infidelity, believing that bad things do not happen to good people. In other instances, self-blame may help victims of infidelity to regain a sense of control of the shattered marital partnership. Self-blame allows the betrayed partner to continue to experience a sense of "oneness" by hoping to repair the marriage to an intact state (Gordon & Baucom, 1998). Although this strategy might temporarily reduce anxiety, it also increases negative self-perception—in other words, shame.

PROMOTING FORGIVENESS IN THE FACE OF SHAME

The therapist should always be cautious to avoid provoking shame-related feelings, especially when dealing with infidelity. As stated earlier, direct confrontation is circumvented. Interrupt arguments and verbal attacks. Explain the rationale for maintaining a stable emotional climate and assiduously control the expression of intense affect. It is essential that both partners feel safe within the therapeutic process and trust the authority of the therapist. For instance, postpone discussion of embarrassing issues until a strong rapport has been established. Offer partners a method of signaling a timeout when they are feeling too much emotional intensity or unreasonable attack.

Clients cooperate when given a rationale for therapeutic interventions. They also work well when given explanations that normalize feelings. In cases of infidelity, these interventions are repeated often, because partners feel overwhelmed or "crazy" from the emotional turmoil they are experiencing. In one conjoint session, the betrayed husband explained that he had waited to raise very disturbing questions until within the protective atmosphere of the therapist's office. In this instance, the wife exhibited shame-based defensive behaviors and often refused to discuss an affair. The husband was so eager to gain information that he began to bombard her with questions. The therapist explained that it is understandable that the husband should want an explanation for his wife's behavior, but it was important to refrain from overwhelming the wife with too many queries. The therapist normalized this man's anxiety and insecurity, explaining that his reactions were common after the revelation of an affair. The wife was reassured that the therapist would help to maintain balance and not let things get "out of hand." The couple cooperated and proceeded cautiously.

Because shame is a predominant emotion in dealing with infidelity, the couple should be educated about how this emotion manifests itself. Shame itself should be discussed, and shame-based feelings surrounding sex, humiliation, betrayal, and vulnerability should be explored. Clarify the difference between guilt and shame, normalizing the benefits of guilt in the process of forgiveness. Explain that shame produces behaviors that interfere with healing after infidelity. Encourage the partners to refrain from accusing the other of negative personality attributes such as "She's a liar" or "He's a hypocrite." Instead, illustrate the use of specific behaviors that should be cited when registering a complaint. For instance, help the partner to ask a question instead, such as "Did you lie to me when . . ." or "Your actions did not make sense to me when. . . ." Explain that verbal attacks reinforce shame and prevent progress.

In general, shame causes individuals to attribute their failings to causes that are global, internal, and invariant: "I must deserve this pain," "I am no good," "I do not deserve to live." By using therapeutic reframes, the clinician helps the partner to develop a more reality-based assessment of the causes of the presenting problem. Encourage discussion of concepts that are specific, external, and changeable. In this way, partners who are feeling shame are distracted from lashing out in humiliated rage or withdrawing in self-focused humiliation. Instead, they are helped to experience legitimate guilt for specific, measurable transgressions. In the presence of genuine remorse, the unfaithful partner can promise behavior change and seek forgiveness. Empathy and compassion in the betrayed partner are therefore more likely.

Accusatory Suffering

Accusatory suffering results from an individual's perception of having been the casualty of an injustice (Seagull & Seagull, 1991). In cases of infidelity, this emotion often coexists with anger and fear. Accusatory suffering is one of the most tenacious and troublesome sentiments that we have encountered in working with infidelity. Protracted agony in the betrayed partner impedes resolution of the affair because it polarizes the couple into fixed positions of offender and victim. As long as the hurt partner sustains anguish, the partner who had the affair is kept outside of the dyad; interdependence and unity are therefore precluded.

Accusatory suffering is a consequence of intense traumatization of the betrayed partner after the revelation of an affair. Typically, this partner unconsciously fears that "full recovery from the psychic trauma associated with victimization would somehow exonerate the perpetrator from blame" (Seagull & Seagull, 1991, p. 16). An added element is the belief that if the suffering ceases, the victim will have little right to justifiable anger. In cases of infidelity, continued agony is often a strategy to hold the offender account-able for the betrayal and breach of trust. In fact, a full recovery from the trauma of infidelity could deny betrayed partners their "rights" as victims or the "moral high ground" that they have acquired because their partners transgressed. They attempt to reestablish balance in their relationships by placing themselves in the "one-up" position, which is difficult to relinquish (Fitness, 2001).

The reasons for the betrayed partner's reluctance to give up suffering are numerous. One reason is the perceived loss of support from family, friends, and others who have extended help to the victim of infidelity. We have often seen the anguished partner attempting to win the influence of family and friends by propagating the intimate details of the betrayal. In Chapter 6 we discussed the dangers of sharing with children inappropriate information about the unfaithful partner. Unfortunately, this happens too often. Some-times, the intractable rage and pain in the betrayed partner represent an attempt to acquire enough power to self-protect. Another motivation for sustained suffering is the desire for revenge. Perversely, some partners who most readily agree to reconciliation following a case of infidelity are locked into accusatory suffering in order to punish the partner once the tables have been turned. This stance can be a powerful obstacle to therapy generally and forgiveness work specifically. Wounded partners need to decide which they want more: to punish their unfaithful partner, or to free themselves from the emotional distress of the infidelity.

WORKING WITH ACCUSATORY SUFFERING

In severe cases of accusatory suffering, symptoms of rumination, agitation, insomnia, weight loss, sadness, and irritability can immobilize the betrayed partner. These reactions can persist long after the infidelity is terminated and the other partner is ready to work on the marriage. Allow sufficient time for the wounded partner to explore and understand this suffering in individual sessions. In addition to supporting the betrayed partner, this strategy allows the therapist to control the emotional climate of the conjoint sessions in an effort to reduce the damaging effects of shame in the partner who had the affair. Include occasional individual sessions until the couple is ready to proceed in regularly scheduled conjoint therapy. The wounded partner must have sufficient opportunity to deal with the accusatory suffering and the concomitant emotions such as rage. However, the amount of time is not the same for every client; thus, clinical judgment is essential. Preexisting individual risk factors must also be considered.

When betrayed partners trust that their pain is understood, explain that protracted suffering will interfere with the progression of treatment and preclude resolution of the marital problems. Using the strength of the therapeutic alliance, discuss the conditions that would be necessary for the suffering to cease. Various dimensions need to be considered, such as time, support systems, and acknowledgment that the offending partner is appropriately remorseful. We sometimes recommend a psychiatric consultation for psychotropic medications if such symptoms are refractory to therapy. The timing of the recommendation is critical in addition to the acknowledgment that the therapist is not trying to absolve the unfaithful partner by medicating the wounded partner. If necessary, encourage responsibility by asking if this partner wishes to continue suffering or is willing to consider medications that could provide relief. Suggest that the consultation with the psychiatrist is an attempt to help alleviate suffering and that the actual decision to use medications is between the psychiatrist and the client. The SSRI (serum seratonin reuptake inhibitor) antidepressants are often helpful for treating these symptoms.

Attempt to assess the reasons for protracted suffering in each case. Present hypotheses to the partner and seek agreement. Encourage insight, develop cognitive techniques that could provide relief, and discuss behavioral remedies such as guided imagery or relaxation techniques. Utilize a combination of individual and conjoint sessions in order to allow for expression of the suffering without stirring up too much paralyzing shame in the guilty partner. Encourage patience in the guilty partner while attempting to establish boundaries in the wounded partner's expression of accusatory suffering. Carefully use a combination of empathy and limit-setting. Explain that, over time, accusatory suffering in the betrayed partner can become as destructive to the relationship as the infidelity has been.

In one couple, the aggrieved wife confronted family members and friends, telling them of her husband's transgressions. She went through his social calendar and, prior to scheduled recreational outings such as tennis or golf, contacted his friends, requesting that they try to convince him that he was wrong to hurt her so badly. In more subtle ways, she undermined his authority and credibility with their children. The therapist expressed empathy for the pain and suffering of the wife, but warned that her actions could drive her husband further away from resolution of the infidelity Also, the betrayed woman was educated about the negative consequences of accusatory suffering. Nonetheless, she persisted. The accusatory suffering and related boundary violations restimulated so much shame and humiliation in the guilty husband that he refused to attend conjoint sessions. Eventually, he pursued a divorce.

In other situations, the combination of support and limit setting is enough to interrupt the accusatory suffering. The therapist must provide encouragement for this partner, control the emotional climate of the sessions, and manage the degree of exposure of the betrayed partner to protracted rage and pain. Flexibility is essential.

Anger and Fear

The crisis of infidelity produces fear in the betrayed partner. Feelings of uncertainty, mistrust, doubt, concern, and pessimism abruptly replace the stability and predictability that were once provided by the relationship. Fear is related to unanticipated doubt about the marriage, the future, and other assumed foci of security. Anger is a manifestation of fear (Worthington, 1998). Partners who are angry or fearful are still passionately connected to the offense and are therefore willing to speak to these feelings in therapy. In contrast, depressed, apathetic, or hateful partners are often unable to productively work with forgiveness until they have gained sufficient strength to confront their anger or fear (Worthington & Wade, 1999).

WORKING WITH ANGER AND FEAR

In Chapter 4 we discussed that the therapist can expect protracted anger in the betrayed partner after the revelation of infidelity. If the anger does not abate after a reasonable course of treatment, specific interventions may be necessary. Always respond calmly to anger, and empathize by using reframes that equate anger with fear. For instance, ask angry partners what they fear most. This technique often interrupts the anger and gets to the source of the pain. Another, similar technique is to simply assume that anger is often a manifestation of fear, and thus speak to the fear without addressing the anger.

Sometimes the betrayed individual has difficulty letting go of the infidelity and, consequently, the anger. If the anger phase has not abated within 6 months of treatment and appears to be as strong as ever, then this partner may have an underlying psychological risk factor such as a personality disorder. Such partners will continue to recall every vivid detail of the affair as if it had just occurred. One case representing this pattern stands out. Mark was a 62-year-old man who had been married for 20 years. For most of the marriage, the couple had been unhappy. His wife was frustrated about the marital discord, but did not think she could leave him because they had two children who were still at home. Her choice was to have an affair. Mark's anger and quest for details about the affair did not subside, despite the therapist's efforts to get him to focus on feelings. The therapy eventually shifted to why he was having such difficulty letting go and gently moved into his obsessional patterns. Realizing that he was fixated, he decided to work through it by painting a series of canvasses depicting the affair. When he was finished with the paintings, the obsession about the affair ended.

Educating couples about anger is another invaluable strategy. Explain that anger serves an important self-protective function and exists in healthy individuals. It usually occurs in the face of unmet needs or a perceived threat to the individual's security. It cannot be ignored, bypassed, or left unresolved without creating negative consequences for the individual or the relationship. Several theoretical models can be used for the purpose of helping couples to examine their predominant style of dealing with anger. For instance, Fitzgibbons (1998) offered three ways in which people typically experience anger:

- Expressing the anger directly.
- Forgiving the unmet need or perceived threat.
- Denying the anger.

There are two common misconceptions about anger (Fitzgibbons, 1998). The first is that expressing anger is the only effective way to deal with it. Many clients have learned only that unresolved resentment is damaging. This belief causes individuals to express all anger that is felt or imagined. It is important to consider the consequences of unfettered expression of the anger associated with infidelity. How much venting of rage is necessary? What response will such an intense expression provoke in the partner who was unfaithful? Many relationships simply cannot recover from such an unregulated release.

The second misconception is that anger is an unacceptable emotion. Some individuals are socialized to believe that anger should not be directed toward a family member or loved one. Such individuals often have difficulty becoming aware of their own anger because it is not felt or perceived. They often find themselves stuck in denial or passive-aggressive behaviors. Partners should be educated to the process of denial and taught to recognize evidence of anger in themselves and others. Once partners learn to recognize cues or internal signals of incremental levels of anger, they should be encouraged to discuss them in a safe, supportive environment. Often, they are surprised to discover considerable amount anger surrounding the presenting problems in counseling as well as other relational issues from the past.

One example is a 40-year-old man who grew increasingly angry with his wife of 15 years. She was frustrated and angry that her husband was not present and available to her. He reported that she was often critical at home, and that she sometimes publicly humiliated him at social gatherings. Nonetheless, he was unaware that over time her criticisms and aggressiveness had become intolerable. One day, he announced that he could no longer remain in the marriage. The shocked wife became even more outraged and aggressive. In fact, she would not accept his decision to leave the marriage and remained in an agitated state of denial for some time. The therapist worked to help her realize that attempts to control his behavior could only produce anger in her husband. Simultaneously, the therapist helped the husband to recognize that he had grown increasingly angry without realizing it, and that he showed his resentment behaviorally without discussing it sufficiently to resolution. For instance, he spent more and more time avoiding his wife and family, using work as a justification. He agreed that this and other behaviors were warning signals of his increasing resentment. Therapy focused on helping him to identify physical and behavioral manifestations of incrementally increasing levels of anger in an effort to replace his typically "all or none" response. He was also helped to verbally express his anger before it became overwhelming. Each partner examined intergenerational and individual factors that influenced their anger management styles. The couple was supported in behaving autonomously within the partnership, limiting their enmeshment, and sharing power and control without attempting to influence the other through disengagement or humiliation. Therapy is ongoing.

Conclusion

Treatment of infidelity is often blocked by the exacerbation of one or more barriers to forgiveness. The therapist might assume that a couple is unable to resolve the damage when in fact the case is workable. In some situations, forgiveness is impossible; however, couples that appear refractory to treatment might need more aggressive, tenacious strategies before resolution is to occur. Once the emotional barriers to forgiveness are identified, the therapy progresses through a series of steps to ensure their removal. Often, one or more of the steps will need to be repeated, especially in ostensibly intractable cases.

Once forgiveness has occurred and resolution of infidelity has been successfully completed, the couple is ready for the final phase of treatment. The couple now has an understanding of the factors that contributed to the betrayal, and they have worked through the infidelity itself. The final phase of treatment is to help ensure that infidelity will not occur again. The underlying causes and predisposing conditions are addressed in detail. This phase requires a restructuring of the couple's relationship. In the following chapters, we discuss some of the common factors contributing to infidelity and their treatment.

11

❀ ❀ ❀

The Final Phase of Therapy: Treating Factors that Trigger Infidelity

IN THE EARLIER CHAPTERS OF THIS TEXT, WE IDENTIFIED and discussed a number of circumstances that contribute to infidelity. Using the intersystems approach, the risk factors can be organized under three areas of vulnerability: relational discord, individual issues, and intergenerational influences on marriage and committed relationships. Additionally, we recommended strategies for managing the confusion and damage that result from the discovery of infidelity. These strategies include a unique emphasis on the necessity of forgiveness. Nonetheless, all of the aforementioned therapeutic principles are insufficient if one or both partners believe that the infidelity might happen again. Thus, to complete the therapeutic course, the couple must be reassured that the underlying problems have been addressed. Unequivocally, the betrayed partner must believe with some degree of certainty that the causative factors have been treated.

We have emphasized throughout the text that the partners have a right to know the therapist's ideas about the plan of treatment. They will be less fearful and more apt to cooperate if they are informed at each juncture. Furthermore, if couples understand the structure of therapy from the beginning, then they will know what to expect as the treatment unfolds. They will be assured that the objective is not solely about getting beyond the infidelity. Moreover, the partners will trust that the way to preclude future infidelity is to restructure the intimate relationship, eliminating the risk factors that contributed to the affair in the first place.

Many factors can play a part in the occurrence of infidelity. However, the early chapters of this volume demonstrated that typically a few themes or problems are common. Fortunately, these difficulties are not foreign to couples therapists and can be treated effectively. Some of the most common motivators for infidelity include:

- The inability to develop intimacy in the relationship.
- Problems with commitment.
- The lack of passion.
- Ineffectiveness in resolving conflict and anger.
- Sexual addiction.
- Life cycle transitions.
- Psychiatric illness.
- Fears about intimacy, dependency, or trust.
- A value system that gives priority to pleasure and excitement over loyalty and faithfulness.

AN INTIMACY-BASED TREATMENT APPROACH

This section deals with factors that cause a lack of intimacy, which is a major contributor to infidelity. Additionally, we describe how intimacy problems may be understood within the context of a relationship. Much of what therapists treat as marital pathology is an intimacy-based problem. For example, two common issues contributing to infidelity are a lack of intimacy in the relationship and a need to exit a marriage. Most people consciously believe that they want intimacy in their relationships, but may unconsciously sabotage the partnership when too much intimacy occurs. In other words, one or both parties might be uncomfortable with intimacy or commitment. Additionally, because each partner may bring fears to the relationship, they protect each other in not getting too close. Unfortunately, the couple may recognize these fears only after a considerable amount of time together.

The concept of intimacy has been extensively investigated in the field of family studies. Much of the empirical literature is theoretical rather than clinical in orientation. Schaefer and Olson (1981) described various typologies. They argued that intimacy was not a single phenomenon, but instead a constellation of behaviors. Altogether, they identified seven types of intimacy. However, marital and family therapists only cautiously embraced this concept in their work, because the majority of empirical research was not clinically applicable. Prager (1997) dealt exclusively with the notion of intimacy in *The Psychology of Intimacy*, a noteworthy example of meaningful attention to the theoretical. Finally, Sternberg (1986) refined a theoretically and empirically based model of adult (romantic) love into a clinically useful model of intimacy. We rely heavily on this work and add our own ideas to help explain couple pathology. We next describe the three components of the Sternberg model.

STERNBERG'S MODEL OF LOVE

Commitment, intimacy, and passion are the three equally important components of Sternberg's (1986, 1997) triangular theory of love. Couples find this model intuitively true. Therapists can use this paradigm to observe how well partners function in each area. For example, a couple may experience a problem in one sphere that is isolated from the other two, or this problem may significantly affect one or both other components. Definitions of the components follow.

Commitment is the intellectual decision to live with another person in an exclusive relationship. Heterosexual couples commonly express commitment through engagement, marriage, and couple fidelity. Additionally, we have found that two indices of commitment are predictive of a good clinical outcome when dealing with infidelity: commitment to an intimate relationship and commitment to the process of therapy. Couples who are committed to each other and to their work in therapy are usually successful in their treatment.

Passion is a motivational component that draws the two people together. Passion is not solely sexual; it encompasses a sense of romance, sex, physical attraction, and the desire to be with the other person.

Intimacy is clearly the most complex part of the triangle of love. It includes many characteristics, such as:

- Feeling a sense of closeness.
- Being connected or bonded.
- Having a sense of welfare for the other person.
- Wanting happiness for the other person.
- Regarding the other person highly.
- Being able to count on the other person in time of need.
- Sharing oneself.

- Talking personally, especially about feelings.
- Providing emotional support.
- Being honest and empathic, and so on.

Any human relationship seeks definition by identifying aspirations, expectations, and other parameters. This need for definition is true of relationships such as teacher–student, employer–employee, parent–child, male–female, husband–wife, or dating partner–dating partner. Committed relationships function best when the partners have reached consensus about the relationship's meaning or significance. By using Sternberg's (1986, 1997) model, the therapist can help the partners to define their relationship, assess areas of strength and weakness, and establish treatment goals that maximize strengths and address areas of deficiency.

The first step in using the triangular theory of love is to explain why it is necessary. The therapist must reframe infidelity as an intimacy-based problem. Next, in order for this model to be most productive, the couple must understand it. A brief description by the therapist is usually sufficient. The partners should be able to connect the motivation for the affair to a lack of commitment, intimacy, or passion. These areas of intimacy can be addressed using six general questions:

- *Do both partners desire all three components as described in the triangle?* The therapist begins by asking partners to define the general notion of love or intimacy as it applies to their relationship. Note the similarities and differences between the disparate definitions. Ask the partners if they desire all three components of love. Ask each to consider if the other person wants each of the three components.

- *Does each partner want the same level of intensity for each of the three components?* Once it is established that the partners want some or all of the three components of the model, the therapist asks about the degree to which they want each of these three ingredients. Note areas of agreement or disagreement in desire levels or expectations. For instance, some partners expect a high measure of passion in the relationship whereas others do not.

- *How much togetherness and individuation does each partner want in the relationship?* Every couple must find a balance between closeness and distance. From a developmental perspective, during the formative part of a relationship couples are constantly striving to find ways to be together. They will make dates, call each other, e-mail, and spend time talking or doing activities together. Once they have established a sense of commitment, they must decide how they will function as individuals without feeling smothered or a losing their sense of identity within the context of the relationship. The most important part of the discussion is for the couple to plan the need for each individual to act autonomously. We help with this process through psychoeducation about issues such as enmeshment and differentiation.

- *What prevents the partners from being able to identify and / or express the three components openly and freely?* The three concepts are not difficult to grasp intellectually. However, demonstrating them emotionally or behaviorally may be arduous, regardless of the actual intelligence of the individuals. Sometimes, the individuals may have rarely seen this behavior during their development; it is difficult to demonstrate something that was not internalized. Alternately, a partner may feel embarrassed or incompetent about expressing some of these components because of learned messages about acceptable behavior. The therapist will find the attachment genogram (DeMaria et al., 1999) useful in helping the couple to understand what was modeled and learned within the family of origin. This is especially important when a partner is unable to express any of the components.

  The individual's cultural and social milieu will also play a significant role. Typically, men are socialized to be self-sufficient, strong, and unemotional. They often avoid expressing affective material because feelings are equated with weakness, incompetence, and vulnerability. Commonly, women value sharing emotions. They may feel disappointed and angry when their expectations are not met, resulting in relational discord. Sometimes, women blame themselves for their partner's lack of affection. Alternately, they can feel left out, rejected, unappreciated, useless, and emotionally frustrated.

- *Does each partner have a realistic perception of what love involves?* Some partners overvalue one part of the triangle and undervalue the other two. A common example is the belief that in a committed relationship, expressing passion or promoting intimacy are unnecessary. We have heard statements such as "I'm still here after 20 years of marriage." Unfortunately, the sole focus is on the fact that they are together, ignoring other essential aspects of love. Other people tend to equate love with sex, arguing that they stay together with their partners because the sex is so great. They underestimate the negative impact of frequent arguments and long-standing resentment. Some partners will idealize or distort one of the components, especially intimacy. They think that intimacy involves constant togetherness, a blending of mind and soul, or emotional enmeshment. Sometimes the expectations seem realistic, whereas at other times individuals may want so much of one of these components that they have set themselves up for constant frustration, disappointment, and anger.

- *Does each partner have a realistic perception of what he or she can actually offer?* At times, a discrepancy exists between what individuals believe they can provide and actual behavior. There appear to be at least two common scenarios. The first occurs when partners have different definitions for a component. One believes he or she is providing the behavior in question, but the other disagrees. For example, one man argued that he was intimate with his wife, and he offered an example of exchanged backrubs. His wife's response was that he never told her how he felt (a lack of emotional intimacy). Furthermore, she was unaware of his intentions because of his lack of verbal communication. He presumed he was giving her the behavior we were discussing, whereas she was frustrated that she had never received the behavior that she had asked him to provide. The second scenario is when the person wants to impart the behavior, but lacks the personal capacity to do so. A husband, for example, may say that he wants to share his feelings with his wife. However, he has never seen feelings expressed in his family and has never expressed feelings himself. A wife, for example, may say she wants to be more sexual but suffers from primary lack of desire. It is unlikely that she will be able to change her level of desire. She might be able to have sex more frequently, but it would probably be without desire.

This last question raises a more general issue regarding the capacity for change. Partners sometimes talk about the triangle of love with great facility, but may have limited capacity to express or experience its components. Ideally, therapists would like to see each partner make adjustments so that definitions are more congruent and the couple is working in synchrony. Nonetheless, couples who cannot accomplish this goal may be helped to see that despite their differences or limitations, they do have a good deal in common and on balance the relationship is worth continuing.

Treating Commitment Problems

Commitment to the Marriage

We have stated previously that the issue of commitment to the marriage or primary relationship is of critical importance. The degree of each partner's commitment must be assessed as early in treatment as possible. The couple will want to discuss the infidelity; therefore, the therapist must be sensitive to their needs. However, couples enter therapy in one of several positions vis-à-vis the marriage. The ideal situation is when both are committed to their relationship—then the therapy can proceed without having to make commitment a priority issue. However, one or both partners may be ambivalent, tenuous, or unequally committed such that one wants to leave and the other stay. Under these circumstances, the therapist must commence by focusing on enhancing the commitment in the couple's relationship.

Commitment to the relationship may be a problem in and of itself, or one that is related to other parts of the triangle. For example, if a couple has lacked intimacy over a long period of time, the level of commitment may have diminished, thus placing the couple at risk for infidelity. Therapists can employ several strategies to address the cause of the commitment problem. The first tactic is to discuss each partner's respective definitions of the concept of commitment. These questions can be used to facilitate discussion:

- Do the partners share the same definition of commitment?
- What does it mean to be committed in the current relationship?
- What are the advantages and disadvantages of being in a committed relationship?
- When they married or started dating, did the partners expect that the relationship would be permanent?
- Do they have a history of ending relationships easily, many sequential relationships, abrupt ending of friendships, anger within relationships, or multiple divorces?
- What have they learned about commitment in their families of origin?
- Were their parents committed? How was the commitment demonstrated?
- Did their parents separate or divorce?
- Is there a history of infidelity in the family?

Kelley (1983) reviewed basic research conducted on the process of commitment at both the intrapsychic and interpersonal levels. Some of his research has clinical utility for enhancing commitment in couples. Another tactic is to improve commitment is by changing the rewards-cost balance by altering the ratio in favor of rewards. Gottman (1994a, 1994b) also showed that in functioning intimate relationships there is a ratio of at least five positive to every negative interaction. This principle can be used in several ways. By the time most couples enter therapy, their interactions have become mostly pessimistic and they tend to think of the relationship being negative. The therapist can interrupt this dynamic by helping the couple to remember what attracted them to each other and what they liked about the relationship in the beginning. This discussion helps the partners revive positive thoughts of and about each other. Next, the therapist can ask them a behaviorally oriented question concerning what is positive about the current relationship, and have the couple list those items. Many couples will report that little is positive. They could then be asked to reinstate some of the positive things they used to do, and to start thinking about things they can currently do.

We use an exercise called the "three As" (affirmation, appreciation, and affection) to promote optimism and commitment:

- *Affirming* the importance of the relationship and the positive feelings of love, care, concern, and so on.
- *Appreciating* what one likes about the other person and the things that they he or she does.
- *Affection*, or the nonsexual expression of feelings of warmth and liking.

At this stage of treatment, the therapist may ask the couple to try to increase all three areas, but the mostly likely change will be in their ability to express appreciation. Often, we ask each partner to make at least three appreciative statements or actions each day. Finally, the couple is asked to think about the future. For example, "Would you want to stay in this marriage if it is like it was years ago?" Most couples will say yes, and then the discussion can focus on how they can work on getting back to having the kind of relationship they once enjoyed.

A third tactic to increase commitment is to review the strategy of recalling irretrievable investments, discussed in detail previously in Chapter 6. Essentially, the couple is asked to summon up the many ways in which they define themselves as a cohesive union, stressing the accompanying sense of we-ness replete with recreational activities, pet names, rituals, and so on. Couples do not normally think about this loss when they consider behavior that could threaten the marriage or when they plan to end a marriage.

The final factor in increasing commitment deals with the attractiveness of alternatives. Some partners entertain a version of an escape fantasy or a belief that they will readily find another relationship that is better than their current relationship. Unfaithful partners may assume that their affair relationships are going to be ideal for them. These people fail to realize that an affair is generally quite positive and untouched by the monotony of daily living. It is often about fun, sharing good times, and being engulfed in intense feelings of love or lust. When the affair relationship becomes public and the partners begin to deal with the daily problems of life, the quality may change dramatically.

The betrayed partner may attempt to find another relationship quickly in order to circumvent the pain, feelings of abandonment, and other hurtful emotions that were stimulated by the infidelity. In our experience, the end of any marriage is accompanied by a period of grief and hesitancy to become reinvolved in a committed relationship. The most common situation is that the person will have to date extensively in order to find an acceptable match. Those who begin with idealized expectations are most likely to be disappointed. The other fact that is often overlooked is that both partners contributed to the problems in the marriage. Establishing a new relationship without understanding and having dealt with those problems means the new relationship will also have problems.

A 50-year-old woman entered treatment just before separating from her husband of 25 years. Their marriage was much like a sibling partnership in which each enjoyed activity with the other person but the couple was rarely sexually intimate. Nonetheless, they had built a life together and there were many losses resulting from the separation. The client had the support of family and friends, particularly a coworker and his wife. Following the separation, she became emotionally close to her colleague and they sexualized the relationship. Admittedly, she wanted to feel desired, attractive, and worthwhile. Additionally, this woman fantasized about marrying her lover and sometimes placed herself and her lover in situations that could lead to discovery of the affair. The therapist repeatedly warned that her behavior could precipitate a crisis that would be equal to or worse than the marital separation. In addition, she was reminded that the affair was a reprieve from feelings of grief and pain over the marital demise. Continuing the affair was extremely self-destructive and hurtful to the other persons involved. She was redirected to deal with the vulnerabilities within herself and the marriage that led to the separation. The therapist offered reality-based examples of individuals who complicated their lives by marrying their affair partners. Fortunately, she agreed to cease the sexual involvement and explore the individual and relational concerns that needed attention.

Another one of our clients, a 28-year-old woman, was filled with notions about a better relationship with another partner. She attempted to find relational happiness in each of her three marriages (and one long-standing committed relationship). She had ended each relationship with an affair. In the present marriage, she was also unfaithful. In each case, she lost her sexual desire within about 6 months of the start of the relationship. Although she had great hopes and expectations for each new relationship, the pattern kept repeating. She finally accepted the fact that the problem must be hers, and entered therapy.

Commitment to Treatment

The second area of commitment pertains to therapy. The couple must take responsibility for working within the context of therapy, even if they decide that the outcome will be separation rather than reconciliation. The therapist is responsible for providing information about the course of treatment in order to help the couple develop realistic expectations about the process, length, and outcome of treatment. If the couple is committed to treatment, they will not terminate prior to completion. After a few sessions, partners usually have a sense if the therapy is moving them toward reconciliation, forgiveness, and eventually rebuilding the marriage. These issues are usually openly discussed. When the partners do not offer information about the progress and direction, the therapist must promote such discussions. If couples cannot work out their issues and choose to separate, the therapist must switch roles from marital facilitator to divorce mediator. When this occurs, the therapist helps the couple to separate with the least amount of hurt, examining how they reached this point, and how to deal with children.

TREATING PROBLEMS WITH PASSION

Some forms of infidelity are more sexual than others. Additionally, some are motivated by sexual frustration. The most common situation is when one of the partners lacks desire or when there is a great discrepancy in levels of sexual desire. The partner with the higher level of desire may begin to feel frustrated, angry, resentful, and rejected. These feelings are intensified if the partner also thinks the condition is hopeless and is unable to express feelings about it. Lack of sexual desire—or hypoactive sexual desire disorder (HSD)—is a common clinical phenomenon. The most widespread variety of this problem is when one partner lacks sexual desire for the established or marital partner, but may feel desire toward others. The complexity of this difficulty cannot be overstated. HSD is usually multidetermined and requires a mix of various approaches, including the integration of couple and sex therapy. The reader who is treating a couple for whom HSD is one of the motivating factors for infidelity should consult Weeks and Gambescia (2002). In brief, the two most common relational factors contributing to lack of desire are feeling of loss (including a sense of loss of self or lack of control) and anger or resentment toward the partner over an extended period. Treatment involves traditional sex therapy, couple therapy, as well as behavioral and cognitive techniques in both the assessment and treatment of the problem.

In a recent case, a couple struggled with the lack of sexual desire and low sexual frequency. The husband was frustrated and unhappy with his wife's apparent indifference about sex. She was dissatisfied with the quality of sexual relations and, over time, became more disinterested. The wife's unhappiness ostensibly was related to the fact that he was a premature ejaculator and they never made love for more than a few minutes. In addition, they had developed a pattern of avoiding sensual intimacy during sex. The rushed quality and lack of enjoyment exacerbated the problem only further. She wanted him to last longer so that she could have an orgasm, and complained bitterly about his lack of ejaculatory control. As more history was taken, the complexity of the problem increased. Her focus on the husband's inadequacy distracted the couple from addressing her anorgasmia. In this instance, the lack of sexual desire was simply the presenting problem or tip of the iceberg. This couple had deeper issues involving intimacy and commitment. When the therapist asked the couple what might happen if they did not get this problem resolved, the husband commented that it would lead to an affair, divorce, or both. The sexual problems became the justification for anticipated subsequent affairs if they were not resolved.

Dealing With Underlying Fears of Intimacy

Underlying fears of intimacy are common (Weeks & Treat, 1992, 2001). Every couple must confront the question of how much closeness and distance they can comfortably tolerate in their relationship. Many couples have difficulty with unresolved fears about emotional closeness. Typically, it is difficult to articulate such fears, and thus they are enacted behaviorally. In fact, we believe that much of marital pathology can be accounted for by these underlying fears. Thus, identifying and thoroughly treating the intimacy fears will prevent reoccurrence of infidelity.

As human beings, we are biologically predisposed to react to fear by either fighting or fleeing. Consequently, when partners fear intimacy, they need behavioral tactics to promote a comfortable emotional distance from the other partner. Sometimes anger, discord, or arguing can help partners to keep at a safe emotional distance. Other manifestations include overworking, becoming involved in hobbies or other activities such as the computer, or attaching oneself to another person or persons. Sometimes, the sole purpose of the infidelity may be to regulate the distance in the marriage.

Intimacy fears have many variations. It is helpful to describe the more common presentations in order to help the couple understand the concept and identify their own areas of vulnerability. These can include (but are not limited to) fear about:

- Feeling anger.
- The loss of control.
- Dependency.

- Rejection or abandonment.
- Feelings.
- Exposure.

The fear of intimacy is often expressed through anger, animosity, or conflicted styles of interaction with others. Hostility serves to keep the intimate partner at a distance, thereby "protecting" the fearful partner from the dreaded closeness. Anger is a commonly experienced emotion, yet many individuals are uncomfortable experiencing or expressing it. Some are so uneasy with anger that they suppress or repress it. This dynamic feeds into passive-aggressive behaviors such as lateness or forgetting. In addition, unexpressed anger is a major cause of the lack of sexual desire. The partner with low desire becomes indifferent to sexual intimacy and thereby avoids opportunities for closeness (see Weeks and Gambescia, 2002, for a detailed description of the role of anger in HSD). Certain individuals have problems controlling anger and suffer from bouts of agitation or rage, especially with intimate partners. Others fear that they are not able to appropriately articulate anger or resolve the disagreements that precipitate it. Regardless, appropriate expression of anger is a normal part of any human relationship, and circumventing anger precludes conflict resolution (L'Abate & McHenry, 1983).

The fear of losing control is another common manifestation of the unconscious fear of intimacy. In this presentation, the person fears being oppressed by another person and thus resists closeness. The deeper manifestation of this fear is the belief that the intimate partner has already taken so much control that personal identity has been altered.

In one of our cases, a 32-year-old married woman with two children had no sexual desire for her husband. The husband was involved in the religious movement known as Promise Keepers, and believed that men should be in charge of their families. The wife viewed him as exceedingly controlling, and resented his efforts to dominate her. The more power and influence he imposed, the more she resisted because she feared she would lose her identity. The wife came to believe that the only power she had was to distance herself emotionally from the relationship. Eventually, she met a man in her church who listened to and respected her, and their emotional relationship gradually grew into an affair.

The fear of emotional dependency is another underlying factor that can predispose an individual to infidelity. Dependent partners usually do not think of having an affair, because they would not want to risk losing their spouses. However, partners who have an underlying fear of being too dependent must unconsciously find some way to maintain distance in order to counteract their intense dependency needs. Infidelity becomes a way of creating distance in the relationship. For example, a couple entered treatment because the husband wanted a divorce after 20 years of marriage. He had been extremely dependent on his mother and then his wife—in fact, enmeshed in both relationships. He sought independence through work-related travel. Finally, he met another woman and began an affair, switching his dependence from one woman to another.

Fears of rejection or abandonment can also play a role in many forms of infidelity. Normally, feelings of rejection and abandonment are associated with one's parents. However, some partners experience adult rejection and abandonment. Whenever the trauma occurs, it leaves people with the defense that they never want to be in that position again. Thus, they unconsciously think that it is better to reject first in order to protect themselves. In one case, the husband requested a divorce after being married for 20 years. He had a critical, rejecting father and a mother who could not protect him from the ravages of his father. Within the previous few years, his wife had become progressively resentful, angry, and rejecting. During arguments, she had threatened to divorce her husband several times. In addition, she had become publicly critical and sexually rejecting. Some of her anger was lifelong, but the more acute versions were about the husband's difficult work schedule. Fearing rejection, he began an emotionally intimate relationship with another woman that eventually became sexualized. He gave numerous justifications for his actions that all resulted from a perceived fear of abandonment. Thus, he terminated the marriage when it appeared that his wife would reject him.

Infidelity can also be motivated by the fear of feelings. This presentation often occurs in persons with obsessive-compulsive personality structures who appear to be affectivity restricted and cognitively oriented. They wish to experience feelings but unconsciously fear them. In many cases, they will select a partner who is more affective or even histrionic and then begin to be critical of that partner's feelings. This is a classic case of projective identification because one rejects in the other what is unacceptable to the self. In other words, such individuals renounce their feelings, and then project these disclaimed feelings onto their partners and negatively identify with them. Once a partner becomes a source of projective identification, the relationship quickly diminishes. A typical maladaptive solution is to form another relationship in which it will be acceptable to express and compartmentalize some feelings.

In one case, the husband often became enraged when his wife demonstrated affect of any sort. He criticized her for being childlike and immature. He could not tolerate feelings in himself, and was exquisitely sensitive to and critical of affect displayed by his wife. In another case, a woman was fearful of feelings about herself. This fear had prevented her from enjoying mature and reciprocal relationships. Rachel was an attractive, divorced, 46-year-old, successful professional. She had a family history of rejection and abandonment, resulting in a low self-esteem. She overcompensated at work because she underestimated her intellectual capacity. In her marital relationship, she shut down emotionally. During the marriage and thereafter, she compartmentalized her feelings, experiencing them in only in affairs. Typically, Rachel would attach herself to men she presumed to be powerful, attractive, intelligent, successful, and special, hoping to acquire vicariously some of their perceived assets. In each case, the men rejected her, because she was too needy.

The final factor that can motivate infidelity is the fear of exposure. This fear has also been called the imposter syndrome. People experiencing this condition feel that they have fooled or tricked another person into thinking that they are worthy of love when in fact they feel unlovable. In relationships, they will hide behind work and other activities in order to maintain emotional distance. For example, Harry, 58, believed that he was an imposter. He thought that if his wife knew what he was like, she would find him unlovable. Thus, he told her very little about his life in order to keep up the pretense and retain her love. Harry became involved in multiple affairs for several reasons. One was that he needed to prove that he could interest women who were attractive and desired by other men. Attracting these women thus meant, to Harry, that he was a desirable man with good qualities. In these relationships, he expressed loving feelings, thinking that he was revealing himself when, in fact, he hid behind a profuse display of affection.

A number of techniques can be used to work with the fears of intimacy and thereby prevent a reoccurrence of future betrayals. They are addressed in the sections that follow.

Normalize Intimacy Fears

It is useful to normalize the fear of intimacy, because this strategy counteracts pessimism and promotes the joining process. As we said earlier, pessimism serves as a barrier to productive therapy. Therapists need to assure the couple that they can provide help and support because they possess skills and experience. Explain that intimacy fears are very common in couples, and that these worries have many different manifestations. Also, ask the couple to think about their own meaning of intimacy and to have a probing discussion of their definitions. This includes helping them to break the concept down into components that could be implemented in their relationship. The smaller components are more palatable and easy to operationalize into behaviorally objective components. The partners can discuss areas of agreement and disagreement in what they consider intimate behavior. Finally, ask each partner to draw two circles, representing the self and the partner, and depict through the amount of overlap of the circles the perceived level of intimacy in the relationship. Then lay sketches out and discuss them in order to gain a more complete understanding of what they actually mean. This simple technique reveals considerable information. For example, the husband might draw his circles barely touching, and the wife might draw hers overlapping to indicate the current level of intimacy. Next, ask each partner to illustrate the desired level of intimacy using the circle drawings.

Think Systemically

The therapist should keep in mind the systemic principles explained earlier in the text. Fears of intimacy are usually interlocking and reciprocal. Whereas one partner might present the ostensible barriers to intimacy, the other usually mirrors a complementary fear. For example, one partner might fear abandonment and the other might fear dependency. It is important from a systemic perspective to uncover the interlocking patterns that keep the couple stuck.

Use the Six Questions Exploring Sternberg's Model of Love

The six questions mentioned earlier in this chapter pertain to commitment, intimacy, and passion in committed relationships. This therapeutic tool will facilitate an understanding of the areas of strength and weakness for each couple. The couple should talk about these issues in session and continue discussions at home using homework assignments. The insight gained will make the concepts more concrete, understandable, and workable. Once the problem areas have been targeted, the therapist can begin to work on developing strength in one or more of these areas.

Explore Expectations

Unmet and frustrated expectations often contribute to occurrences of infidelity. In many cases, the unfaithful partner discussed being chronically frustrated with an unmet expectation. Often, men express sexual frustration and women complain about the lack of intimacy. However, any number of other disappointed expectations can create a breeding ground for infidelity, such as childrearing, in-laws, division of labor, and so on.

Everyone enters a relationship with certain expectations that result from experiences within their families of origin. Likewise, every relationship carries undeniable expectations; if not realized, disappointment and frustration occur. Sager (1976) developed a useful way of conceptualizing and exploring levels of expectations in a relationship:

- Those that the partner was clearly aware of and verbalized to the other partner.
- Those that the partner was clearly aware of but did not verbalize to the other partner.
- Those that are beyond the awareness of the partner and therefore could not be verbalized.

The first category represents conscious expectations, which can be openly discussed. The second and third categories of expectations are more problematic. The third category is especially difficult, because the partner wants something, does not know what it is, and thus cannot communicate it to the other partner. Hence, the expectation is often not realized, creating disappointment, frustration, and anger. In practical terms, the therapist can explain this system to the couple and ask that they spend time each week identifying what they want to give and receive from their partner. A further refinement is to ask them to think about what they want for themselves, the marriage, and the family. A useful technique is to ask partners to explain how the other person disappointed them. This brings the expectation from an unconscious or preconscious realm to a level of conscious expression. Obviously, some expectations are "normal" or beneficial to the relationship, and others are unrealistic and unhealthy. The therapist can help the couple to identify expectations, decide if they are beneficial for the relationship, implement the desired expectations, and eliminate the problematic ones.

Margie and Ralph, in their early 20s, sought treatment because of disagreements about parenting their 2-year-old child. They lived in a rural area, and Ralph worked as a fire fighter. It quickly became apparent that many other problems existed, including unmet expectations. They reported that Ralph had had an emotional affair (although Margie suspected it was also sexual) after the birth of their child. Ostensibly, the affair had been terminated. Ralph enjoyed hunting as a recreational activity and liked to socialize with his single friends when not working. He expected that he would continue to enjoy the freedom that he had had before marriage. In this way, he appeared immature to Margie, who, on the other hand, assumed that Ralph would undertake the responsibilities of a husband and father and would share household chores equitably. In addition, she had the unconscious expectation that Ralph would play a parental role in their marriage and take care of her. Although quite competent, she would frequently act helpless, such as not being able to drive herself places, and expecting Ralph to take her. He responded to her unconscious expectations by feeling smothered, and he justified spending time away from home by complaining about her neediness.

Promote Communication

Effective communication is essential in developing greater levels of intimacy. However, many couples have not mastered this facility. They may intellectually know the skills but not be able to use them for a variety of reasons. This fact then leads to miscommunication, misunderstanding, and a feeling of lack of connection or intimacy. By the time the couple enters therapy, many of their assumptions about each other have become negative. A negative assumption will usually lead to misinterpretation of the other partner's intentions and ultimately to an avoidance of conversation. Furthermore, the partners will come to expect that every discussion will be like the last, a supposition that intensifies their sense of helplessness and hopelessness. If the couple is to reverse the downward spiral, they must begin to change their assumptions and think more positively.

CONCLUSION

The final phase of treatment encompasses more than helping the couple to recover from infidelity—The underlying risk factors that contributed to the betrayals must be identified and eliminated. Thus, the relationship is restructured to help the couple achieve more satisfaction and a greater experience of intimacy. The treatment chapters discussed a systematic approach that is extremely effective in preventing relapse. In fact, we believe that many marriages affected by infidelity can be salvaged through a systemic rather than traditional approach. A great deal of time and effort is required to successfully treat infidelity. Partners need to understand the plan of treatment, develop realistic expectations about therapy, and be willing to commit themselves to complete the process.

In Chapter 12, the final chapter of this volume, we will continue with an intimacy-based approach to the treatment of infidelity. Techniques and strategies that we commonly use to facilitate and improve communication are be reviewed. Many of these tactics address the communication problems that typically create distance in a relationship and interfere with intimacy. Treating these intimacy-based problems will reduce the risk of recurrence.

12

✾ ✾ ✾

Concluding Techniques: Promoting Intimacy Through Communication

IN THE PREVIOUS CHAPTER, WE INTRODUCED AN INTIMACY-BASED model for the treatment of infidelity. In many cases, intimacy problems contribute to the development and maintenance of relational dissatisfaction and infidelity. Communication is a fundamental element of intimacy; therefore, problems in this area will interfere with the development and maintenance of emotional closeness. Without a foundation of clear communication, the couple is at risk for betrayals of intimacy and will not have the skills required to repair the damage created by infidelity. In this chapter, we describe several treatment approaches for promoting productive communication between partners. Therapists can use these techniques with couples working on a wide array of problems, especially with those wanting to prevent relapses of infidelity. The five approaches that we discuss in this chapter address various aspects of communication, such as the essential ingredients, different levels, recognition and correction of barriers, and effective conflict resolution. This list is not exhaustive, yet it provides the reader with some sense of how to intervene at a systemic level.

Five Essential Ingredients
Commitment

Throughout the text, we have emphasized the essential nature of commitment to the marriage and to treatment. Partners must articulate, as clearly as possible, their level of commitment, because commitment cannot be assumed. This step is critical for assessment purposes, as is coaching the partners to express their feelings about the relationship. Having two committed partners at the outset is ideal, but, in some cases, one or both will be ambivalent, or one will want to leave and the other will want to stay. When the latter situations are at hand, the therapist may need to spend a significant amount of time on this issue in order to determine a course of action.

In one case, the couple had been in treatment for several months. The husband had little sexual desire for his wife of 10 years, although he admitted that she was attractive and sexually responsive. The treatment progressed slowly and was interrupted whenever he sabotaged by refusing to attend sessions. The therapist suspected infidelity. The husband denied it and the wife agreed, by suggesting that he was not sophisticated enough to sustain a marital relationship, let alone an affair. Nonetheless, the issue of his commitment was addressed, along with other relational factors that contributed to their lack of intimacy. In addition, there were significant communication problems between the partners, specifically, the conflict-avoidant husband's tendency to stonewall discussion of affect-laden material. Often, the wife enabled his style of conflict resolution by making jokes about him and explaining that he was limited. She had her fears of abandonment, which led her to avoid the very serious issues that contributed to their lack of intimacy. The wife eventually became suspicious and discovered that he had been having an affair for several years. Despite efforts by the therapist to explore and help to resolve the affair, the husband—through a variety of intransigent tactics—continued to demonstrate a lack of commitment to the marriage and treatment. Eventually, the therapist stopped conjoint treatment due to the husband's apparent lack of commitment, and referred each person for individual therapy. Eventually, the wife discovered an Internet trail that gave credible evidence of the husband's affiliation with prostitutes. The couple divorced.

If the commitment level is low but not absent, treatment can proceed. We often recommend that the partners act "as if" there were greater commitment than actually exists. This strategy helps to interrupt pessimism and negativity, allows for behavioral rehearsals of the desired outcome, and promotes goodwill. The therapist can then realistically discuss the treatment plan and time frame, although cautioning that therapy may be difficult at times. A premature termination will not be in the best interest of the relationship.

In one situation, the wife was certain that she could not remain in the marriage after discovering that her husband had been unfaithful. The therapist recommended the previously mentioned strategy in order to promote engagement in treatment and counteract hopelessness. This couple remains in treatment 18 months later, and is now working to resolve the underlying problems that contributed to their lack of intimacy. They are deeply committed and working effectively on reestablishing sexual intimacy.

Goodwill

A common occurrence in the treatment of infidelity is for a partner to have negative or faulty assumptions about the other's intentions. Such presumptions are rarely verified; thus, the faulty belief persists and communication is halted. To interrupt this negative spiral, the therapist must help the couple to examine their pattern of communication for evidence of faulty or negative assumptions. Then, ask each partner to presuppose that the other's intentions are good, even if a statement is ambiguous, and continue to reinforce this leap of faith. Next, help the partners to discuss and probe each statement in order to determine the actual content and significance of the communication. In our experience, the intention is usually good, although the comment might seem awkward or negative. Sometimes a lack of skill or anxiety can distort the message so much that the receiver is wounded when no offense is intended. In one case, the angry husband insisted that his wife was acting in a selfish manner by contributing less than the anticipated amount to their discussions about her affair. Upon clarification, they realized that she was feeling tremendous guilt for hurting him and was not intentionally withholding her emotions. In another case, the wife accused her spouse of being hostile because he rarely completed household tasks when it was his responsibility. He had problems with organization and never intended to frustrate his wife. They discussed and found remedies for some of the specific behavioral difficulties. Moreover, she was able to recognize that although his course of action might sometimes be annoying, his intent was not malevolent.

Understanding

After the repeated experience of miscommunication and misunderstanding, couples are inclined to give up rather than persist at grasping the message. In order to promote understanding, the therapist can explain that communication is an imperfect process, even when people think they have expressed an idea clearly. Remind the couple that understanding involves the feeling or affective tone as well as the content. Suggest that the couple must avoid avoidance; they will never make progress without trying. Additionally, remind them that communication is a learned skill and that only with continued practice and discipline will they be able to untangle miscommunication. Another couple suffered because their methods of resolving conflict often led to heated arguments. They felt hopeless and frustrated about their inability to avoid quarreling. In treatment, they discovered that many disputes resulted from misunderstandings about the communication. Each felt misunderstood, and this emotion contributed to a lack of goodwill toward each other. The therapist coached them to dissect each interchange into two categories, affect (or the feelings of each partner), and content. The partners learned to explore the underlying feelings before attempting to resolve problems. This strategy provided a great deal of relief, and allowed them to progress to other communications work.

Process

Process refers to how the communication is expressed. It includes nonverbal behaviors such as body language, and dimensions of verbal communication such as voice loudness, inflection, tone of voice, and so on. Many couples find it challenging to note the process of communication. The therapist can teach the skill in session by reinforcing it through many trials. Process thinking is more mature, differentiated, abstract, and self-reflective.

One way to begin is to have couples distinguish between process and content. The therapist can coach the partners to describe the manifest level of a communication and then to add process comments. It is necessary to slow down the pace in order for each partner to observe the process before offering an immediate reply or rebuttal. In the case of the husband who had organizational problems, the wife brought up a specific issue in session. He became anxious and responded to her observations with humor. She told him that his verbal response was understandable, but that his joking made no sense to her. Instead of personalizing his reaction, she demonstrated differentiation by asking him about it. This interrupted a potential argument about a situation that she perceived as humorless. The therapist helped him to discuss his feelings and then to return to the topic at hand.

Circularity

The concept of circularity is a quintessential component of systems thinking. It presupposes that spouses react to each other and in doing so influence their partners by their own reactions. Thus, the behaviors are reciprocal or interlocking. To encourage systemic thinking in the couple, ask the partners to observe how their behaviors fit together even when it is not obvious at first glance. They are to look for the impact that their conduct has on the other person and vice versa, keeping track of the process as it unfolds. Help them to see the nonlinear nature of communication, emphasizing that there are no beginnings and endings—instead, their interactions occur within a loop or circle in which one stimulates the other, and so forth. Circularity is one of the most difficult concepts for a couple to grasp, and they need much direction from the systemic therapist to use this powerful idea.

Levels of Communication

Often, couples feel that something is missing when they talk. Communication that occurs on a superficial level will not promote a sense of intimacy. Bernal and Barker (1979) developed a schema that offers a simple way to comprehend and explain the levels of communication to the couple. There are five levels, and each will promote a different depth of intimacy. In some situations, a superficial level of communication is adequate; however, for the fullest experience of emotional closeness, a deeper level is required.

- *Objects* communication comprises an impartial, detached, or impersonal accounting of events, details, and descriptions. It involves sharing of factual data only, as if the person were reading a newspaper article. Self-reflective thinking and feelings about the information are absent.

- *Individual* communication is a reflexive interchange that occurs in reaction to something or someone else. Thus, people are unaware of their responsibility for actions, feeling, or beliefs, or how these responses trigger reactions in their partners and perpetuate conflict. Instead, such people blame their partners for the perceived cause of the conflict. For example, a wife might say that she could not feel close because her husband is always pushing her away. This partner is disavowing her own feelings, and failing to see the interlocking nature of the issue. Individual communication is limited, because it is linear in nature and tries to assign cause or blame. Human interactions are more complicated than that. It is more productive to think in terms of circularity when attempting to resolve conflict. We find that couples enjoy working with systemic thinking once they have some comfort with the idea.

- *Transactional* communication enables partners to respond to each other's behavior in a noninflammatory way. This level is marked by the introduction of "I statements," which demonstrate ownership of thoughts and feelings, and possession of greater subjective awareness. These statements reflect more differentiation and less enmeshment. Moreover, the couple is beginning to see the circularity of their interactions. For example, a man might say that he understands why his wife feels so alone by connecting her aloneness to his own emotional experience. He might recognize that he pulls back emotionally and in response she becomes angry, which makes him shut down more. Thus, transactional communication is circular.

- The *relational* level is an extension of the transactional. Interactions are based on commonly held assumptions about the operating rules of the relationship. Another way to describe this level is that the partners are now capable of meta-communicating about their relationship. They can talk about how they talk with significant depth and understanding. Marsha and Dave, a dual-career couple, had gradually devoted more emotional energy to their respective careers than they did to their relationship. They experienced conflict as their emotional distance increased. Their pattern of communication reflected their feelings of frustration and agitation; Dave would stonewall and Marsha would criticize. This pattern escalated until they barely spoke. They did not realize that their styles of communication exacerbated their discord; therefore, feeling intimate became difficult or impossible. The treatment centered on helping them to recognize how their form of communication was destructive. This involved helping Marsha and Dave to communicate about their communication.

- The *contextual* level adds the dimensions of history and background to the communication. The partners can talk about relationship problems and also understand how these patterns evolved. Moreover, they are helped to recognize that some of their patterns were learned within their families of origin and expressed in their relationship. For example, contextual communication enables the partners to discuss the underlying fears of intimacy learned in their families, and how these fears played a part in choosing each other. This understanding will defuse their anger and help them to make sense of some of their reflexive actions. The couple learns that they must communicate at deeper levels in order for feelings of intimacy to emerge. This kind of cognitive and emotional self-disclosure is an essential ingredient of intimacy.

Recognizing Common Barriers to Intimate Communication

Couples are typically unaware of their use of problematic communication. Furthermore, they do not intuitively understand the connection between communication and intimacy. Thus, it is the responsibility of the therapist to teach this principle to the couple and help them to monitor their use of such patterns. Progress in this area is incremental, because old habits are difficult to break. Moreover, when couples are under stress, they are particularly prone to return to dysfunctional styles of communication rather than use the newer, more adaptive styles. The following list discusses a few of the more common dysfunctional modes of communication.

- *Mind reading* occurs when one partner claims to know what the other is thinking, feeling, or intending to say. Despite overwhelming evidence to the contrary, mind readers will maintain their stance because they have convinced themselves that they are right. Thus, they deflect contrary information and do not consider the other person's perceptions. The consequences of mind reading are often disastrous, resulting in incorrect assumptions, increased frustration between partners, halted communication, and ultimately a state of emotional disconnection.

- *Personalizing* is a defensive form of communication in which the receiver perceives offense when it is not necessarily intended. The partner who personalizes is exquisitely sensitive to criticism and feels personally attacked when a problem is brought up. Instead of dealing with the problem at hand, people who personalize defend themselves. Their unknowing partners feel alienated, misunderstood, and unloved, often concluding that they cannot be intimate with someone who is out to attack them. In one couple, the husband was sensitive to criticism. In his family of origin, his father's anger was unpredictable and the son never knew when he might be attacked. In one session, his wife expressed her concern about finances. Instead of asking her to discuss her feelings about finances, he launched into a diatribe about his earnings over the previous few years. The bewildered wife cried and explained that she felt hopeless. This couple often had difficulty in exploring and resolving problems because of the husband's defensiveness.

- *Distraction* is another problem in communication and a barrier to intimacy. First, a message is sent or a problem is brought up. The responding partner does not react to the issue at hand and instead changes the subject. This defense is often expressed as a countercomplaint or attack. For instance, a wife wanted to discuss her husband's lack of sexual desire for her. He responded by complaining about her body, stating that she was too thin. He then commented that she had emotional issues with her mother and that she was far from perfect. The nondefensive partner felt misunderstood and unloved. Distraction often causes the partner to become angry, hurt, and frustrated, or to establish distance in self-defense.

- *Polarizing language* places the partners at extreme positions. Imbalance and distance are maintained within the system by using "all or none" thinking. Thus, if one partner is right the other has to be wrong, or if one is good then the other is bad. The perceptions, beliefs, or opinions of the other spouse cannot enter the equation. When both partners use polarization, there is constant strife and an attitude of trying to win rather than to compromise.

Gottman (1994a, 1994b) studied couples communication within a laboratory setting for many years, and concluded that four styles of interchange can damage the level of intimacy to the point of divorce. A therapist can share this list of barriers to intimate communication in order to help partners monitor and interrupt their use of these destructive patterns:

- *Criticism* refers to attacking the partner's personality rather than the problem.
- *Contempt* involves making statements designed to insult or hurt one's partner.
- *Defensiveness* consists of avoiding responsibility for one's own actions by using denial, excuses, "yes-butting," blaming, or overtalking the other partner.
- *Stonewalling* means not listening to or accepting what the other partner says. Stonewalling strategies include leaving a discussion, changing the subject, or just not responding.

Basic Techniques for Facilitating Intimate Communication

Sometimes basic strategies are the most successful. Throughout the years, we have returned to three effective and reliable techniques. They facilitate intimate communication, enhance goodwill, and promote optimism. Although they are elementary, the therapist can use these strategies in a variety of situations, including therapeutic work around infidelity.

- *"I" statements* involve speaking for oneself in a direct and nonjudgmental way. The content of the message can involve thoughts, feelings, wishes, desires, complaints, and so on that are offered in a noninflammatory manner. An "I" statement reduces defensive communication and is a way of giving part of oneself to another person. The partner implicitly assumes that the other can be trusted with something that is important or intimate. Teaching couples to use this strategy can be challenging, however. It helps to suggest that they do not use "I" statements to bash or blame a partner—for example, "I feel that you are a liar" (or some other negative personality characteristic). This is obviously misuse of the technique. One recommended way to use the "I" statement constructively is to employ a phrase such as "I feel ____ about . . ." (a behavior, situation, problem, etc.). Later, help the partners to express a request from each other regarding with a specific example.

- *Reflective listening* is an active process that begins by taking note of a statement or series of statements. The receiver restates the content and reflects back the feeling tone of the message. The sender then comments on accuracy or corrects the restatement in order to ensure that the message received was in fact the message sent. At the end of this series of interactions, the receiver is free to respond and the process begins again. This sort of transaction is more complicated than mere listening and repeating. Reflective listening is a caring, nonjudgmental gesture that opens the door for further communication and feelings of we-ness. It demonstrates an active interest in understanding the partner.

- *Validation* is the process of putting one's opinions aside in order to listen to another person's message without interjecting bias. It is a response that indicates that a message was received, nothing more. There is no counterargument to the problem or complaint. Validation does not imply agreement; instead, it involves understanding a statement and the psychological context in which it emerged. People can verify that they heard and understood the message by using phrases such as "I understand" or "I get it."

COMMUNICATING CONFLICT AND ANGER

Situations involving infidelity evoke intense anger. Problematic conflict-resolution styles can often worsen the crisis. Families of origin and personality traits strongly influence how a person learns to communicate anger. By the time couples seek counseling, they usually have a number of ineffective communication habits that interfere with resolving discord. The therapist must help the couple to recognize their ineffective methods of arguing or expressing anger. Approaches that are more effective must be learned and substituted. We ask both partners to list their bad habits in expressing anger, and then ask them to alternately share these items without responding to the other person's list. Then, we ask each partner to discuss the other person's most bothersome habits. Suggest that the partners use "I" language when they respond, such as "I felt frightened when you said. . . ." Help them to recognize and accept that the other person's perception is the focal point, not whether a particular habit is justified. The partners then rank order their bad habits so that special attention can be given to the few that are the most common or destructive. The next step is to negotiate a more palatable version of expressing anger or conflict by developing alternative responses and strategies. We also recommend some guidelines for the expression of angry feelings in the form of a list of do's and don'ts.

Dos and Don'ts

- Don't complain for the sake of complaining. Instead, think about the change you want and ask for it specifically, without expressing raw anger.
- Ask for a reasonable change or one that you think your partner is capable of making.
- Start small and work toward larger change.
- Never assume that you know how your partner is going to respond. If you presuppose a negative response, you will be angry at the outset and not get what you need from your partner.
- Don't make sweeping, labeling judgments about your partner's feelings and wants.
- Never discount your partner's feelings or intensity of emotion.
- Don't use sarcasm, contempt, criticism, stonewalling, or defensiveness.
- Confine yourself to one issue at a time, without cross-complaining.
- Express all your feelings about the conflict, not just your anger.
- Validate your partner's feelings.
- Remember that the ultimate goal of conflict is compromise, not winning.
- There are no totally objective realities in a relationship; instead, there are subjective feelings and beliefs about an issue.

This list is by no means comprehensive. Ask the couple to refine and customize it to their relationship. The next step is to teach the skills of fair fighting. We present fair fighting in two stages. For a more comprehensive version, see Weeks and Treat (2001). We recommend giving to the couple a handout detailing the steps, to help the couple get the sequence firmly fixed.

Fair Fighting

STAGE 1

When a couple has a dilemma, they really have two problems—the dilemma itself and their feelings about it. We recommend separating the two com-

ponents before attempting to solve the problem. During Stage 1, the participants concentrate on feelings. Couples will usually shortchange the feelings.
Remind them that the first rule of fair fighting is that the feelings about the
problem take priority. Explain the importance of giving sufficient time to
express all their feelings. The next step is for the partner to use reflective
listening to understand and validate the feelings from the other person's
perspective. Once the partner who brings up the complaint feels sufficiently
understood, the couple can move to the next step. Stage 1 allows the other
partner time for talking about how he or she feels about the problem, and
his or her own emotions about how the partner feels. These steps are not
easy and require practice within the therapy setting with the facilitation of
the therapist. The therapist must prevent partners from interrupting or mis-
interpreting each other's messages.

There are two reasons for separating the feelings from the dilemma. First,
the partner who has the conflict needs to reflect on the problem and be able
to state it objectively. Second, the feelings about the problem must be recognized and understood. It helps to assign a numeric level to designate intensity, in order to add this dimension when talking about how the feeling is
experienced. These strategies allow time for the partner to modulate his or
her anger. Then help the partner to understand the basis for the feeling by
recognizing the thoughts (cognitions) that fuel it. The feelings must be
exposed and addressed, otherwise the couple will continue to be frustrated.

Sometimes, the strategies involved in Stage 1 will be sufficient for resolving the conflict. This is especially true when the individual is struggling with
a dilemma that does not involve the partner, such as a problem at work or
with a friend or parent. The second stage is useful when a problem is relational and when compromise is needed.

STAGE 2

During the second stage, the partner with the problem proposes a solution
first and the couple discusses it. The other partner may counter with another
possible solution and they consider that solution. The partners may
exchange ideas until they mutually agree that one solution appears to be the
best. At that point, they must discuss implementation using behaviorally
objective terminology. The couple understands the specific behaviors
required of each to accomplish the expected outcome. They try the accepted
solution for a week or two, and then reevaluate how well it is working. They
may need to make adjustments or change solutions. The final part of Stage
2 is to for the couple to comment on how they cooperated with each other
and to congratulate each other on sticking to the rules of constructive conflict
resolution.

Couples will not be able to immediately use these skills. They should begin the session with issues that are least emotionally laden and therefore more likely to be successfully resolved. The therapist assigns working on an issue at home only after the couple demonstrates some success in session. The emphasis should be on creating success, not failure. If the couple resists doing the skills-based assignments at home, then a number of explanations may be applicable. The most common is that the therapist may have asked them to go too quickly, or that they may need more coaching. Another explanation is that the couple may still need to work on their negative attitudes toward conflict, or that they may continue to be caught in their pattern of avoidance regarding conflict.

Some disagreements take many hours to untangle. Most couples do not understand this fact and expect that conflict resolution will be relatively expeditious. Make them understand that conflict cannot always be resolved quickly. Lengthy arguments can be punctuated into more manageable segment using timeouts. Timeouts enable the couple to suspend the discussion until their emotions are less intense. Either partner may call a timeout without question for a period of 20 minutes or longer. Gottman's (1994a, 1994b) research demonstrated that it takes an average of 20 minutes to calm down sufficiently from an agitated physiologic state to think rationally. The person who calls the timeout is expected to resume the discussion after the pre-scribed period. Timeouts should be used sparingly and only to move the conversation forward.

The successful use of anger management and conflict resolution strategies will reduce overall resentment and increase the couple's sense of optimism about the relationship and resentment. Moreover, good communication assures the couple that some of the problems that contributed to having the affair are being addressed.

Conclusion

We believe that intelligible and empathic communication is a pivotal component of intimacy. In this chapter, we reviewed a number of basic communication techniques that will effectively promote intimacy in couples dealing with infidelity. The techniques we recommend cannot be used in a vacuum—they must be integrated with other strategies designed specifically for treating infidelity, such as promoting forgiveness and helping the couple to think systemically. The therapist must be familiar and comfortable with a number of treatment strategies and demonstrate flexibility with their application in order to increase the likelihood of successful resolution.

The treatment of infidelity challenges the clinical skills and the personal values of the therapist. This is overridingly due to the damaging force of infidelity on relationships (Olson et al., 2002). The emotional milieu of the sessions is often intense, fluctuating, and overwhelming. Moreover, therapists must constantly monitor and understand their own values and countertransference issues. Unrecognized areas of conflict in the therapist, particularly with respect to intimacy, can be easily triggered in cases of infidelity. A defensive rather than empathic response can adversely affect treatment.

Repairing damage and rebuilding the couple's intimate relationship is at the heart of our intersystemic treatment of affairs and other intimacy transgressions. This approach is comprehensive, integrative, and contextual. Infidelity is a highly complex phenomenon with multiple dimensions that must be understood for each situation. This volume is designed to help therapists better understand the intricacies, dimensions, and dilemmas of treating infidelity, and to provide a myriad of strategies that can lead to successful and rewarding outcomes for couples.

References

Agnew, C. R. (2000). Cognitive interdependence and the experience of relationship loss. In J. H. Harvey & E. D. Miller (Eds.), *Loss and trauma: General close relationship perspectives* (pp. 385–398). Philadelphia: Brunner-Routledge.

Agnew, C. R., & Gephart, J. M. (2000). Testing the rules of commitment enhancement: Separating fact from fiction. *Representative Research in Social Psychology, 24,* 41–47.

Agnew, C. R., Van Lange, P., Rusbult, C. E., & Langston, C. A. (1998). Cognitive interdependence: Commitment and the mental representation of close relationships. *Journal of Personality and Social Psychology, 74*(4), 939–954.

Alberti, R., & Emmons, M. (1990). *Your perfect right.* San Luis Obispo, CA: Impact.

Al-Mabuk, R. H., Enright, R. D., & Cardis, P. A. (1995). Forgiveness education with parentally love-deprived adolescents. *Journal of Moral Education, 24*(4), 427–444.

American Psychiatric Association. (1994). *Diagnostic and statistical manual of mental disorders* (4th ed.). Washington, DC: Author.

Arriaga, X. B., & Agnew, C. R. (2001). Being committed: Affective, cognitive, and conative components of relationship commitment. *Personality & Social Psychology Bulletin, 27*(9), 1190–1203.

Athanasiou, R., Shaver, P., & Tavris, C. (1970). Sex. *Psychology Today, 4*(2), 37–52.

Athrons, C. (1995). *The good divorce: Keeping your family together when your marriage comes apart.* New York: HarperCollins.

Atwater, L. (1979). Getting involved: Women's transition to first extramarital sex. *Alternative Lifestyles, 2*(1), 33–68.

Atwood, J. D., & Seifer, M. (1997). Extramarital affairs and constructed meanings: A social constructionist therapeutic approach. *American Journal of Family Therapy, 25*(1), 55–75.

Balswick, J., & Balswick, J. (1999). Extramarital affairs: Causes, consequences, & recovery. *Marriage & Family: A Christian Journal, 2*(4), 419–426.

Baumeister, R. F., Exline, J. J., & Sommer, K. L. (1998). The victim role, grudge theory, and two dimensions of forgiveness. In E. L. Worthington, Jr. (Ed.), *Dimensions of forgiveness: Psychological research and theological speculations* (pp. 79–104). Philadelphia: Templeton Foundation.

Baumeister, R. F., Stillwell, A. M., & Heatherton, T. F. (1995). Interpersonal aspects of guilt: Evidence from narrative studies. In J. P. Tangney & K. W. Fischer (Eds.), *Self-conscious emotions: The psychology of shame, guilt, embarrassment, and pride* (pp. 255–273). New York: Guilford.

Baumeister, R. F., Stillwell, A. M., & Wotman, S. R. (1990). Victim and perpetrator accounts of interpersonal conflict: Autobiographical narratives about anger. *Journal of Personality and Social Psychology, 59*(5), 994–1005.

Beach, S., Jouriles, E., & O'Leary, D. (1985). Extramarital sex: Impact on depression and commitment in couples seeking marital therapy. *Journal of Sex and Marital Therapy, 11*(2), 99–108.

Beck, A., & Freeman A. (1990). *Cognitive therapy of personality disorders*. New York: Guilford.

Bernal, G., & Barker, J. (1979). Toward a metacommunication framework of couples intervention. *Family Process, 18*, 293–302.

Berry, J. W., & Worthington, E. L., Jr., (2001). Forgiveness, relationship quality, stress while imagining relationship events, and physical and mental health [Special issue]. *Journal of Counseling Psychology, 48*(4), 447–455.

Berry, J. W., Worthington, E. L. Jr., & Parrott, L., III. (2001). Dispositional forgiveness: Development and construct validity of the Transgression Narrative Test of Forgiveness (TNTF). *Personality & Social Psychology Bulletin, 27*(10), 1277–1290.

Betzig, L. (1989). Causes of conjugal dissolution: A cross-cultural study. *Current Anthropology, 30*(5), 654–676.

Billy, J. O. G., Tanfer, K., Grady, W. R., & Klepinger, S. H. (1993). The sexual behavior of men in the United States. *Family Planning Perspectives, 25*, 52–60.

Blackman, M. C., & Stubbs, E. (2001) Apologies: Genuine admissions of blameworthiness or scripted, sympathetic responses? *Psychological Reports: Special Issue; 88*(1), 45–50.

Boekhout, B., Hendrick, S., & Hendrick, C. (1999). Relationship infidelity: A loss perspective. *Journal of Personal & Interpersonal Loss, 4*(2), 97–114.

Boon, S., & Sulsky, L. (1997). Attributions of blame and forgiveness in romantic relationships: A policy-capturing study. *Journal of Social Behavior & Personality, 12*(1), 19–44.

Booth, A., & Dabbs, J. (1993). Testosterone and men's marriages. *Social Forces, 72*(2), 463–477.

Botwin, C. (1994). *Tempted women: The passions, perils, and agonies of female infidelity*. New York: William Morrow.

Broucek, F. J. (1997). Shame: Early developmental issues. In M. R. Lansky & A. P. Morrison (Eds.), *The widening scope of shame* (pp. 41–62). Hillsdale, NJ: Analytic Press.

Brown, E. (1991a). Dealing with secret affairs in psychotherapy. In L. Vande-Creek, T. Jackson, & S. Knapp (Eds.), *Innovations in clinical practice: A source book* (Vol. 12, pp. 133–145). Sarasota, FL: Professional Resource Exchange.

Brown, E. (1991b). *Patterns of infidelity and their treatment.* New York: Brunner / Mazel.

Bumpass, L., Sweet, J., & Cherlin, A. (1991). The role of cohabitation in declining rates of marriage. *Journal of Marriage and the Family, 53,* 913–927.

Butler, M. H., Dahlin, S. K., & Fife, S. T. (2002). "Languaging" factors affecting clients' acceptance of forgiveness intervention in marital therapy. *Journal of Marital & Family Therapy, 28*(3), 285–298.

Buunk, B. (1988). The extramarital behavioral intentions scale. In C. Davis, W. Yarber, & S. Davis (Eds.), *Sexually related measures. A compendium.* (pp. 99–100). Lake Mills, IA: Graphic Publishing.

Buunk, B. (1995). Sex, self-esteem, dependency, and extradyadic sexual experience as related to jealousy responses. *Journal of Social and Personal Relationships, 12*(1), 147–153.

Buunk, B., & Bakker, A. (1995). Extradyadic sex: The role of descriptive and injunctive norms. *Journal of Sex Research, 32*(4), 313–318.

Buunk, B., & Van Yperen, N. (1989). Social comparison, equality, and relationship satisfaction: Gender differences over a ten-year period. *Social Justice Research, 3,* 151–180.

Buunk, B., & Van Yperen, N. (1991). Referential comparisons, relationship comparisons and exchange orientation: Their relations to marital satisfaction. *Personality and Social Psychology Bulletin, 17,* 709–717.

Cano, A., & O'Leary, K. (1997). Romantic jealousy and affairs: Research and implications for couple therapy. *Journal of Sex and Marital Therapy, 23*(4), 249–275.

Cano, A., & O'Leary, K. (2000). Infidelity and separations precipitate major depressive episodes and symptoms of nonspecific depression and anxiety. *Journal of Consulting and Clinical Psychology, 68*(5), 774–781.

Carnes, P. (1991). *Don't call it love: Recovery from sexual addiction.* New York: Bantam.

Carnes, P. (1992). *Out of the shadows: Understanding sexual addiction* (2nd ed.). Minneapolis, MN: Compcare.

Charny, I. (1992). Catering and not catering affairs: The proper and improper pursuit of extramarital relationships. In I. W. Charny (Ed.), *Existential / dialectical marital therapy* (pp. 220–244). New York: Brunner / Mazel.

Charny, I., & Parnass, S. (1995). The impact of extramarital relationships on the continuation of marriages. *Journal of Sex and Marital Therapy, 21*(2), 100–115.

Choi, K. H., Catania, J. A., & Dolcini, M. M. (1994). Extramarital sex and HIV risk behavior among U.S. adults: Results from the National AIDS Behavioral Survey. *American Journal of Public Health, 84*(12), 2003–2007.

Christensen, A., Jacobson, N. S., & Babcock, J. C. (1995). Integrative behavioral couple therapy. In N. S. Jacobson & A. S. Gurman (Eds.), *Clinical handbook of couple therapy* (pp. 31–64). New York: Guilford.

Christopher, F. S., & Sprecher, S. (2000). Sexuality in marriage, dating, and other relationships: A decade review. *Journal of Marriage and the Family, 62*(4), 999–1018.

Clarkberg, M., Stolzenberg, R., & Waite, L. (1995). Attitudes, values, and entrance into cohabitational rather than marital unions. *Social Forces, 51,* 609–633.

Coleman, P. (1998). The process of forgiveness in marriage and the family. In R.

Enright & J. North (Eds.), *Exploring forgiveness* (pp. 75–95). Madison: University of Wisconsin Press.

Cooper, A., Delmonico, D., & Burg, R. (2000). Cybersex users, abusers, and compulsives: The dark side of the force. *Sexual Addiction and Compulsivity, 7*(1–2), 5–30.

Cottone, R., & Mannis, J. (1996). Uncovering secret extramarital affairs in marriage counseling. *Family Journal, 4*(2), 109–116.

Couch, L., Jones, W. H., & Moore, D. S. (1999). Buffering the effects of betrayal: The role of apology, forgiveness and commitment. In J. M. Adams, & W. H. Jones (Eds.), *Handbook of interpersonal commitment and relationship stability* (pp. 451–469). New York: Kluwer Academic / Plenum.

Coyle, C. T., & Enright, R. D. (1998). Forgiveness education with adult learners. In C. M. Smith & T. Pourchot (Eds.), *Adult learning and development: Perspectives from educational psychology* (pp. 219–238). Mahwah, NJ: Erlbaum.

Daly, M., & Wilson, M. (1988). *Homicide.* Hawthorne, NY: Aldine de Gruyter.

Darby, B. W., & Schlenker, B. R. (1982). Children's reactions to apologies. *Journal of Personality and Social Psychology, 43*(4), 742–753.

DeMaria, R., Weeks, G., & Hof, L. (1999). *Focused genograms: Intergenerational assessment of individuals, couples, and families.* Philadelphia: Brunner / Mazel.

Denton, R., & Martin, M. (1998). Defining forgiveness: An empirical exploration of process and role. *American Journal of Family Therapy, 26*(4), 281–292.

DiBlasio, F. A. (2000). Decision-based forgiveness treatment in cases of marital infidelity. *Psychotherapy, 37*(2), 149–158.

Dolcini, M., Catania, J., Coates, T., Stall, R., Hudes, E., Gagnon, J., & Pollack, L. (1993). Demographic characteristics of heterosexuals with multiple partners: The national AIDS behavior surveys. *Family Planning Perspectives, 25*, 208–214.

Doyle, G. (1999). Forgiveness as an intrapsychic process. *Psychotherapy, 36*(2), 190–198.

Drigotas, S., & Barta, W. (2001). The cheating heart: Scientific explorations of infidelity. *Current Directions in Psychological Science, 10*(5), 177–180.

Emmons, R. (2000). Personality and forgiveness. In M. McCullough, K. Pargament, & C. Thoresen (Eds.), *Forgiveness: Theory, research and practice* (pp. 156–179). New York: Guilford.

Enright, R. D. (1996). Counseling with the forgiveness triad: On forgiving, receiving, forgiveness, and self-forgiveness. *Counseling and Values, 40*(2), 107–126.

Enright, R. D., & Coyle, C. T. (1998). Researching the process model of forgiveness within psychological interventions. In E. L. Worthington, Jr. (Ed.), *Dimensions of forgiveness: Psychological research and theological perspectives* (pp. 139–161). Philadelphia: Templeton Foundation.

Enright, R. D., Easton, D. L., Golden, S., Sarinopoulos, I., & Freedman, S. (1992). Interpersonal forgiveness within the helping professions: An attempt to resolve differences of opinion. *Counseling and Values, 36*(2), 84–103.

Enright, R., & Fitzgibbons, R. P. (2000). *Helping clients forgive: An empirical guide for resolving anger and restoring hope.* Washington, DC: American Psychological Association.

Enright, R. D., & North, J. (Eds.). (1998). *Exploring forgiveness.* Madison: University of Wisconsin Press.

Exline, J., & Baumeister, R. (2000). Expressing forgiveness and repentance: Benefits and barriers. In M. McCullogh, K. Pargament, & C. Thoresen (Eds.), *Forgiveness: Theory, research and practice* (pp. 133–156). New York: Guilford.

Farmer, S. (1989). Effects of parental separation and divorce on children. In G. R. Weeks (Ed.), *Treating couples: The intersystem model of the Marriage Council of Philadelphia* (pp. 258–284). New York: Brunner / Mazel.

Fincham, F. D. (2000). The kiss of porcupines: From attributing responsibility to forgiving. *Personal Relationships, 7,* 1–23.

Finlayson, A:, Sealy J., & Martin, P. (2001). The differential diagnosis of problematic hypersexuality. *Sexual Addiction and Compulsivity, 8*(3–4), 241–251.

Fitness, J. (2001). Betrayal, rejection, revenge, and forgiveness: An interpersonal script approach. In M. R. Leary (Ed.), *Interpersonal rejection* (pp. 73–103). New York: Oxford University Press.

Fitzgibbons, R. P. (1986). The cognitive and emotive uses of forgiveness in the treatment of anger. *Psychotherapy, 23,* 629–633.

Fitzgibbons, R. P. (1998). Anger and the healing power of forgiveness. In R. Enright & J. North (Eds.), *Exploring forgiveness* (pp. 63–75). Madison: University of Wisconsin Press.

Flanagan, B. (1992). *Forgiving the unforgivable: Overcoming the bitter legacy of intimate wounds.* New York: Macmillan.

Forste, R., & Tanfer, K. (1996). Sexual exclusivity among dating, cohabiting, and married women. *Journal of Marriage and the Family, 58*(1), 33–47.

Fow, N. (1996). The phenomenology of forgiveness. *Journal of Phenomenological Psychology, 27*(2), 219–233.

Francis, J. L. (1977). Toward the management of heterosexual jealousy. *Journal of Marriage and Family Counseling, 3,* 61–69.

Franklin, K. M., Janoff-Bulman, R., & Roberts, J. E. (1990). Long-term impact of parental divorce on optimism and trust: Changes in general assumptions or narrow beliefs? *Journal of Personality and Social Psychology, 59,* 743–755.

Freedman, S. R. (2000). Creating an expanded view: How therapists can help their clients forgive. *Journal of Family Psychotherapy, 11*(1), 87–82.

Geiss, S. K., & O'Leary, K. D. (1981). Therapist ratings of frequency and severity of marital problems: Implications for research. *Journal of Marital and Family Therapy, 7*(4), 515–520.

Gelso, C. J., & Carter, J. A. (1985). The relationship in counseling and psychotherapy: Components, consequences and theoretical antecedents. *Counseling Psychologist, 13*(2), 155–243.

Glass, S., & Staehel, J. C. (2003). *Not "just friends": Protect your relationship from infidelity and heal the trauma of betrayal.* New York: Free Press.

Glass, S., & Wright, T. (1977). The relationship of extramarital sex, length of marriage, and sex differences on marital satisfaction and romanticism: Athanasiou's data reanalyzed. *Journal of Marriage and the Family, 39*(4), 691–703.

Glass, S., & Wright, T. (1985). Sex differences in type of extramarital involvement and marital dissatisfaction. *Sex Roles, 12*(9–10), 1101–1120.

Glass, S., & Wright, T. (1992). Justifications for extramarital relationships: The association between attitudes, behaviors, and gender. *Journal of Sex Research, 29*(3), 361–387.

Glass, S., & Wright, T. (1997). Reconstructing marriages after the trauma of infidelity. In W. K. Halford & H. J. Markman (Eds.), *Clinical handbook of marriage and couples interventions* (pp. 471–507). New York: Wiley.

Gold, G. J., & Weiner, B. (2000). Remorse, confession, group identity and expectancies about repeating a transgression. *Basic & Applied Social Psychology, 22*(4), 291–300.

Goldhor-Lerner, H. (1985). *The dance of anger*. New York: HarperCollins.

Goldhor-Lerner, H. (1989). *The dance of intimacy: A woman's guide to courageous acts of change in key relationships*. New York: Harper & Row.

Gonzales, M. H., Pederson, J. H., Manning, D. J., & Wetter, D. W. (1990). Pardon my gaffe: Effects of sex, status, and consequence severity on accounts. *Journal of Personality and Social Psychology, 58*(4), 610–612.

Goodman, A. (2001). What's in a name? Terminology for designating a syndrome of driven sexual behavior. *Sexual Addiction and Compulsivity, 8*(3–4), 191–213.

Gordon, K. C., & Baucom, D. H. (1998). Understanding betrayals in marriage: A synthesized model of forgiveness. *Family Process, 37*(4), 425–429.

Gordon, K. C., Baucom, D. H., & Snyder, D. K. (2000). The use of forgiveness in marital therapy. In M. McCullogh, K. Pargament, & C. Thoresen (Eds.), *Forgiveness: Theory, research and practice* (pp. 203–228). New York: Guilford.

Gottman, J. (1994a). *What predicts divorce? The relationship between marital process and marital outcomes*. Hillsdale, NJ: Erlbaum.

Gottman, J. (1994b). *Why marriages succeed or fail*. New York: Simon & Schuster.

Griffin, D. (1999). Forgiveness as an intrapsychic process. *Psychotherapy, 36*(2), 190–198.

Hansen, G. (1987). Extradyadic relations during courtship. *Journal of Sex Research, 23*(3), 382–390.

Hargrave, T. D. (1994). *Families and forgiveness: Healing wounds in the intergenerational family*. New York: Brunner / Mazel.

Hewitt, J. P., & Stokes, R. (1975). Disclaimers. *American Sociological Review, 40*, 1–11.

Hodgins, H. S., Liebeskind, E., & Schwartz, W. (1996). Getting out of hot water. Facework in social predicaments. *Journal of Personality and Social Psychology, 71*, 300–314.

Humphrey, F. G. (1982). Extramarital affairs: Clinical approaches in marital therapy. *Psychiatric Clinics of North America, 5*(3), 581–593.

Humphrey, F. G. (1985). *Extramarital affairs and their treatment by AAMFT therapist*. Paper presented at the meeting of the American Association of Marriage and Family Therapy, New York, October 19.

Humphrey, F. (1987). Treating extramarital sexual relationships in sex and couples therapy. In G. Weeks & L. Hof (Eds.), *Integrating sex and marital therapy: A clinical guide* (pp. 149–170). New York: Brunner / Mazel.

Humphrey, F., & Strong, F. (1976). *Treatment of extramarital sexual relationships as reported by clinical members of AAMFC*. Paper presented at the meeting of the Northeastern American Association of Marriage and Family Counselors, Hartford, CT, May 22.

Hunt, M. (1974). *Sexual behavior in the 1970's*. Chicago: Playboy Press.

Hurlbert, D. (1992). Factors influencing a woman's decision to end an extramarital sexual relationship. *Journal of Sex and Marital Therapy, 18*(2), 104–113.

Irving, L. M., & Cannon R. (2000). Starving for hope: Goals, agency, and pathways in the development and treatment of eating disorders. In C. R. Snyder (Ed.), *Handbook of hope: Theory, measures, and applications* (pp. 261–283). San Diego: Academic Press.

Jacobson, N. S., & Christensen, A. (1996). *Integrative couple therapy: Promoting acceptance and change*. New York: Norton.

Janoff-Bulman, R. (1992). *Shattered assumptions: Towards a new psychology of trauma*. New York: Free Press.

Janoff-Bulman, R., & Frantz, C. (1996). The loss of illusions: The potent legacy of trauma. *Journal of Personal and Interpersonal Loss, 1*, 133–150.

John, O. P., & Robins, R. W. (1994). Accuracy and bias in self-perception: Individual differences in self-enhancement and the role of narcissism. *Journal of Personality and Social Psychology, 66*(1), 206–219.

Johnson, R. (1970). Extramarital sexual intercourse: A methodological note. *Journal of Marriage and Family, 32*(2), 279–282.

Karpel, M. (1980). Family secrets: I. Conceptual and ethical issues in the relational context II. Ethical and practical consideration in therapeutic management. *Family Process, 19*, 295–306.

Kassinove, H. (1995). *Anger disorders: Definition, diagnosis, and treatment*. Washington, DC: Taylor & Francis.

Kelley, H. (1983). Love & commitment. In H. Kelley, E. Berscheid, A. Christensen, J. Harvey, G. Levinger, E. McClintock, L. Paplau, & D. Petersons (Eds.), *Close relationships* (pp. 265–314). New York: W.H. Freeman.

Kelln, B. R., & Ellard, J. H. (1999). An equity theory analysis of the impact of forgiveness and retribution on transgressor compliance. *Personality & Social Psychology Bulletin, 25*(7), 864–872.

Kernberg, O. (1990). Countertransference. In R. Langs (Ed.), *Classics in psychoanalytic techniques* (pp. 207–216). New York: Jason Aronson.

Kinsey, A. C., Pomeroy, W. B. & Martin, C. E. (1948). *Sexual behavior in the human male*. Philadelphia: W.B. Saunders.

Kinsey, A. C., Pomeroy, W. B., Martin, C. E., & Gebhard, P. H. (1953). *Sexual behavior in the human female*. Philadelphia: W.B. Saunders.

Klausner, E. J., Snyder, C. R., & Cheavens, J. (2000). A hope-based group treatment for depressed older adult outpatients. In G. M. Williamson, D. R. Shaffer, & P. A. Parmalee (Eds.), *Physical illness and depression in older adults: A handbook of theory, research, and practice* (pp. 295–310). New York: Kluwer Academic / Plenum.

Koerner, K., Jacobson, N. S., & Christensen, A. (1994). Emotional acceptance in integrative behavioral couple therapy. In S. C. Hayes, N. S. Jacobson, V. M. Follette, & M. J. Dougher (Eds.), *Acceptance and change: Content and context in psychotherapy* (pp. 109–118). Reno, NV: Context Press.

L'Abate, L., & McHenry, S. (1983). *Handbook of marital interventions*. New York: Grune & Stratton.

Larzelere, R. E., & Huston, T.L. (1980). The dyadic trust scale: Toward understanding interpersonal trust in close relationships. *Journal of Marriage and the Family, 42*, 595–604.

Laumann, E., Gagnon, J. H., Michael, R. T., & Michaels, S. (1994). *The social organization of sexuality: Sexual practices in the United States*. Chicago: University of Chicago Press.

Lawson, A. (1988). *Adultery: An analysis of love and betrayal*. New York: Basic.

Leedes, R. (2001). Three most important criteria in diagnosing sexual addictions: Obsession, obsession, and obsession. *Sexual Addiction and Compulsivity, 8*(3–4), 215–226.

Leigh, B. C., Temple, M. T., & Trocki, K. F. (1993). The sexual behavior of U.S. adults: Results from a national survey. *American Journal of Public Health, 83*(10), 1400–1408.

Lenthall, G. (1977). Marital satisfaction and marital stability. *Journal of Marrital and Family Therapy, 3*(4), 25–32.

Levine, S. B. (1998). Extramarital sexual affairs. *Journal of Sex & Marital Therapy, 24*(3), 207–216.

Lopez, S. J., Floyd, R. K., Ulven, J. C., & Snyder, C. R. (2000). Hope therapy: Helping clients build a house of hope. In C. R. Snyder (Ed.), *Handbook of hope: Theory, measures, and applications* (pp. 123–150). San Diego: Academic Press.

Lusterman, D. D. (1995). Treating marital infidelity. In R. H. Mikesell, D. D. Lusterman, & S. H. McDaniel (Eds.), *Integrating family therapy: Handbook of family psychology and systems theory* (pp. 259–269). Washington, DC: American Psychological Association.

Lusterman, D. (1998). *Infidelity: A survival guide.* Oakland, CA: New Harbinger.

Malcolm W. M., & Greenberg, L. S. (2000). Forgiveness as a process of change in individual psychotherapy. In M. McCullogh, K. Pargament, & C. Thoresen (Eds.), *Forgiveness: Theory, research and practice* (pp. 179–203). New York: Guilford.

Mamalakis, P. M. (2001). Painting a bigger picture: Forgiveness therapy with pre-marital infidelity: A case study [Special issue]. *Journal of Family Psychotherapy, 12*(1), 39–54.

Manley, G., & Koehler, J. (2001). Sexual behavior disorders: Proposed new classification in the DSM-V. *Sexual Addiction and Compulsivity, 8*(3–4), 253–265.

Marett, K. M. (1990). Extramarital affairs: A birelational model for their assessment. *Family Therapy, 17*(1), 21–28.

Maykovich, M. D. (1976). Attitudes versus behavior in extramarital sexual relations. *Journal of Marriage and the Family, 38*(4), 693–699.

McCarthy, B. (2002). Sexual secrets, trauma, and dysfunction. *Journal of Sex and Marital Therapy, 28,* 353–359.

McCormick, N., Brannigan, G., & LaPlante, M. (1984). Social desirability in the bedroom: Role of approval motivation in sexual relationships. *Sex Roles, 11*(3–4), 303–314.

McCullough, M. E. (2000). Forgiveness as human strength: Theory, measurement, and links to well-being. *Journal of Social and Clinical Psychology, 19*(1), 43–55.

McCullough, M. E. (2001). Forgiveness: Who does it and how do they do it? *Current Directions in Psychological Science, 10*(6), 194–197.

McCullough, M. E., Exline, J. J., & Baumeister, R. F. (1998). An annotated bibliography of research on forgiveness and related topics. In E. L. Worthington, Jr. (Ed.), *Dimensions of forgiveness: Psychological research and theological speculations* (pp. 193–317). Philadelphia: Templeton Foundation Press

McCullough, M., Hoyt, W., & Rachal, K. (2000). What we know (and need to know) about assessing forgiveness constructs. In M. McCullogh, K. Pargament, & C. Thoresen (Eds.), *Forgiveness: Theory, research and practice* (pp. 65–91). New York: Guilford.

McCullough, M. E., Worthington, E. L., Jr., & Rachal, K. C. (1997). Interpersonal forgiving in close relationships. *Journal of Personality and Social Psychology, 73*(2), 321–336.

McLaughlin, M. L., Cody, M. J., & Rosenstein, N. E. (1983). Account sequences in conversations between strangers. *Communication Monographs, 50,* 102–125.

Miller, W. I. (1993). *Humiliation.* Ithaca, NY: Cornell University Press.

Millon, T. (1999). *Personality—guided therapy.* New York: Wiley.

Mitchell, C. E. (1989). Effects of apology on marital and family relationships. *Family Therapy, 16*(3), 283–287.

Moultrup, D. (1990). *Husbands, wives, and lovers: The emotional system of the extramarital affair.* New York: Guilford.

Nass, G. D., Libby, R. W., & Fisher, M. P. (1981). *Sexual choices.* Belmont, CA: Wadsworth.

North, J. (1987). Wrongdoing and forgiveness. *Philosophy, 62,* 499–508.

North, J. (1998). The "ideal" of forgiveness: A philosopher's exploration. In R. D. Enright & J. North (Eds.), *Exploring forgiveness* (pp. 15–45). Madison: University of Wisconsin Press.

Ohbuchi, K., Kameda, M., & Agarie, N. (1989). Apology as aggression control: Its role in mediating appraisal of and response to harm. *Journal of Personality and Social Psychology, 56*(2), 219–227.

Olson, M., Russell, C., Higgins-Kessler, M., & Miller, R. (2002). Emotional processes following disclosure of an extramarital affair. *Journal of Marital and Family Therapy, 28*(4), 423–434.

Penn, C., Hernandez, S., & Bermudez, M. (1997). Using a cross-cultural perspective to understand infidelity in couples therapy. *American Journal of Family Therapy, 25*(2), 169–185.

Pittman, F. (1989). *Private lies: Infidelities and the betrayal of intimacy.* New York: Norton.

Pittman, F. (1993). Beyond betrayal: Life after infidelity. *Psychology Today, 33,* 78–82.

Pittman, F., & Wagers, T. P. (1995). Crises of infidelity. In N. S. Jacobson & A. S. Gurman (Eds.), *Clinical handbook of couple therapy* (pp. 295–316). New York: Guilford.

Prager, K. (1997). *The psychology of intimacy.* New York: Guilford.

Prins, K., Buunk, B., & Van Yperen, N. (1993). Equity, normative disapproval and extramarital relationships. *Journal of Social and Personal Relationships, 10*(1), 39–53.

Reiss, I., Anderson, R., & Sponaugle, G. (1980). A multivariate model of the determinants of extramarital sexual permissiveness. *Journal of Marriage and the Family, 42*(2), 395–411.

Rempel, J. K., Holmes, J. G., & Zanna, M. P. (1985). Trust in close relationships. *Journal of Personality and Social Psychology, 49,* 95–112.

Rhodes, S. (1984). Extramarital affairs: Clinical issues in therapy. *Social Casework: The Journal of Contemporary Social Work, 65*(9), 541–546.

Rose, S., & Frieze, I. (1989). Young singles' scripts for a first date. *Gender and Society, 3*(2), 258–268.

Rosenau, D. (1998). Extramarital affairs: Therapeutic understanding and clinical interventions. *Marriage & Family: A Christian Journal, 1*(4), 355–368.

Rotter, J. B. (1967). A new scale for the measurement of interpersonal trust. *Journal of Personality, 35,* 651–665.

Rusbult, C. E., Arriaga, X. B., & Agnew, C. R. (2001). Interdependence in close relationships. In G. J. O. Fletcher & M. S. Clark (Eds.), *Blackwell handbook of social psycholgy: Vol 2. Interpersonal processes* (pp. 359–387). Oxford, UK: Blackwell.

Rusbult, C. E., Bissonnette, V. L., Arriaga, X. B., & Cox, C. L. (1998). Accommodation processes in the early years of marriage. In T. N. Bradbury (Ed.), *The developmental course of marital dysfunction* (pp. 74–113). New York: Cambridge University Press.

Rusbult, C. E., & Buunk, B. P. (1993). Commitment process in close relationships: An interdependence analysis [Special issue: Relational maintenance]. *Journal of Social & Personal Relationships, 10*(2), 175–204.

Sager, C. (1976). *Marriage contracts and couples therapy: Hidden forces in intimate relationships.* New York: Brunner / Mazel.

Sager, C., & Hunt, B. (1979). *Intimate partners: Hidden patterns in love relationships.* New York: McGraw-Hill.

Saunders, J. M., & Edwards, J. N. (1984). Extramarital sexuality: A predictive model of permissive attitudes. *Journal of Marriage and the Family, 46,* 825–835.

Schaefer, M., & Olson, D. (1981). Assessment of intimacy: The PAIR inventory. *Journal of Marital and Family Therapy, 7,* 47–60.

Scher, S. J., & Darley, J. M. (1997). How effective are the things people say to apologize? Effects of the realization of the apology speech act. *Journal of Psycholinguistic Research, 26*(1), 127–140.

Schlenker, B. R. (1980). *Impression management: The self-concept social identity, and interpersonal relations.* New York: Brooks / Cole.

Schneider, C. D. (2000). What it means to be sorry: The power of apology in mediation. *Mediation Quarterly, 17*(3), 265–280.

Schneider, J. (2000). Effects of cybersex addiction on the family: Results of a survey. *Sexual Addiction and Compulsivity, 7*(1–2), 31–58.

Schwartz, G. S., Kane, T. R., Joseph, J. M., & Tedeschi, J. T. (1978). The effects of post-transgression remorse on perceived aggression, attribution of intent, and level of punishment. *Journal of Social and Clinical Psychology, 17,* 293–297.

Seagull, E. A., & Seagull A. A. (1991). Healing the wound that must not heal: Psychotherapy with survivors of domestic violence. *Psychotherapy, 28*(1), 16–20.

Seal, D., Agostinelli, G., & Hannett, C. (1994). Extradyadic romantic involvement: Moderating effects of sociosexuality and gender. *Sex Roles, 31*(1–2), 1–22.

Sells, J., & Hargrave, T. (1998). Forgiveness: A review of the theoretical and empirical literature. *Journal of Family Therapy, 20,* 21–26.

Semin, G. R., & Manstead, A. S. R. (1983). *The accountability of conduct: A social psychological analysis.* London: Academic Press.

Shaw, J. (1997). Treatment rationale for internet infidelity. *Journal of Sex Education and Therapy, 22*(1), 29–34.

Sheppard, V., Nelson, E., & Andreoli-Mathie, V. (1995). Dating relationships and infidelity: Attitudes and behaviors. *Journal of Sex and Marital Therapy, 21*(3), 202–212.

Silverstein, J. (1998). Countertransference in marital therapy for infidelity. *Journal of Sex and Marital Therapy, 24*(4), 293–301.

Simpson, J., & Gangestad, S. (1992). Sociosexuality and romantic partner choice. *Journal of Personality, 60*(1), 31–51.

Singh, B., Walton, B., & William S, J. (1976). Extramarital sexual permissiveness: Conditions and contingencies. *Journal of Marriage and the Family, 38*(4), 701–710.

Smith, T. (1991). Adult sexual behavior in 1989: Number of partners, frequency of intercourse and risk of AIDS. *Family Planning Perspective, 23,* 102–107.

Smith, T. (1994). Attitudes toward sexual permissiveness: Trends, correlates, and behavioral connections. In A. S. Rossi (Ed.), *Sexuality across the life course* (pp. 63–97). Chicago: University of Chicago Press.

Snyder, C. R. (1994). *The psychology of hope: You can get there from here.* New York: Free Press.

Snyder, C. R. (Ed.). (2000). *Handbook of hope: Theory, measures & applications.* New York: Academic Press.

Snyder, C. R., & Taylor, J. (2000). Hope as a common factor across psychotherapy approaches: A lesson from the Dodo's verdict. In C. R. Snyder (Ed.), *Handbook of hope: Theory, measures & applications* (pp. 89–103). New York: Academic Press.

Solomon, M., & Siegel, J. (1997). *Countertransference in couples therapy.* New York: Norton.

Spanier, G., & Margolis, R. (1983). Marital separation and extramarital sexual behavior. *Journal of Sex Research, 19*(1), 23–48.

Sprecher, S., Regan, P., & McKinney, K. (1998). Beliefs about the outcomes of extramarital sexual relationships as a function of the gender of the "cheating spouse." *Sex Roles, 38*(3–4), 301–311.

Sprenkle, D. H., & Weis, D. L. (1978). Extramarital sexuality: Implications for marital therapists. *Journal of Sex & Marital Therapy, 4*(4), 279–291.

Spring, J. A. (1996). *After the affair: Healing the pain and rebuilding the trust when a partner has been unfaithful.* New York: HarperCollins.

Spring, J. A. (1999). After the affair, rebuilding trust and personal intimacy. *Issues in Psychoanalytic Psychology, 21*(1–2), 53–62.

Steiner, C. (2000). Apology: The transactional analysis of fundamental exchange. *Transactional Analysis Journal, 30*(2), 145–149.

Sternberg, R. (1986). A triangular theory of love. *Psychological Review, 93*(2), 119–135.

Sternberg, R. (1997). Construct validation of a triangular love scale. *European Journal of Social Psychology, 27*(3), 313–335.

Stevens, B. (1986). A Jungian perspective on transference and countertransference. *Contemporary Psychoanalysis, 22,* 185–201.

Stiff, J. B., Kim, H. J., & Ramesh, C. N. (1992). Truth biases and aroused suspicion in relational deception. *Communication Research, 19*(3), 326–345.

Strean, H. (1976). The extramarital affair: A psychoanalytic view. *Psychoanalytic Review, 63*(1), 101–113.

Strean, H. (1980). *The extramarital affair.* New York: Free Press.

Strean, H. (2000). *The extramarital affair.* Northvale, NJ: Jason Aronson.

Strong, S., & Claiborn, C. (1982). *Change through interaction: Social psychological processes of counseling and psychotherapy.* New York: Wiley.

Taibbi, R. (1983). Handling extramarital affairs in clinical treatment. *Social Casework: The Journal of Contemporary Social Work, 64*(4), 200–204.

Tangney, J. P. (1991). Moral affect: The good, the bad, and the ugly. *Journal of Personality and Social Psychology, 61,* 598–607.

Tangney, J. P. (1995). Shame and guilt in interpersonal relationship. In J. P. Tangney & K. W. Fischer (Eds.), *Self-conscious emotions: The psychology of shame, guilt, embarrassment and pride* (pp. 114–142). New York: Guilford.

Tangney, J. P., Miller, R. S., Flicker, L., & Barlow, D. H. (1996). Are shame, guilt, and embarrassment distinct emotions? *Journal of Personality and Social Psychology, 70*(6), 1256–1269.

Tavuchis, N. (1991). *Mea culpa: A sociology of apology and reconciliation.* Stanford, CA: Stanford University Press.

Tedeschi, J. T., & Norman, N. (1985). The self and social power. In B. R. Schlenker (Ed.), *The self and social life.* New York: McGraw-Hill.

Tedeschi, J. T., & Riess, M. (1981). Predicaments and verbal tactics of impression management. In C. Antaki (Ed.), *Ordinary language explanations of social behavior* (pp. 156–187). London: Academic Press.

Thompson, A. (1983). Extramarital sex: A review of the research literature. *Journal of Sex Research, 19*(1), 1–22.

Thompson, A. (1984). Extramarital sexual crisis: Common themes and therapy implications. *Journal of Sex and Marital Therapy, 10*(4), 239–253.

Treas, J., & Giesen, D. (2000). Sexual infidelity among married cohabiting Americans. *Journal of Marriage and the Family, 62*, 48–60.

Turner, M. (1995). Addictions in marital / relationship therapy. In G. R. Weeks & L. Hof (Eds.), *Integrative solutions: Treating common problems in couples therapy* (pp. 124–147). New York: Brunner / Mazel.

Van den Eijnden, R., Regina, J., Buunk, B., & Bosveld, W. (2000). Feeling similar or feeling unique: How men and women perceive their own sexual behaviors. *Personality & Social Psychology Bulletin, 26*(12), 1540–1549.

Van Lange, P. A. M., Agnew, C. R., Harinck, F., & Steemers, G. E. M. (1997). From game to theory to real life: How social value orientation affects willingness to sacrifice in ongoing close relationships. *Journal of Personality and Social Psychology, 73*(6), 1330–1344.

Walster, E., Traupmann, J., & Walster, W. (1978). Equity and extramarital sexuality. *Archives of Sexual Behavior, 7*(2), 127–142.

Weeks, G. (1977). Toward a dialectical approach to intervention. *Human Development, 20*(5), 277–292.

Weeks, G. (1986). Individual-system dialectic. *American Journal of Family Therapy, 14*(1), 5–12.

Weeks, G. R. (Ed.). (1989).*Treating couples: The intersystem model of the Marriage Council of Philadelphia*. New York: Brunner / Mazel.

Weeks, G. R. (1994). The intersystem model: An integrative approach to treatment. In G. R. Weeks & L. Hof (Eds.), *The marital relationship therapy casebook: Theory and application of the intersystem model* (pp. 3–34). New York: Brunner / Mazel.

Weeks, G., & Gambescia, N. (2000). *Erectile dysfunction: Integrating couple therapy, sex therapy, and medical treatment*. New York: Norton.

Weeks, G., & Gambescia, N. (2002). *Hypoactive sexual desire: Integrating sex and couple therapy*. New York: Norton.

Weeks, G. R. & Hof, L. (Eds.). (1995). *Integrative solutions: Treating common problems in couples therapy*. New York: Brunner / Mazel.

Weeks, G. R., & Treat, S. (1992). *Couples in treatment: Techniques and approaches for effective practice*. New York: Brunner / Mazel.

Weeks, G. R., & Treat, S. (2001). *Couples in treatment: Techniques and approaches for effective practice* (2nd ed.). Philadelphia: Brunner / Routledge.

Westfall, A. (1989). Extramarital sex: The treatment of the couple. In G. R. Weeks (Ed.), *Treating couples: The intersystem model of the Marriage Council of Philadelphia* (pp. 163–190). New York: Brunner / Mazel.

Westfall, A. (1995). Working through the extramarital trauma: An exploration of common themes. In G. R. Weeks & L. Hof (Eds.), *Integrative solutions: Treating common problems in couples therapy* (pp. 148–194). New York: Brunner / Mazel.

Whisman, M., Dixon, A., & Johnson, B. (1997). Therapist's perspectives of couple problems and treatment issues in couple therapy. *Journal of Family Psychology, 11*(3), 361–366.

Wiederman, M. W. (1997). Extramarital sex: Prevalence and correlates in a national survey. *The Journal of Sex Research, 34*(2), 167–174.

Wiggins, J., & Lederer, D. (1984). Differential antecedents of infidelity in marriage. *American Mental Health Counselors Association Journal, 6*(4), 152–161.

Witvliet, C., vanOyen, C., Ludwig, T. E., & Vander Laan, K. L. (2001). Granting forgiveness or harboring grudges: Implications for emotion, physiology, and health [Special issue]. *Psychological Science, 121*(2), 117–123.

Worthington, E. L., Jr. (1998). An empathy-humility-commitment model of forgiveness applied within family dyads. *Journal of Family Therapy, 20,* 59–76.

Worthington, E. L., Jr., Sandage, S. J., & Berry, J. W. (2000). Group interventions to promote forgiveness: What researchers and clinicians ought to know. In M. E. McCullough, K. I. Paragment, & C. Thoresen (Eds.), *Forgiveness: Theory, research, and practice* (pp. 228–253). New York: Guilford.

Worthington, E. L., Jr., & Wade, N. (1999). The psychology of unforgiveness and forgiveness and implications for clinical practice. *Journal of Social and Clinical Psychology, 18*(4), 385–418.

Yablonsky, L. (1979). *The extra-sex factor: Why over half of America's married men play around.* New York: Times Books.

Young, K., Griffin-Shelly, E., Cooper, A., O'Mara, J., & Buchanan, J. (2000). Online infidelity: A new dimension in couple relationships with implications for evaluation and treatment. *Sexual Addiction and Compulsivity, 7*(1–2), 59–74.

Index